THE LAST
SPEAKERS

THE LAST
SPEAKERS

THE QUEST TO SAVE THE WORLD'S MOST
ENDANGERED LANGUAGES

K. DAVID HARRISON

NATIONAL GEOGRAPHIC

WASHINGTON, D.C.

Published by the National Geographic Society
1145 17th Street N.W., Washington, D.C. 20036

Library of Congress Cataloging-in-Publication Data

Harrison, K. David.
The last speakers : the quest to save the world's most endangered languages / K. David Harrison.
   p. cm.
Includes bibliographical references.
ISBN 978-1-4262-0461-6 (hardcover : alk. paper)
1. Endangered languages. 2. Language attrition. 3. Language maintenance. 4. Linguistic change. 5. Linguistic minorities. 6. Sociolinguistics. I. Title.
P40.5.E53H37 2010
408.9--dc22

2010014720

Contents page, Chris Rainier/National Geographic Enduring Voices Project; 18, Courtesy of Ironbound Films; 25, David M. Harrison; 50, K. David Harrison; 65, Kelly J. Richardson; 67, Kelly J. Richardson; 79, Gregory Anderson; 96, K. David Harrison; 108, Anna Luisa Daigneault; 113, Chris Rainier/National Geographic Enduring Voices Project; 122, K. David Harrison; 145, K. David Harrison; 157, Chris Rainier/National Geographic Enduring Voices Project; 188, Katherine Vincent; 199, K. David Harrison; 206, Thomas Hegenbart/Contact Press Images; 227, Thomas Hegenbart/Contact Press Images; 251, K. David Harrison, courtesy Ramona Dick and Alan Yu; 259, Courtesy of Swarthmore College Linguistics Department.

Photo insert: 1 (top), Source: Living Tongues Institute for Endangered Languages; 1 (bottom), Chris Rainier/National Geographic Enduring Voices Project; 2, K. David Harrison; 3 (both), Chris Rainier/National Geographic Enduring Voices Project; 4 (both), Kelly J. Richardson; 5 (top), Chris Rainier/National Geographic Enduring Voices Project; 5 (bottom), K. David Harrison; 6 (top), K, David Harrison; 6 (bottom), Chris Rainier/National Geographic Enduring Voices Project; 7 (both), Chris Rainier/National Geographic Enduring Voices Project; 8, Chris Rainier/National Geographic Enduring Voices Project.

The National Geographic Society is one of the world's largest nonprofit scientific and educational organizations. Founded in 1888 to "increase and diffuse geographic knowledge," the Society works to inspire people to care about the planet. It reaches more than 325 million people worldwide each month through its official journal, *National Geographic*, and other magazines; National Geographic Channel; television documentaries; music; radio; films; books; DVDs; maps; exhibitions; school publishing programs; interactive media; and merchandise. National Geographic has funded more than 9,000 scientific research, conservation and exploration projects and supports an education program combating geographic illiteracy.

For more information, please call 1-800-NGS LINE (647-5463) or write to the following address:

National Geographic Society
1145 17th Street N.W.
Washington, D.C. 20036-4688 U.S.A.

Visit us online at www.nationalgeographic.com

For information about special discounts for bulk purchases, please contact
National Geographic Books Special Sales: ngspecsales@ngs.org

For rights or permissions inquiries, please contact National Geographic Books
Subsidiary Rights: ngbookrights@ngs.org

Interior design: Cameron Zotter and Al Morrow

Printed in the United States of America

10/WCPF/1

For Khiem H. Tang

Koro speaker, near Bana village,
Arunachal Pradesh, India

CONTENTS

*Dying languages succumb
more discreetly. Village by village
they go under—no shouting,
no watery ruckus.
Just a simple, sudden absence.
It takes a shrewd eye to spot
these silent catastrophes,
and a frugal, determined heart
to intervene.*

—John Goulet

{INTRODUCTION}

MY JOURNEY AS A SCIENTIST exploring the world's vanishing languages has taken me from the Siberian forests to the Bolivian Altiplano, from a fast-food restaurant in Michigan to a trailer park in Utah. In all these places I've listened to last speakers—dignified elders—who hold in their minds a significant portion of humanity's intellectual wealth.

Though it belongs solely to them and has inestimable value to their people, they do not hoard it. They are often eager to share it, sometimes because they find so few of their own people willing to listen. What can we learn from these languages before they go extinct? And why should we lift a finger to help rescue them?

As the last speakers converse, they spin out individual strands of a vast web of knowledge, a noosphere of possibilities that encircles all of us. They tell how their ancestors calculated accurately the passing of seasons without clocks or calendars, how humans adapted to hostile environments from the Arctic to Amazonia.

We imagine eureka moments taking place in modern laboratories or in classical civilizations. But key insights of biology, pharmacology, genetics, and navigation arose and persisted solely by word of mouth, in small, unwritten tongues. This web of knowledge contains feats of human ingenuity—epics, myths, rituals—that celebrate and interpret our existence.

Pundits argue that linguistic differences are little more than random drift, minor variations in meaning and pronunciation that emerge over time (the British say "lorry," Americans "truck"; Tuesday is CHOOZ-day for Brits, TOOZ-day for Americans).

These differences reveal—some claim—nothing unique about our souls or minds. But that's like saying that the Pyramid of Cheops differs from Notre Dame Cathedral only by stone-cutting techniques that evolved randomly in different times and places, revealing nothing unique in the ancient Egyptian or medieval French imagination.

All cultures encode their genius in verbal monuments, while considerably fewer do so in stone edifices. We might as well proclaim human history banal, and human genius of no value to our survival.

The fate of languages is interlinked with that of species, as they undergo parallel extinctions. Scientific knowledge is comparable for both domains, with an estimated 80 percent of plant and animal species unknown to science and 80 percent of languages yet to be documented. But species and ecosystems unknown to science are well known to local people, whose languages encode not only names for things but also complex interrelations among them.

Packaged in ways that resist direct translation, this knowledge dissipates when people shift to speaking global tongues. What the Kallawaya of Bolivia know about medicinal plants, how the Yupik of Alaska name 99 distinct sea ice formations, how the Tofa of Siberia classify reindeer—entire domains of ancient knowledge, only scantily documented, are rapidly eroding.

INTRODUCTION

Linguistic survivors—the last speakers whom I profile throughout this book—hold the fates of languages in their minds and mouths.

Johnny Hill Jr., a Chemehuevi Indian of Arizona, spent much of his life working in construction and farming. Now retired, he serves as an elected tribal council member of the Colorado River Indian Tribes and works to promote the Chemehuevi language.[1] Designated a "last speaker" of Chemehuevi, Johnny told his story in the 2008 Sundance documentary film *The Linguists*.

Raised by his grandmother who spoke only Chemehuevi, Johnny learned English at school seeking a path out of isolation. At the other end of his life span, Johnny finds himself linguistically isolated once again. "I have to talk to myself," he explains resignedly. "There's nobody left to talk to. All the elders have passed on, so I talk to myself. . . . That's just how it is."

Johnny has tried to teach his children and others in the tribe. "Trouble is," he says with a sigh, "they say they want to learn it, but when it comes time to do the work, nobody comes around."

Speakers react differently to loss—from indifference to despair—and adopt diverse strategies. Some blame governments or globalization, others blame themselves. Around the world, a growing wave of language activists works to revitalize their threatened tongues. Positive attitudes are the single most powerful force keeping languages alive, while negative ones can doom them.

Two dozen *language hotspots*—a term derived from biodiversity hotspots, referring to places where small languages both abound and are endangered—have now been identified globally. With funding from the National Geographic Society, my effort to map and visit all the hotspots, and to record as many last speakers there as possible, is well under way. Around the globe, numerous scientists and indigenous language activists are mounting similar efforts. But recording is not enough, we must also work to revitalize small languages.

New technologies are being mobilized to the cause. A Torres Strait Islander in Australia told me: "Our language is standing still. We need to make it relevant to today's society. We need to create new words, because right now we can't say 'computer.'"

The lowly text message may lift obscure tongues to new levels of prestige. Translated software may help them cross the digital divide. Hip-hop performed in threatened tongues, as I've heard among young speakers of Aka in India, infuses new vitality.

Language revitalization will prove to be one of the most consequential social trends of coming decades. This push-back against globalization will profoundly influence human intellectual life, deciding the fate of ancient knowledge.

Listening to the elders, I am astonished by how little we know and how vast human knowledge is. We find ancient systems of knowledge—in many cases more sophisticated than what modern science knows—about the natural world, plants, fish, weather patterns, sea ice, and landscapes. We find amusing stories of reindeer, bears and fishes, weather patterns and stars, healing plants, mythical yeti-like beasts, and world-creating ducks. In short, we find a mental catalog of mankind's attempts to make sense of the world and harness its resources for human survival. The elders' stories often contain a history of the first contact between an indigenous people and colonial Europeans, an encounter that has driven most of the world's languages to the very brink of existence.

What hubris allows us, cocooned comfortably in our cyberworld, to think that we have nothing to learn from people who a generation ago were hunter-gatherers? What they know—which we've forgotten or never knew—may someday save us.

This book consists partly of my findings in diverse locations where I've made recordings of some of the world's most obscure tongues. It is also a concerned global citizen's op-ed piece, urging readers to consider the dire consequences of knowledge loss and help reverse it. Finally, it is a channel for voices of elders around the world—voices otherwise seldom heard—who have shared with me their insights and their struggles to protect vanishing cultures.

We live at a time when we can still hear their voices, albeit muted, sharing knowledge in 7,000 different ways of speaking.

WHY SHOULD WE VALUE LANGUAGES?

Everyone values their mother tongue, and few people would be willing to part with it. Even if you ask a bilingual person which of his two languages he'd prefer to forgo, he is loath to choose one, sensing a loss regardless of the choice. Yet we live in a society that curiously undervalues bilingualism. Millions of schoolchildren spend countless hours drilling the verb forms of Spanish, while just a classroom or corridor away, millions of other children who speak Spanish with their parents at home and could be fully bilingual are shamed for having a slight accent and intimidated into giving up their Spanish. "English Only" is one of the most intellectually ruinous notions ever perpetuated upon American society, and one of the most historically naïve. We have always been a multilingual society, even before we were a nation.

When I speak to public school classes in my home city of Philadelphia, I ask for a show of hands: Who speaks another language at home, or hears it from their parents? In a typical tenth-grade Philadelphia classroom I find Albanian (both Gheg and Tosk varieties), Serbian, Hmong, Vietnamese, Malayalam, Polish, and Ukrainian. Spanish is of course ubiquitous, but students less often admit they speak it. The students' faces always reflect their surprise when they look around and marvel at the deep knowledge base of languages right there in their classroom. As their less-than-fluent teacher of Spanish drills them tediously on the irregular verbs, the other languages are withering for lack of use. Imagine the kind of games these kids could play creating parallel translations into many tongues, or the wealth of metaphors and wise sayings they could share.

Language plays a role in forming a strong personal identity, and diversity can be seen to threaten group cohesiveness. If the American project has indeed been a melting pot, that accounts for immigrant families' rapid abandonment of their heritage languages. Our society is linguistically less like a tossed salad, in which the distinct parts retain their individual shapes and textures while contributing flavor, and more like a soup, in which each ingredient is melted and masked by others. At the same time we devalue bilingualism, we spend millions of dollars to teach kids a rudimentary form of classroom French that will guarantee disdain when they try to order at a Paris McDonald's. Yet the problem is spread more widely than that. The Army lacks Arabic linguists and the CIA Kurdish specialists. Meanwhile, many bright American kids grow up speaking Arabic or Kurdish at home, but are made to feel ashamed of that fact in our educational system.

In one often repeated story, a Native American girl in Oklahoma raises her hand when the teacher asks, "Who here can speak a foreign language?" She replies: "I can. English," incurring the teacher's disapproval. Yet for her—indeed, for all Native Americans—English is a foreign language. The power of their native tongues has lingered all over the land, as shown in rivers such as the Chattahoochee, Monongahela, and Susquehanna. Rarely do newcomers rename rivers; they merely mangle the old pronunciation. For instance, in Ojibwe *misi-ziibi* means "Great River."

Languages abound in local knowledge, information that is not written down anywhere, that is not possessed by a single individual but is socially distributed. The problem of local knowledge was brought to the fore by F. A. Hayek in his work in economics, but it has a powerful parallel to language. He wrote:

Today it is almost heresy to suggest that scientific knowledge is not the sum of all knowledge. But a little reflection will show that there is beyond question a body of very important but unorganized knowledge which cannot possibly be called scientific in the sense of knowledge of general rules: the knowledge of the particular circumstances of time and place.[2]

Though Hayek was not necessarily referring to indigenous peoples, his view of knowledge, like mine, assumes that most of it is hidden, "unorganized," off the books, residing in people's minds. This vast body of knowledge exceeds what we like to think of as scientific (or book) knowledge.

By amassing this knowledge, and distributing it within a society so that it can survive the lifetime of any one individual, humans build up their cultures. Many of the rules and principles we unconsciously follow (how to greet someone, what is the common good, when to speak, whom to follow) are based on cultural learning that is transmitted to us, often with no awareness on our part, largely via language. We know more than our brain contains by virtue of being a member of a society. As Hayek points out:

We make constant use of formulas, symbols, and rules whose meaning we do not understand and through the use of which we avail ourselves of the assistance of knowledge which individually we do not possess. We have developed these practices and institutions by building upon habits and institutions which have proved successful in their own sphere and which have in turn become the foundation of the civilization we have built up.

In the chapters ahead, we will visit remote communities in Australia, India, Papua New Guinea, and Bolivia. Each one gives a vivid example of how language connects humans to the local environment. If these local ties dissolve, our entire species has less connection to Earth, less ability to sustainably manage our resources, less knowledge of how to care for our planet. From the outback deserts to the Pacific Ocean's coral reefs, from the Andean glaciers to the Himalayan foothills, we find major stress points of human impact on ecosystems we don't fully understand. Endangered languages hold the key to a fuller understanding of these ecosystems and humankind's place in them.

We're now facing what I call a triple threat of extinction. Species and ecosystems are in collapse, while the traditional systems of knowledge about those species and ecosystems are vanishing as the small, unwritten languages that contain them disappear. Every one of the languages discussed in this book, and every story from the mouths of the last speakers, contains knowledge that is highly specialized and unique, holding keys to human adaptation in diverse environments and clues to our continued survival on this planet.

Linguists have been tardy to sound the alarm for dying languages, and even now we are not doing all that we could. We are far behind our colleagues in conservation biology in persuading the general public. Our scientific field is in many ways blinkered by our own theories and skewed priorities. One of the great discoveries of modern linguistics is that language is a part of the human genetic code—that all humans are programmed to know a language. The theory of universal grammar posits that all languages, at some deep level, share certain fundamental properties, which helps explain why any human child can effortlessly learn whatever language she hears during infancy, be it Icelandic or Igbo. Generations of linguists have been trained to search for these universals, constructing elaborate theories, all the while overlooking the particulars of individual tongues.

This notion of universality has a detrimental flip side, because it leads many linguists to view languages as essentially interchangeable, all equally expressive, each simply a different way of saying the same thing.[3] Linguists have also focused on the *structure* of languages, elements like suffixes and prefixes, word order and case marking. The fixation on grammatical structures has eclipsed our view of what people have to say and has prevented us from fully seeing how each tongue is adapted to a unique society and habitat. In my work, I try to shift from possible universal properties shared by all tongues to focus on the deep differences among them. Rather than *how* people speak (how their languages build words and sentences), I concentrate on *what* they say, and on the very diverse bodies of knowledge held by different societies. Once focused on difference instead of what is shared in common, and on the what instead of the how, we see each individual language as having inestimable value that cannot be replaced.

As I travel the globe, working always as part of a team, I seek to learn more about the deeper connection between landscapes and languages. Many elders I meet are determined to recall and pass on remnants of knowledge. By sharing, they bestow on me the responsibility to care about it and to care for it. Many of these voices, and the stories they share, have never been heard outside of remote villages and backwaters where the speakers live. I take this opportunity to give their voices, now fading, a global megaphone, a rapt audience, an attentive hearing.

Though many small tongues will cease to be spoken and the knowledge they contain erased, the situation is not all dire. I see hope in a vibrant global movement to reclaim and enliven small tongues. A determined push-back against the steamroller of globalization is happening right now. I hear it in Mohawk-language kindergartens, Navajo pop music, and Ojibwe Facebook postings. These familiar media present new and powerful platforms for

Johnny Hill Jr., a last speaker of the Chemehuevi language of Arizona, as he appeared in the film The Linguists.

many of the world's smallest languages. Their speakers, also wired global citizens, cleverly apply new media to sustain ancient words. Rather than viewing technology and globalization as threats, they dive into the information sea, using it to buoy their languages to new heights.

I have been dismayed to find indifference in the very communities where languages are most threatened, but also heartened to see individuals undertaking heroic efforts to sustain heritage languages. An elderly Aboriginal lady, Thelma Sadler, teaches youngsters in western Australia the names for local plants in her Yawuru language. Young men in a mountain village in India perform hip-hop in Aka, a language spoken by barely a thousand people. These language warriors reject the false choice of globalization that says people have to give up small languages and speak only big ones. Their resistance gives hope for language revitalization efforts worldwide.

Along the way, I've met many mentors, role models, and heroes who have been doing this kind of work for ages. My heroes are the elders, last speakers like Johnny Hill Jr. in Arizona and Vasya Gabov in Siberia. These guardians of unique knowledge possess the wisdom and generosity of spirit to share some of that knowledge with us, and by their generosity, they reach out through us to touch a global audience with their words.

This is a story of survival and awakening. My personal encounters with last speakers inspired me to write this book. What they taught me far surpassed what I was able to learn while earning a doctorate in linguistics at Yale. What they know about the natural world often exceeds information accumulated by scientists. The speakers' own stories and passions cry out before an ominous shadow of extinction. At the same time, they may signal a global reawakening to the value of languages and thus portend that all we have learned about our world will inform how we wish to live here.

{ CHAPTER ONE }

BECOMING A LINGUIST

Even though it is the demise of earthly forests that elicits our concern, we must bear in mind that as culture-dwellers we do not live so much in forests of trees as in forests of words. And the source of the blight that afflicts the earth's forests must be sought in the word-forests—that is, in the world we articulate.

—Neil Evernden, *The Natural Alien*

WHO EXACTLY IS A LINGUIST? The general public has little idea of what we do or why it matters. Some think a linguist is a word pundit or grammar maven, doling out advice about correct usage or obscure word origins. The U.S. government uses the term to refer to translators or experts, as in "Arabic linguist." Many people think it means a polyglot who can order beer in any of 25 vernaculars.

The reality is both more banal and more exciting. Banal because a linguist is simply a scientist of language. He has tools just as a biologist has a microscope, or a physicist a particle accelerator. For linguists, the basic tools are a trained ear (able to hear and transcribe exotic sounds); an ability to analyze a language by breaking it down into meaningful bits (often with the help of computer programs that turn audible speech into a visual representation of the sound wave); a thorough knowledge of many hundreds, if not thousands, of scholarly works on the topic; and often a Ph.D.

With these tools, acquired by long study, a linguist can be dropped into a village anywhere in the world, with no more than a notebook and pencil and a good recording device, and begin work. Chances are, whichever of the 7,000 dots on a world map one of us might land on, the language will not yet have been adequately documented or described, and perhaps never before recorded. Though the tools are minimal and the preparation intense, we thrive on the exciting possibility of encountering words entirely new and unknown to science.

Unlike an entomologist who collects butterflies, the linguist always has an abundance of speech to study at any location and need not chase it down. But like the butterfly collector, if the linguist just sits in one place studying whatever is at hand, he will never discover the full range of possibilities.

Linguists strive to see both forest and tree. Language is the element in which we—and much of our conscious thought—exists, and since we can't really step outside of it, we can sometimes more easily make sense of a foreign language than our own. The tiniest elements may be scrutinized. An entire dissertation may explore the vowel sound that appears in the French word *de* as in "pas de deux," or a lengthy scholarly article be devoted to the English "dude," as in "Dude, where's my car?"[1]

But the forest also matters, and linguists like to tackle big questions such as how and when language arose in our human species. Can apes be taught symbolic communication systems akin to language, or does that set us apart from the apes? What are the origins of diversity—if not the biblical tower of Babel, how and when did all the world's languages diverge along their very different trajectories? Are there basic building blocks that all human languages, whether spoken by the mouth or signed with one's hands, share—and if so, what are they and what can they reveal about human cognition?

Becoming a linguist can take many pathways. Mine started early and wended its way through Siberia, Yale University, and other locales around the globe. Some people show unusual prowess at a young age, and may even be linguistic savants. I was not one of those, but according to my mother, my career path may have begun in the womb. I was still four months from being born when my parents attended the Summer Institute of Linguistics, which trains missionary-linguists.[2]

Missionaries have done much of the basic work on undescribed languages, typically by spending many years living in communities to produce a dictionary and Bible translation. This mission is part of a larger agenda to convert people to a particular sect, and missionaries from all types of churches may be found around the world. Though disdained by many academic linguists, missionary work often provides the first or only existing description for many of the world's languages.

My early years were filled with heroic tales told by missionaries on furlough from their field sites. I had missionary aunts, uncles, and cousins in the Belgian Congo (later Zaire), missionary friends in the Philippines, and fellow "MKs" (missionary kids) in Haiti and Ghana as pen pals. Our refrigerator at home was covered with "prayer cards"—photos of missionaries and their families, with little maps showing where they were serving. So, my early exposure to languages and linguistics was through the prism of missionary work.

Of course, missionaries do more than learn languages. They may provide basic medical and educational services, proselytize new converts to the faith, and over the long term, translate portions of the Bible into obscure tongues. My first role models as linguists were missionary Bible translators. I used to collect little pamphlets like the Gospel of John in Sinhala and marvel at the ability to translate. I also pondered some of the classic dilemmas in missionary translation, such as how to render important theo-logical concepts like the "lamb of God" into a culture that pos-sessed no obvious equivalent (for Arctic cultures, I learned "lamb of God" is sometimes rendered as "God's seal pup").

My parents attended the Summer Institute, where my mother recalls struggling with a course in phonetics, learning to pronounce strange sounds, clicks, and trills. Other courses taught them how to analyze the grammar and begin Bible translation. The language they studied was Cree, a difficult Algonquian language that is spread widely across Canada with an estimated 34,000 speakers. My parents were assigned by their mission organization to work with the Ermineskin Cree Nation in Alberta, Canada, a small First Nation community. I was born there, and so I heard plenty of Cree from a young age, from everyday talk to gospel hymns. I was dubbed *napasis,* meaning "little boy." But none of the vocabulary stuck once Cree vanished from my life at age three, when my family moved back to the United States. Though I listened to those Cree gospel songs for years afterward, playing them on a hand-cranked record player, I never picked up any more Cree.

I did not become a missionary, either, mainly because I did not find answers to my deepest questions in dogmatic religion. Unlike many of my colleagues, however, I do not regard mis-sionary work with hostility or as necessarily detrimental to indig-enous cultures. Cultures are strong and resilient, perfectly capable of choosing to believe or disbelieve salvation stories brought by missionaries. No one can really force anyone to believe anything they don't want to. But religion can exert a strong appeal to cer-tain individuals, and I've visited villages where all the inhabitants have fervently converted to a religion that was brought to them recently by outsiders.

My own goals are very different, and some have described my work as being a "reverse missionary." I visit indigenous cultures

John and Mina Currie, of the Ermineskin Cree Nation near Hobbema, Alberta, Canada, shown here in traditional dress in 1967.

not to bring them an alien ideology, to convert, or to advocate that they abandon their beliefs and adopt others. Rather, I go to celebrate, promote, and soak up their knowledge and beliefs. I've been converted, quite willingly, to *their* worldview.

I'm often asked in rural villages, especially in places like rural India where it is common for an entire village to have adopted evangelical Christianity en masse, if I am a Christian. When I reply no, they are surprised, even shocked. Since these villages adopted Christianity from white (often European or Australian) missionaries, they have a notion that all white people must be Christians. They identify Christianity with progress and civilization. Of course, multiple agendas are at work here. One strategic reason the indigenous people of India adopt Christianity is that it allows them to signal a stark difference between themselves and the Hindus who dominate them and, indeed, most political discourse in India. They would never consider converting to

Hinduism, since that would mean the end of their distinct cultural identity.

My next early attempt at learning a language was American Sign Language. ASL has nothing in common with English; its grammar is as foreign as Japanese. The language is spoken with gestures of the hands and face instead of the vocal tract. Deaf people in the United States can be either Deaf (written with a capital *D*), meaning they share a common culture and speak ASL as their primary language, or deaf (small *d*), meaning they cannot hear but have been mainstreamed or are outside of Deaf culture and do not speak ASL fluently.

My father is considered deaf with a small *d*. He had severe hearing loss at birth, but rejected deaf boarding school at an early age and chose to mainstream in hearing society. With the help of hearing aids and expert lip-reading skills, his deafness often passes unnoticed, and he has become an accomplished preacher and public motivational speaker. Still, my family found itself connected to the Deaf/deaf community through my father, and we spent hours learning ASL.

This language, spoken with the hands, is as expressive and beautiful as any spoken language. As a child I experienced ASL as a mysterious power, one that allowed people to communicate across a crowded room, yet at the same time separated them from the society at large. Because deaf people are considered "handicapped," signing also has negative connotations. I was somewhat embarrassed by my father's deafness, which hindered my learning of ASL. I also forgot most of what I had learned of ASL as I grew older. Ironically, at my first real field site as a young professional linguist, I was placed with a mixed deaf and hearing family that used signs to communicate.

How many languages do I speak? This is a frequent question people ask, and one many linguists detest. I don't mind it, but the answer may surprise some. Depending on what "speak" means, I can handle five or six and can understand and read another half dozen. That total is not impressive at all if compared with a famous linguistic savant, a young man identified by the pseudonym Christopher. Studied by linguists, Christopher is described as being able to communicate in 15 to 20 languages, though developmentally disabled in other respects.[3] Nor does my polylingualism come close to the abilities of the many indigenous elders I've met over the years who command nine or ten. I am not a polyglot, though I can mimic sounds and break down words into grammatical structures.

I grew up monolingual, a language bumpkin—a fact I will always regret. Besides hearing Cree as a toddler and learning a few songs in German class in third grade, I had no formal training until high school French class. That was a dreary affair, and I continued to flail ineffectively in college. All I really learned was that I cannot learn in a classroom environment. I wish I was a language whiz, but the most I can say is that I love listening to languages and trying to make sense of them.

I discovered my language aptitude only during my senior year in college, when I ended up as an exchange student in Poland by sheer chance. Poland had communist chic then—in 1988, it was gray and cold, free of any advertising or color, and quite poor. People stood in line to buy toilet paper or, rarely, small oranges that arrived on ships from Cuba. Meat was rationed.

The Poles didn't know what to make of our group of six American students who showed up one winter day in the city of Poznań, unable to communicate. I used hand gestures to talk to my roommate, who had no English. The reception desk ladies chuckled at my attempts to ask for my room key. I was in 916, so at least twice a day I had to approach the desk, clear my throat, and say *"dziewięćset szesnaście"* (je-vyen-set-shesh-NASH-che).

They nicknamed me "Smurf" due to my funny pronunciation. But over three months, an amazing transformation occurred. I managed to find a circle of Polish friends who had almost no English and who were patient enough to include me in their activities and talk to me. I began to absorb the language day by day, mastering the crazy sibilants, the nasal vowels, and the odd way of saying "it fell me" instead of "I dropped it."

Once I learned Polish, I traveled the Eastern Bloc and realized it was home to many related languages—Czech, Slovak, Russian, Ukrainian, Lemko. I could understand between 40 and 70 percent of these, based on their similarities to Polish. The notion of a language "family" was a major epiphany for me: once you learn one member, you have a big head start on the others, and you can see interesting historical connections. I should mention, though, how pitfalls and false cognates can lead you astray: *zhygat'* in Russian means to light a fire, while a word that sounds alike in Polish means to vomit.

Still, even Slavic languages, for all their complexities, represent a sister branch on the expansive Indo-European family language tree, related to English, German, Greek, Latin, Spanish, and even Hindi. Indo-European is a family (linguists call it a "stock") of several hundred related tongues. It is vast in terms of both geographic spread (from India to Iran to Russia to England to Canada to Argentina) and population (with as many as three billion speakers). Nevertheless, it is but one branch on the tree of human languages, with only a small fraction of the diversity.

As soon as one moves outside of the Indo-European, all bets are off, bizarre and unfamiliar structures abound, and assumptions about how languages work must be set firmly aside. Non-Indo-European tongues can also be more difficult to learn because it is difficult to break out of familiar patterns and understand radically different ways of organizing information.

Having found a topic that stirred my interest, I decided to find out more about this field called linguistics. I had no idea that my graduate school studies would send me to one of the most remote regions of the world. Nor did I suspect I would specialize in the world's smallest languages. All I knew was that I had found a mission of my own.

{CHAPTER TWO}

SIBERIA CALLING

We are all far from home.
Language is our caravan bell.

—Rumi (trans. Coleman Barks)

STRETCHING EASTWARD FROM MOSCOW lies a vast land that spans eight time zones. Most people think of it as a barren, snowy wasteland, or place of exile for dissidents. Yet Siberia would be the place I came of age as a scholar and a linguist and forged lasting intellectual and emotional connections. The many adventures I had there radically shifted my view of language and gave me a whole new understanding of how people organize knowledge and communicate.

My original semester as an exchange student in Eastern Europe somehow morphed into a five-year sojourn, and I began to explore the peripheries. I used to loiter at the Kazan' railway station in Moscow, watching trains arrive from Baku and other exotic places and listening to some of the minority languages of Russia. I visited the local mosque to hear Tatar spoken, and the fruit market to hear Georgian spoken by the watermelon vendors. I felt drawn eastward, but visa and legal restrictions on foreigners held me back.

Finally, one day in 1996, I heard that travel restrictions had been lifted. On a whim, I packed my backpack and went directly to Kazan' station. I stood in line clutching $200 in rubles and, when it was my turn, asked for a ticket to Tuva. The surly ticket clerk behind the window, without looking up, said, "There's no such place." When I persisted, she assumed that I was simply mispronouncing Tula, a Russian city where samovars are made. I shouted back at her through the little gap in the ticket window, insisting that a place called T-u-v-a did exist and thinking to myself that she could verify it if she would only heave her bulk up out of the chair and look at the enormous map of Russia on the wall behind her. People behind me in the queue tried to shoo me away, grumbling that I was delaying their purchases. However, being loudly rude in Russia, and with an American accent, sometimes gets results. I stuck to the ticket window, and eventually we reached an understanding. The ticket vendor sold me a train ticket to Abakan, the nearest city to Tuva where trains go.

Tuva had captivated my imagination by the simple fact that, in the late 20th century, people there still lived as nomads, in collapsible felt houses, making their own ropes, saddles, cheese, and wool. Protected by mountains, with no railroads, few airplanes, and no paved roads leading in or out, many Tuvans migrate seasonally, following their animal herds to greener pastures. I couldn't wait to see it with my own eyes.

I boarded my train in Moscow, and 2,500 miles later emerged sleepily before dawn in Abakan. Four days of clackety-clack, sharing a small, four-bunk sleeping compartment with a family of three and watching the monotonous Siberian forest-scape of birches rolling by, gave me plenty of time to prepare. I had read cover to cover the somewhat outdated but only existing grammar of Tuvan, written in the 1960s by Soviet scholars. And though I could not speak or understand much Tuvan, I could at least envision the elegant word structures and knew how to assemble smaller pieces to build longer words like *teve-ler-ivis-ten,* meaning "from our camels."

In Abakan, I hopped in a shared taxi to cross the mountain pass to Tuva. "This road is built on human bones," the driver solemnly declared, recounting that forced Stalinist labor camps had been located here. A tiny statelet absorbed into the Russian Federation, Tuva is culturally one part Russian and three parts Central Asian nomadic, with a strong dash of Mongolian flavor and influence. It contains some of the world's wildest and most magnificent combinations of animals and landscapes: wolves frolicking in mountain pastures, Bactrian camels loaded with bundles plodding across snowdrifts, saddled reindeer treading single file through dense alpine forests, yaks charging each other on the high plains.

Tuvans are perhaps most famous for their throat singing, a technique that sounds like whistles, barber's clippers, and fog-horns all emanating from a single vocal tract. Tuva also has its share of grim Soviet traditions: asbestos mines spewing dust, corrupt bureaucrats, secret police who view all outsiders as spies, rampant alcoholism and violence.

We arrived road-weary in Kyzyl, Tuva's capital, a dismal collection of Soviet-era cement block buildings, with an imposing central square adorned by a large theater and a pointing Lenin statue. The local joke is that Lenin's outstretched arm is hailing a taxi. Kyzyl was all turned out for "Policemen's Day," and the streets were filled with uniformed officers on horseback. I befriended a few of them and was invited to the yurt village outside the city to see horse races and wrestling and eat the local fare (sheep were slaughtered and prepared by convicts who had been let out for a day to assist in the festivities).

At the yurt camp, I realized quickly that knowing Russian was both an asset and a handicap in Tuva. With my Slavic appearance, people were loath to speak anything other than Russian to me. Being an American was also a mixed blessing. I was the first foreigner many Tuvans had ever encountered, which made them eager to talk to me. At the same time, many told me directly that they knew I was a CIA spy. I did not deny it—what good would that do? But I resolved to spend less time with the Tuvan police and more time with the nomads on my next visit.

A few days later, I returned to Moscow, with a nearly expired visa and in a hurry to leave the country. But Tuva left an impression on me like no other place, and I knew I would have to return. My first visit to Tuva in 1996 had lasted barely 72 hours. But I went back to Yale determined to come back and immerse myself in the language. I would need two years of planning and some crucial training in graduate school, but I resolved to come back prepared, with the tools and time to study Tuvan seriously.

When I asked my dissertation committee in 1997 for permission to spend a year in the field studying Tuvan, they sensibly asked me what I might expect to learn or discover there. At that time, Tuvan was poorly documented and no linguistic recordings were available. The only published grammar of the language was that obscure Soviet one, written in Russian and likely to be incomplete and outdated in terms of the kinds of questions modern linguists ask. A brief handbook of Tuvan written in English was compiled from second- and thirdhand sources by a scholar who had never set eyes on a Tuvan or heard a single word of the language uttered.

Tuva itself was a mystery, having been shut off from much of the world, with foreigners denied visas to travel there during most of the Soviet period. The land had become an object of fascination for Nobel Prize–winning physicist Richard Feynman, who long dreamed of going there. He finally managed to wrest permission from Soviet authorities, but died before he was able to go. The first American to gain access to Tuva, in 1988, was musicologist

Ted Levin, who went on to launch the now famous Tuvan throat singing as a major cultural export from Tuva to the West. While throat singing is the most iconic part of Tuvan culture, I found the character of Tuvans revealed in their deep veneration of the Earth, their unique synthesis of animism and Buddhism, and their rich tradition of myths and stories. I chose to school myself in the language and listen to the stories and songs, while living the local nomadic lifeways as much as I could.

One of my role models was an intrepid Finnish linguist named Matthias Alexander Castrén (1813–1853), who spent his most vibrant years (1845–1849) tramping around Siberia. Covering vast distances under extreme conditions, this intrepid scholar would spend a few weeks here and there with various families and isolated tribes. He had to hunt his own food, build his own campfires, and forage for every calorie he consumed. Despite these hardships, he managed to collect thousands of words and sentences from such languages as Forest Nenets and Karagass—the latter now referred to as Tofa, whose last speakers I would encounter 144 years later. In a prodigious body of scholarship, Castrén stitched these words together into a grand tapestry (and many volumes of notes) that gives us perhaps our earliest and most comprehensive view of the linguistic landscape of Asia's cold left shoulder. Castrén was manic in his work, motivated partly by a desire to show that the Finns, whose language was a linguistic oddity in Europe, were connected to peoples deep in the Siberian hinterlands. These linguistic ties placed the Finns as a branch on a larger and more ancient lineage than their Scandinavian and Slavic neighbors, rooting them more deeply in the Arctic cultural landscape. Castrén's years in Siberia produced "a vast addition to previous knowledge," but at the cost of his own health. He died, his great work unfinished, at age 39.[1]

Following in Castrén's bootprints, I wanted to undertake long-term fieldwork, though given the constraints of family life and graduate school, my time commitment was going to be 12–18 months, not five years! The period that I lived in Tuva during 1998–1999 changed me in ways I could not have imagined, not only from the physical rigors but also through the intense interactions I had with people that led to my own intellectual awakening. I returned realizing that I knew much less than I thought I did, and with a new appreciation for the power of culture as a survival tool. My year in Tuva would change my life, my attitudes, and my values. Intellectually, it would forever alter my view of what language is and why even the smallest languages are worthy of careful study.

My professors were patient with me when I could answer them in only vague and speculative terms about what I expected to find in Siberia. In all honesty, I did not know exactly what I might learn there. Tuvan would have—I expected—wonderful complexity just waiting to be described. I knew it had something called "vowel harmony," an intricate sound pattern that would soon become a near obsession for me. It was reported to have special "pharyngeal" vowels, which upon investigation turned out to be pitch accent (a poor man's tone language—whereas Mandarin Chinese contains four tones, Tuvan had just one or two). And it would turn out to have a wonderfully rich system of reduplication, a process that produces words like "willy-nilly" or "helter-skelter," but in a much more productive and meaningful way than in English. This last phenomenon had not been reported previously in the scientific literature, and so my description of it would be an original contribution.

I proposed to bring back these exotic specimens, like so many captured butterflies, and put them—in my dissertation—under the microscope of modern linguistic theory. My professors advised me that my work would have a longer shelf life if it showcased new, original data collected in the field, and I was eager to collect it. While this might seem like a basic premise for any scientific work, the field of linguistics had in fact strayed very far from this ideal. Many scholars were earning their Ph.D.'s on the basis of work that contained no original data at all—only new theoretical analyses of facts someone else had collected. This is armchair linguistics, work done entirely in a library without ever meeting an actual speaker.

None of my professors at Yale could remember the last time anyone had submitted a dissertation based on actual fieldwork, or an attempt to describe a previously undescribed or unrecorded language. I felt a personal calling, since so many of the world's languages remain virtually undocumented and fieldwork can be such an enriching experience. In the decade since I defended my own dissertation, I've been heartened to see more and more young scholars eagerly heading out around the world to do fieldwork.

Before heading out to live in Siberia, I was a pampered graduate student at Yale. I spent my days browsing the vast neo-Gothic Sterling Memorial Library, among shelves of dusty (and mostly unread) grammars of obscure languages, or reading in cafés, or working out at the gym. I had received the best possible training in theoretical linguistics. I knew how to identify any possible speech sounds that might occur in any language, from sibilants to ejectives to clicks. With a trained ear, I could listen to and transcribe any language, writing it down in the International Phonetic Alphabet. I could deconstruct complex words into morphemes, the smallest meaningful parts. I could draw syntax trees, the invisible structures in the mind that allow speakers to build sentences out of words and phrases. With these basic tools, and with patient speakers to provide me with examples, I would be able to understand and describe the grammar of any language. Grammar resides in the mind and can be inductively understood by asking the right questions of a single speaker, typically while that speaker is sitting in a room, patiently answering the linguist's agenda of questions.

That's the method I was taught, and I believed it. But Tuva would challenge much of my received wisdom.

AMONG THE NOMADS

The radical change in my view of language and grammar all started with the daily migrations of a nomadic family of yak herders, and the Tuvan word for "go."

I went to Tuva in January 1998 burdened with heavy winter clothing, survival gear, tape recorders, and various gadgets, all of which I would leave behind when I departed in 1999. My load would be much lightened, in the physical sense. Spiritually and intellectually, however, I became weighed down with the knowledge and cultural wisdom Tuvans shared with me, and with a deep empathy for the problems they face. Tuvans live as a minority people, poor, persecuted, forgotten, at the margins of a once great empire—Russia—which regards them as backward, inferior social parasites. Yet the Tuvans are possessed of great cultural and spiritual wealth—and this is what may ultimately sustain their unique way of life far into the 21st century. From this store of wealth, disguised beneath a shabby exterior, Tuvans shared generously with me. Though I left Tuva with an empty backpack, my mind was bursting from the intensity and wisdom of their worldview and knowledge both esoteric and practical on a vast range of topics, from the fertility of camels to prayers for worshipping tree spirits.

Elderly women told me their life stories. Shamans chanted to heal me when I fell ill. Buddhist lamas prayed for my safe travel and peace of mind. Simple country folk made offerings to the local spirits on my behalf and brought me to bathe in the waters of springs they revere as sacred and healing. Young men patiently kept me in the saddle as I inexpertly attempted to ride along with the horse herds. Old men called me son while they carefully taught me the delicate procedures of slaughtering a goat and carving up its carcass. Old ladies (far stronger of arm than I) showed me how to grind grain on a hand-operated grindstone, churn butter by hand, and distill milk into *araga*—fermented milk alcohol much prized by the nomads. At their winter camp, high in the mountains overlooking the Mongolian border, two young boys, age five or six, became my tutors in the intricacies of Tuvan grammar—gleefully shouting out the names of every object I pointed at and giggling at my tongue-twisted attempts to repeat their words correctly.

Hunters taught me to recognize animal calls and to find the right kind of kindling (the papery inner bark of a birch) to make a survival campfire in the winter forest. In the far west of Tuva, in the Black Lake district, two young brothers dove into shallow, rocky, and unbelievably cold and swift mountain streams with me. Later, we warmed in the sun on the riverbank and drank araga to warm our insides. Its intoxicating effects filled my head with the swirling burble of the water and put me into a kind of trance.

Everywhere I went in Tuva, I was treated as a brother and a son. Amazingly, the Tuvans who hosted me never expected anything in return but my smile, my interest, my efforts to speak and understand the Tuvan language, and my solemn promise to tell people outside of Russia that they exist and are well.

On my arrival in Tuva in 1998, I once again faced the same polite insistence that I was a spy and met lots people who wanted to speak to me only in Russian. So I fled Kyzyl as soon as I could to immerse myself in the language and culture in the countryside. Flying in a decrepit single-engine plane, I reached the remotest corner of Tuva, a place where few people spoke Russian. In my pocket, I carried a letter of introduction addressed to country cousins of my Kyzyl friends. They could never have dreamed an American linguist would be dropped at their doorstep. Yet they reacted with aplomb, offering me, in true Tuvan style, tea before questions.

After five days knocking about the hardscrabble town of Mugur-Aksy befriending locals, I tired of being shadowed by the local police (convinced I was a spy, they began to openly harass my village host family). On the sixth day, I finally met the head of my nomadic host family and seized the opportunity to leave town for the countryside. Eres (meaning "brave") Mongush, a weather-beaten, reticent herder wearing a black sheepskin hat, had ridden into town briefly on errands. With no ceremony and almost no introduction, I set off following Eres on foot for the two-hour walk back to his campsite. The landscape was severe, nubs of brown grass buffeted by tiny pellets of ice, with a crackle in the air. Eres was not a talkative soul, and he stopped just twice to point out sacred spots to me, where we placed stones on an *ovaa* (sacred cairn).

We arrived at the Mongush family campsite, a high, flat, and somewhat sheltered spot with two yurts and a large enclosed stockade. Eres's wife Aylana served tea, but was shy and avoided eye contact with me, while the two six-year-old boys, cousins Marat and Murat, were curiosity personified. Red-cheeked, laughing, and dripping snot from their noses, they had boundless energy. In Tuvan, it is not proper to say that children are beautiful, for fear that the praise will attract malicious spirits who may cause them harm. Children are instead praised by calling them "choo-DECK," meaning "ugly"! The ugly boys bounded gleefully after me wherever I went, even to the toilet (any convenient spot out of sight of the yurt). They tirelessly answered my every question of "What do you call this?" and "What is that?" as if playing a game.

The family's 50 head of yaks, two horses, two dogs, and 200 sheep and goats lived within spitting distance of the yurt, constantly making their presence known through smell and sound. The dogs barked at me, the sheep fled, and the skittish yaks were perturbed by my presence as they licked their salt blocks.

There's nothing romantic about the herding life: it is a relentless struggle. The harsh conditions age people well beyond their years. Eres was only 33, but to me he looked 45. Their daily routine was unvarying. Up at six to stoke the fire, then out to the stockade to let out the yaks and sheep. After morning tea, Eres saddled his horse to drive the herds out to pasture, and he would be gone for at least four hours. Aylana began baking flatbread and sometimes a stew for the main meal, eaten around four o'clock. Marat and Murat helped mind the lambs, collect manure, and fetch water, but had plenty of play time. The grandparents, Aylana's elderly mother and father, lived in an adjacent yurt and helped out with everything, from herding to milking. Nomads enjoy neither vacations nor retirement.

The Mongush family indulged my naive desire to help out by assigning me simple tasks I could not flub. Under Aylana's watchful eye, I was given the task of collecting frozen yak manure patties. On my back, I wore a square wicker basket, and I had a special forked stick. Stacking the collected patties into orderly piles about eight feet high, I would bring them into the house in small batches and chuck them into the stove. Yurts heat up fast when manure is burned, then cool quickly due to the large smoke hole in the roof. I fell into a rhythm: two manure patties on the stove translated into ten minutes of heat, so I would seize the moment to remove my gloves, write notes on what I was hearing, and sip tea.

Dung is precious, and so Eres and his family had words for describing it at various stages. *Miyak* is what plops out steaming onto the ground. After being mashed, dried, flipped, collected, and stacked (special words exist for each of these activities), miyak becomes *argazin*. To the outsider's eye, this is exactly the same substance (manure), except dry. But to Tuvans, it has been magically transformed from something unclean, smelly, and belonging outdoors to something sanitary, safe to handle, and good for boiling tea. Each stage in the metamorphosis of shit, from drying to stacking to kindling, is named and well described in the language. As I jotted down the "shizzle lexicon" in my notebook, the flaming manure warmed my fingertips, the smell permeated my clothing, and I felt closer to nature than I had ever wanted to be. The fire flared when someone came in with a gust of air, the yurt chilled again, and my manure routine would begin anew.

Over the following days, my duties expanded, though goat-herding proved far more challenging. I worked hard to perfect the art of strategic stone-throwing needed to keep goats moving compactly in one direction. Tuvans make special sounds to different animals to induce different mental states and make them compliant. In fact, they have an entire psychology of the domesticate mind—a special repertoire of songs sung to camels when they will not nurse their young, to yaks when calving, to sheep when shearing, and so on. Their animal domestication songs, plaintive and tuneful, combine a stylized mimicry of the animal's own vocalizations with a kind of coded command. Oddly, the animals seem to obey, falling into a kind of trance or pacified state as the song carries on the wind. I was able to learn the songs easily, because they had no meaningful words, only vocables, meaningless syllables that followed a different tune for each animal. For sheep, *tot-pa tot-pa tot-pa;* for goats, *che-che-che-che;* for mares, *huree-sal-sal-sal-huree;* and for the skittish yaks, *hoar-hoar-hoar-hoar* (more on this in chapter 8).

Every evening, the Mongush family and I would huddle around the back of the stove for salty tea and pieces of dried mutton. Some days we'd share a baked flatbread. I usually managed to scrounge up a few pieces of candy for the boys, though my gift of a menthol cough drop sent them sputtering and teary-eyed out of the yurt, unused to the pungent flavor.

I already knew that my hosts were reticent and spoke very little, but on the second night, when the grandparents appeared from the neighboring yurt, an animated conversation broke out between them and Aylana. Trouble was, it was entirely in a sign language. Aylana's mother was Deaf, and the family used a system of what linguists call "home sign": a repertoire of meaningful gestures that allow a family to carry on a simple conversation. Home sign is an early step on the way to developing a full sign language, but the full form arises only if children learn it as their first language.

They seemed to have a repertoire of several dozen signs, if not more, and these were often combined into longer strings of five or six gestures. Seeking a way to understand, I watched the two boys to see what they signed. Their sign utterances were simple and short: TEA (a bowl shape with both hands), AXE (chopping one flat hand across the opposite wrist), YURT (one palm held flat, facing upward, while the other hand formed a curved cuplike shape upside-down above it), and GO (pointing a finger in one direction). Marat and Murat also made sentences, but the largest ones had just two elements: GO HOME, BRING AXE, GIVE TEA. The children's simplicity at the sentence level meant that the Tuvan home sign was not yet a full-fledged language.

The mother and daughter had more signs, and they carried on lengthy conversations, seeming to discuss persons, places, and events removed in time and space. Whether they also had signs for abstract concepts—love, uncertainty, forgetfulness—I did not discover. I was never able to crack the code, fixated as I was on learning spoken Tuvan. I did verify later, from Deaf Tuvans, that a native sign language exists, in scattered locations where there are small numbers of Deaf Tuvans. But it is not taught in any school, and Deaf Tuvans are instead schooled in Russian Sign Language. Tuvan sign and home sign are surely among the world's uncounted and undocumented indigenous sign languages, meriting urgent study. I should point out that many traditional cultures also use hand signs not because of deafness, but to communicate in special circumstances to express things that should not be spoken.

DISCOVERING WORDS

My daily sessions spent huddled by the fire, interspersed with forays outdoors to perform chores, began to yield a small treasure trove of new words in my notebook. The first verb I learned among Tuvan yak herders was "fetch water." The noun for water is *soog,* and *soog-la* is a command, "Fetch water!" Linguists call it a "denominal," a verb built from a noun, "water," plus a simple suffix, -la, that says, "Now I'm a verb." But although -la was an easy suffix to memorize, it turned out to have multiple possible meanings. When attached to *shay,* the word for tea, it did not mean "Fetch tea," but rather "Drink tea." And when attached to *hem,* meaning "river," it did not mean to fetch or drink a river, but rather to travel along or across a river. When attached to *Moskva,* the capital of Russia, it meant to travel via Moscow.

Not only was the -la suffix variable in its meaning, but it also had a chameleon-like quality of constantly changing its pronunciation under the influence of the sounds that surrounded it. This process, called "allomorphy" by linguists, is one of the fundamental mechanisms of grammar we expect to find in all kinds of languages, even English. In Tuvan, verbs look like this:

soog-LA	fetch water
hem-NE	travel along or across a river
moskva-LA	travel via Moscow
is-TE	follow the tracks of an animal

Upon collecting many examples, I found that this chameleon morpheme had a total of *eight* completely different manifestations:

-la, -le, -na, -ne, -ta, -te, -da, and *-de.* The first consonant changed under the influence of the sound that immediately preceded it. The vowel of the suffix was always *a* or *e*, obeying vowel harmony, a topic I will discuss later.

For scientists, these chameleon morphemes present a learnability puzzle. Children learning the language are not observed making mistakes about which form to use. They also manage to figure out, with no explicit instruction, that all eight of these variants are in fact the same entity. Other chameleon morphemes in Tuvan, I would learn, have as many as 16 forms. How children master such complexity, while making few or no errors, is one of the unsolved mysteries of linguistics. Rival theories posit different possibilities, yet the brain remains sufficiently mysterious that we do not know how it accomplishes this task at the age of five or six.

Languages are so much more than just words—they are seedbeds for poetry, semantic networks of possibility. But words are the most graspable entities, and the ones we most commonly think of as making up languages. And so I began by collecting words. This process led to many funny misunderstandings along the way. Once I was pointing to a tree but my speaker gave me the word for "finger," thinking that's what I wanted. And there's the famous problem of segmentation: Tuvan, like many languages, does not divide the arm and the hand into separate entities, so I might think I was getting the word for hand, but actually it meant the arm and hand together. Conversely, many languages have finer distinctions than English. For example, they might have a single word that means "left hand" and another word that means "right hand," but no word that simply means "hand" (since any given hand is always left or right). Days or weeks later, or even never, the linguist may realize what he had written down in his notebook as simply "hand" meant precisely "left hand."

At Swarthmore College, I teach a course called "Field Methods," where we sit down with a speaker of a language that no one in the class, including me, has any knowledge of. The goal is to discover as much as possible of the grammar of the language by asking the right kinds of questions. Though I try to replicate a real field environment, the process is much easier and more efficient in a classroom, with a speaker who knows English. My students and I fill up many pages of notebooks, write examples on the blackboard, and morpheme by morpheme build up a descriptive grammar.

In a real field setting, the challenges are multiplied many times over. No one speaks English, curious neighbors come by to help, dogs bark, chickens cluck, and the whole village gathers around to hear and laugh at the foreigner mispronouncing the language.

Extracting the grammar of a language is like solving a multidimensional jigsaw puzzle, of which some of the pieces may be missing and others you have to carve as you go along. Native speakers of any language can almost never explain *why* something sounds the way it does or is said the way it is. They rely on what we call intuition, or "grammaticality judgment." They just know what sounds right and what doesn't, without knowing why. Grammar is what cognitive scientists call *tacit* knowledge: you know it, but you don't know that you know it and you can't really articulate it. The kinds of so-called English grammar rules we are taught in school ("Never end a sentence with a preposition") are, quite simply, boring and not to be put up with. (The preceding sentence ending with a preposition is fully grammatical.) Such dicta are not grammar, the stuff of deeper thought, but merely style, the artifice of writing.

So how do you plumb the depths of a speaker's mind to retrieve the grammar of Tuvan, Igbo, Inuit, or Sora? And once you've "discovered" the grammar, what use is it to anyone?

In the field, we often start with body parts: ear, eye, nose, hand (oops, right hand). Things you can easily point to. But when you are living in a village, in a local environment, it very quickly becomes apparent why you can never figure out the whole grammar sitting in a classroom. Grammars are diffuse: they grow in gardens, flow along rivers, and float on air. One of the most fascinating sentences I ever collected in the nearly extinct Chulym language was "Worms have eaten our cabbage." Though it was an entirely novel sentence, I understood it immediately. "Worms" was a totally new word to me, "eaten" was familiar, and "cabbage" was recognizable as a loanword from Russian. Never in a hundred hours of classroom work would I have asked for or heard such a sentence. It emerged spontaneously during a walk through the vegetable patch with last speaker Anna Baydasheva, as she thrust a worm-eaten cabbage under my nose for inspection.

Living with the Mongush family in Tuva, I collected such wonderful (and unasked-for) sentences as "The yaks pooped a lot yesterday—go and collect it," or "The crooked-horned yak is licking salt." In rural villages where I conduct much of my fieldwork, I always enjoy doing a photo-shoot walk. I may take a hundred images of local objects—cat, broom, canoe, locust, pebble—and play these on my laptop as a slide show. Each image elicits names for local, culturally relevant objects, as well as the stories behind them. A round pebble I picked up in the forest was not merely a pebble but an omen of good luck from the local spirits. A tiny purple flower was the sign for the sixth lunar month. Two-day-old dried yak poop had a different name than fresh poop.

I began to think of language as existing not only in the head, or perhaps not entirely in the heads of speakers, but in local landscapes, objects, and lifeways. Languages animate objects by giving them names, making them noticeable when we might not otherwise be aware of them. Tuvan has a word *iy* (pronounced like the letter *e*), which indicates the short side of a hill. I had never noticed that hills had a short side. But once I learned the word, I began to study the contours of hills, trying to identify the iy. It turns out that hills are asymmetrical, never perfectly conical, and indeed one of their sides tends to be steeper and shorter than the others. If you are riding a horse, carrying firewood, or herding goats on foot, this is a highly salient concept. You never want to mount a hill from the iy side, as it takes more energy to ascend, and an iy descent is more treacherous, as well. Once you know about the iy, you see it in every hill and identify it automatically, directing your horse, sheep, or footsteps accordingly. This is a perfect example of how language adapts to local environment, by packaging knowledge into ecologically relevant bits. Once you know that there *is* an iy, you don't really have to be told to notice it or to avoid it. You just do. The language has taught you useful information in a covert fashion, without explicit instruction.

Fieldwork is a constant string of "Oh my gosh, they actually have a word for that" moments. Standing on a high ridge in the Altai Mountains, my host Eres pointed down to the valley below, in which I could see numerous perfectly round circles etched into the brown landscape. UFO landings? Crop circles? No, these brown, round depressions, called *honash,* are the footprints of yurts that had been moved when families migrated. They may remain for several seasons or even years. Tuvans feel a great sentiment toward them, even extolling them in song. If they return to the same campsite, they never construct the yurt directly on an old honash, but impress a new one beside it.

So, language's proliferation doesn't stop with just having a word for something. Once in the lexicon, the "mental dictionary," a named concept takes on a life of its own. It contributes to organizing thought and perception. We have no idea how deep this effect goes. If it goes deeper than we suspect, these unique words would render perfect communication among different languages impossible. Each language would remain a singularity of conceptual possibilities. At present, we have no idea how deeply (or shallowly) language may influence thought and perception. But we never will know if we allow most of the world's small tongues to pass into oblivion before they can be studied in their natural habitats.

HOW TO SAY "GO" IN TUVAN

One of the crucial parts of speech to learn in a language, after basic nouns, is a set of common verbs. I thought nothing could be simpler. I had learned to say "water" and "fetch water," since I spent part of every day fetching water. But I also wanted to learn to say simply "go." Yet every time I moved, pantomimed, or pointed to indicate "go," I seemed to elicit a different word. It turned out that learning to say "go" in Tuvan is much more complex than I'd imagined. It requires not only an internal compass but also an acute awareness of the local landscape, even parts of it that may not be visible.

How does one acquire landscape awareness? Nomads are connoisseurs of geographic gossip, which they pass on in casual conversation, songs, stories, and their choice of "go" verbs. They talk frequently about where they have been, where the yaks are roaming, and where the neighbors are. I was amazed to find that my hosts always seemed to know the exact locations of migrating friends and relatives many miles distant.

With tools no more advanced than horses, binoculars, and gossip, the nomads in the community where I stayed managed to keep track of dozens of families, herd movements, and migration schedules. People would answer me with absolute confidence anytime I inquired as to the location or migration date of almost any member of the community. By daily observations

A young Tuvan in his familiar landscape, western Mongolia.

through binoculars, talking about landscapes, and distributing bits of knowledge across domains (religious, aesthetic, acoustic), they kept track of a complex and dynamic system of multiple moving parts.

Tuvans live in a land where level spaces are unusual. Nearly every patch of ground slopes in one direction or another. This provides a framework for orientation—the directions of watersheds and river currents. Though Tuvan does have a general word for go, it is less often used. Most of the time, Tuvans use, as appropriate, verbs meaning "go upstream" *(còkta),* "go downstream" *(bàt),* or "go cross-stream" *(kes).* You'd rarely hear, "I'm going to Mugur-Aksy" (the nearest town to the Mongush family camp), but rather, "I'm upstreaming [or downstreaming] to Mugur-Aksy." Being a visitor rather than a lifelong resident, I was clueless as to what rivers were nearby and in which directions they flowed, so I could never confidently select the correct "go" verb. The Mongushes, on the other hand, could not explain to me the invisible orientation framework that was all around them and underfoot. No one ever said to me, "To say 'go,' you must locate the nearest river, ascertain its direction of flow, then locate your path relative to the current." They simply knew all this information without knowing that they did.

River-based systems are strictly local, leading to confusion. In one village, I got completely conflicting directions from two local ladies. One said (pointing due west), "Go upstream a bit more." Farther along, another lady pointed west again, but told me to go downstream. I realized later that each was referring to a different river as her point of orientation. The Yenisei River, located several miles north of the village over a mountain ridge, was well known to all and served as a general axis of orientation. A much smaller stream, the Khüüls, flowed eastward just south of the village, and could also be used, depending on which way the speaker was facing. My ignorance lay in not knowing the local river systems and (even if I had known them) failing to pick up subtle cues about which river system was being referenced.

Locally embedded systems like Tuvan river-flow orientation may be found in many cultures, where the local landscape takes priority over the more abstract cardinal directions. Such languages force their speakers to specify at all times whether they are moving up, down, or across relative to a stream, mountain, wind, or some other frame of orientation. In order to speak correctly, one must attend to the lay of the land.

For the Mongush family, with their seasonal migrations among the mountain passes in unending pursuit of greener pastures, nothing was more pertinent to their survival than the local landscape. They were finely attuned to notice the tiniest details. In their world, but also in ours, landscapes permeate daily life. Landscapes are sculpted by humans, not just in the obvious physical ways—for example, by building roads or leveling hills—but also in cultural ways. What people pay attention to or name in the landscape may be deeply influenced by the language they speak. This holds especially true for small, indigenous cultures, well adapted by cultural habits to surviving in a particular place. Languages, too, adapt and equip their speakers with tools to describe, divide, and manage the local environment and its resources. Nor is this dynamic limited to small or indigenous cultures. If one Manhattanite says, "I'm cabbing it uptown," another Manhattanite will understand perfectly, but outsiders may need a second to process the use of "cab" as a verb and to figure out what exactly "uptown" refers to.

Living with Tuvans, I learned that languages thus come to reflect local geography, not only in their vocabulary but also in more deeply structural ways, in their grammar. This knowledge is often accumulated over many centuries, and so geographic terms can represent an ancient layer of cultural knowledge encoded in language. Grammar can be "embedded" in the local landscape, and in fact cannot be understood or described in isolation from it. This finding, and similar ones by other scientists, has contributed to an emerging area of study known as "ethnosyntax." This formulation goes against the traditional wisdom in linguistics, within the Chomskyan paradigm, by claiming that knowledge of grammar is not contained solely in mental structures—that is, rules in the mind—but also spills out to encompass the local landscape and cultural habits.

In Ket, a nearly extinct language of Siberia that is a distant relative of Native American languages spoken in Alaska, the verb "to stand" is said in four different ways, depending on what is standing:

dúghìn	for a human or animal (as in *keh't dúghìn,* "a person stands")
dúghàta	for a tree (as in *ohks dúghàta,* "a tree stands")
úyba'ut	for an object (as in *u'y úyba'ut,* "a cradle stands")
hávìta	for a structure (as in *qu's hávìta,* "a tent stands")

52

If this expansive view of grammar is true, then you cannot fully explore a language by simply sitting down with a speaker in a room and asking him questions, as is the current practice in linguistics courses. When I was co-authoring a Tuvan dictionary, I grappled with the problem of what information to include under the entry for "go." To give an accurate and complete definition, I would have had to include not only the descriptions given above, but the very landscapes themselves. Similarly, as the following section describes, languages may lack what we think of as basic terms for colors, and instead have a complex system that describes the colors and patterns of animals. All these ways of encoding local knowledge in language are useful cultural adaptations, and they reveal a uniquely Tuvan worldview.

WHAT COLOR IS YOUR YAK?

One thing I learned about yaks is that they are incredibly skittish animals. They dislike strangers, noises, and camera flashes. The Mongush family's yaks did not allow anyone other than their master, Eres, to approach them. Yet once a day the entire herd, the cows and calves following their leader, an imposing shaggy bull, ambled downhill to the stockade. Here the lactating mothers were tied up and milked, while their mewling calves waited eagerly to suck the leftovers. Leaning on the split-rail fence of the stockade, I spent many hours observing and conversing about yaks. My take-home lesson? Every yak has its own color, and color (like other characteristics such as pattern, horn shape, or personality) provides a system of powerful descriptive detail.

The nomadic Tuvan yak herders have a complex hierarchal system for classifying yaks by the following traits in ascending order of importance: (1) fur color, (2) body pattern, (3) head marking, and (4) individual personality. They use different classifications for horses, goats, sheep, and cows. Mastering the system of yak-naming allows a herder to efficiently pick out or refer to a specific yak from a herd of hundreds. The color-and-pattern naming system is a strict hierarchy, determined by cultural preferences (which yak, horse, or cow colors and patterns Tuvans regard as more desirable, beautiful, or rare). If an animal possesses one or more special traits, you may omit mention of the less special ones, but if an animal has only a common trait, such as fur color (which all animals possess), you must mention it. If a horse or yak possesses one of several recognized body patterns—for example, star-spotted—then it will simply be called by that pattern, and its color need not be mentioned. A horse or yak possessing the highest trait, a spot on the forehead, will be named by that characteristic alone. If two animals each possess a foreheard spot, they will be differentiated by naming the spot plus the next trait down the hierarchy, for example "forehead spot brown stripe." Learning extra labels for animals imposes a slight burden on memory, but as an information-packaging technology, it affords Tuvans great efficiency in breeding and herding.

By spending many hours with Tuvan children, I observed that they do not seem to learn words for colors as abstracts labels for qualia (e.g., colors). Rather, what they learn are a set of concrete labels that subsume both color *and* pattern of specific types of animals. By learning a set of labels and their proper use, the speaker also acquires (with little or no effort) a hierarchal classification scheme. Tuvan children learn their color terms as they learn to distinguish (and herd) domestic animals. This provides an example of how categories we may think of as abstract and universal, like color, are in fact culturally filtered and locally contingent.

Tuvan nomads seem to prize certain colors and patterns for horses, yaks, and goats. Not merely aesthetic, this preference reveals an even deeper knowledge system. As experienced breeders, Tuvans have for centuries practiced genetic modification by selecting and manipulating preferred outward traits. They do so not by understanding the DNA (which is to them invisible and unknown), but by observing how external traits interact and combine. Knowing which are recessive and which dominant, they maximize desired traits by controlling breeding among animals. For example, for a good chance of getting a calf with the highly prized star-spotted pattern, you should mate a solid-colored bull yak with a spotted yak cow.

Gregor Mendel (1822–1884), the father of genetic sciences, experimented with cross-pollination of pea plants and discovered which traits would be passed on, and which of those traits would be dominant or recessive in a particular combination.[2] Mendel did all this without actually seeing or understanding genes themselves. Humans have been practicing folk genetic engineering as long as they have domesticated plants and animals. Tuvans, like most animal-breeding cultures, have not had the luxury of setting their genetic knowledge down in books. Instead, they recruit language—and powerful folk taxonomies like the color/pattern hierarchy—to encode, store, and transmit this knowledge.[3]

Folk taxonomies encapsulate generations of subtle and sophisticated observations about how the pieces of the animal and plant kingdoms fit together, and how they relate to each other and to humans. They differ in which outward traits they use to classify organisms, almost always choosing combinations of multiple traits over single ones. Traits may include appearance, behavior, habitat, impact on humans, or some combination of these. The selection is limited only by the standard of usefulness. Folk taxonomies enable human survival. They arise from humans' keen ability to notice and correlate multiple characteristics and interacting patterns, and put this information to practical use. They typically contain a great deal of hidden, or implicit, information, as well as explicit facts about the plant and animal kingdoms.

Such knowledge is fragile, however, and may be lost in transmission. This is particularly true for cultures without writing, which must take great care to pass on their traditional wisdom. A single word may reflect generations of careful observation of the natural world.

Looking up at this edifice of knowledge, I traced my own intellectual path across the landscape. The academic study of linguistics thrilled me, to be sure, and I reveled in piecing together the multidimensional jigsaw puzzle that is the grammar of a language. But in my studies, I had encountered all this knowledge on paper. Out among the nomads, I found language to have an entirely new heft, texture, smell, and taste. My time in Tuva awakened me to the larger possibilities. I now saw language not just as a way of speaking or a domain of cognition. It was an entire conceptual universe of thought, compactly and efficiently encoded into words. Largely unmapped, this landscape of languages awaited discovery.

{CHAPTER THREE}

THE POWER OF WORDS

*The struggle between dominated and dominant groups for
the right to survive includes what I have called "the ecology
of language." By that I mean that the preservation of language
is a part of human ecology.*

—Einar Haugen

DÖNGGÜR (doong-GUR) is a powerful word. It means "male
domesticated uncastrated rideable reindeer in its third year and
first mating season, but not ready for mating." It is one of dozens of
words that can be expressed in the Tofa language spoken by Siberian reindeer herders, each providing a precise description of a type
of reindeer. This technology allows herders to identify and describe
with a single word what would otherwise require a complex construction. But the Tofa are giving up their ancestral tongue in favor
of Russian—the dominant national language, which doesn't have a
remote equivalent to the word "dönggür." And the Tofa are just one
of hundreds of small communities whose language is endangered.
Working with such groups, I explore how knowledge is encoded in
language, and what exactly is lost—in terms of descriptive power
and survival technologies—when small languages vanish.

Many linguists, including leading thinkers Noam Chomsky
and Steven Pinker, view language in the technical, cognitive sense

as consisting of basic elements. For example, there are *words* (the lexicon) and then there are *mental rules* for building words or combining them into sentences (the grammar). An English speaker, for example, has in her mental dictionary the word "hat," which is simply an arbitrary string of sounds she has learned to associate with an object one wears on one's head. She also has a rule of morphology that tells her the plural is "hats" and a rule of syntax that says when there's an adjective, put it first—"red hat," not "hat red." And she has certain cognitive structures, not learned but thought to be genetic. The knowledge that nouns and adjectives are different parts of speech and that one modifies the other, for example, allows her to understand that red describes a type of hat, but hat does not describe a type of red. This cognitive view, while not incorrect, bypasses much of the knowledge that language actually contains.

As the examples in the last chapter show, languages abound in "cultural knowledge," which is neither genetic nor explicitly learned, but comes to us in an information package—rich and hierarchical in its structure. Any English-speaking child may know the word "uncle," but what does she store in her head as its meaning? An uncle may be a mother's brother, or a father's sister's husband, or perhaps just her parents' adult male friend. The English-speaking child has no explicit linguistic information to indicate these distinct positions in the kinship tree. Why not? We could speculate that since it was not culturally crucial to distinguish these positions, the language did not do so. While our mind readily grasps the various types of uncle, English provides no ready-made, unique labels to distinguish them. Conversely, in cultures like Tofa, with more socially important kinship relations, there exists no general word for uncle. Five different types of uncles would have five completely different labels. By learning these labels, the child implicitly learns that these are distinct kinship roles.

Kinship systems are just the tip of the iceberg. By simply know-ing the word "dönggür," the young Tofa reindeer herder has, at the tip of his tongue, a tool to identify among the herd a specific set of reindeer. Tofa reindeer herders who have switched to speaking Russian can still talk about and herd reindeer, but they lack the labels to do so efficiently. Knowledge their ancestors accumulated over centuries, knowledge that is specifically adapted to the nar-row ecological niche of reindeer herding in south Siberian moun-tain forests, has essentially been lost.

At some deeper level, human cognition may be the same no matter what tongue one speaks. But languages package knowledge in radically different ways, facilitating certain means of conceptu-alizing, naming, and discussing the world. In the case of a young Tofa reindeer herder who no longer speaks his ancestral tongue, the human knowledge base—as manifested in specific ways of describing the world of reindeer—has been impoverished. Arcane bits of knowledge vanish under the pressures of globalization.

Does this matter? While this may seem like a minor loss in the face of modernity and progress, we cannot even fathom what the long-term effects will be. Klaus Toepfer, former executive direc-tor of the United Nations Environment Program (1998–2006), warns: "Indigenous peoples not only have a right to preserve their way of life. But they also hold vital knowledge of the animals and plants with which they live. Enshrined in their cultures and cus-toms are also secrets of how to manage habitats and the land in environmentally friendly, sustainable ways."[1]

We don't really have a grip on how much or what kind of knowledge is out there, uncataloged and unrecorded, existing only in memory. Much of this knowledge concerns animal and plant species, many still undocumented by modern science. The sobering fact that both animal species and human languages are going extinct in tandem portends an impending loss of human knowledge on a scale not seen before. If we hold any hope of understanding and fostering ecodiversity on Earth, we must value vanishing knowledge while it still exists.

WHERE IS A LANGUAGE?

According to the classical theory that is taught in most linguistics classes today, under the influence of Noam Chomsky and his followers, grammar is an invisible set of rules in the mind for combining sounds into words and words into sentences. Yet my struggles to decode spoken Tuvan convinced me that it contains much more than that.

Of course, languages *are* made up of invisible rules in the head, and some of these are likely genetically determined and dictated by the structure of the brain. This brilliant insight by Chomsky— that language cannot be learned by trial and error or by mere learning and observation alone, but rather is part of our DNA— caused a fundamental shift in how linguists viewed language, as important as the Copernican revolution for astronomy.

But it does not the tell whole story, and there are several important gaps to fill. The first gap is *descriptive*—we still lack even a basic scientific description of the vast majority of the world's languages. Many anomalies out there will surprise us once we do notice them, and they will cause us to revise basic assumptions. For example, Urarina, a language spoken by fewer than 3,000 people in the Amazon jungle of Peru, has an unusual way of constructing sentences. An Urarina sentence containing these three elements in the following order:

Kinkajou's bag + steal + spider monkey

is understood to mean, "The spider monkey steals the kinkajou's bag." Urarina places the direct object first, the verb second, and the subject last.[2] Other word-order patterns are much more common. English uses subject-verb-object (SVO), but this is not the only possibility. Turkish and German put the verb last, using subject-object-verb (SOV) order. Welsh, on the other hand, is VSO, putting the verb first, subject second, and object last (read + I + book = "I read the book"). The Urarina OVS word order is vanishingly rare among the world's languages. If not for Urarina and a few other Amazonian languages, scientists might hypothesize—falsely—that OVS word order was cognitively impossible, that the human brain could not process it. Small languages have many more surprises in store for science. Since each new grammar pattern sheds light on how the brain creates language, the loss of even one language may impact a full understanding of human cognition.

Imagine a zoologist describing mammals by looking only at the top hundred most common ones. It would be easier to examine dogs and cats and cows, all of which are composed as the same building blocks as other mammals. But if we did, we'd never know that a mammal could swim (whales), fly (bats), lay eggs (echidnas), use tools (sea otters and orangutans), or have an inflatable balloon growing from its head (male hooded seals).[3] Ignorance of unusual mammals would impoverish our notion of what mammals can be. It is precisely the weird and wonderful exceptions that afford us a full view of the possibilities.

The second gap in our basic knowledge about languages arises because the invisible mental rules (the grammar)—which have been almost the exclusive focus of study among linguists for decades—by themselves do not generate the whole linguistic system. When Chomsky proclaimed language "a window on the mind," an entire research program for the discipline of linguistics was launched. In the 50 years since, this research has already yielded many important insights into human cognition. With his famous sentence "Colorless green ideas sleep furiously," Chomsky demonstrated how linguists can explore complex structures (sounds, phrases, sentences, etc.) even when there is no meaningful content at all. The lack of meaning does not hinder us in our investigation of pristine mental structures, and we ought to distinguish between the two. This has been the conventional wisdom in linguistics for decades.

But although languages certainly contain abstract structures, they evolve and exist to convey information, and that function permeates and influences every level of language. To its critics, including this author, the Chomskyan program has been unduly narrow, overly focused on large global languages, and preoccupied with structure at the expense of content. Linguists' preoccupation with these abstract structures (collectively termed "grammar") has led to a microscopic approach that treats languages like laboratory specimens, utterly divorced from their natural environments, the people who speak them, and the content of those people's thoughts. Like the Tuvan ways of saying "go," the internal grammar *requires* explicit reference to the external world, and dynamically adapts to it. These words arise in the context of rich feedback loops and interactions among themselves, with other brains, and with the external environment.

What's missing in the Chomskyan view of language as a mechanism in the individual brain is the distributed, social nature of language. If only one speaker of a language remains, that language essentially does not exist, because it is missing the fundamental condition: conversation. Grammar is a distributed system of knowledge. Nobody's brain can hold all of English, or Chamacoco, or any other tongue. Language spills out into the world, residing in multiple brains, embedding itself in the local environment, shaped by cultural values and beliefs. It takes on its own mysterious trajectory of change with no one leading it. Such complexities can be thought of as products of emergence, like insect swarming patterns, fireflies flashing in unison, or geese flying in a V-formation, where no rule or leader coordinates the activity, yet a distinct pattern emerges, unplanned. When looking at migrating geese, we may immediately notice the V-formation, since the geese are few in number. But languages are made up of many thousands (in fact an infinite number) of possible forms. Ideally what we would need to collect is every utterance out of the mouth of every speaker, in order to appreciate the full range of possibilities. Of course, that is not possible, but as responsible scientists, we must at least make an effort to encounter as many speakers as possible and to hear as much as they will tell us. That sense of constant discovery is what makes the task of mapping the world's linguistic diversity so exciting. Never knowing what I might hear next keeps pulling me to some of the most remote places on Earth.

MONGOLIA'S HIDDEN PEOPLE

I arrived in Mongolia in the summer of 2000 with high hopes. I was participating in a National Geographic–sponsored expedition led by musicologist Ted Levin, and as our expedition moved farther west from Ulaanbaatar, we left the Mongolian-language area of dominance and approached places where some of Mongolia's tiny and endangered minority languages were spoken. I looked eagerly for small signs of cultural difference: the style of the cloth coverings on the yurts, the brands on horses' flanks. Ted had invited me along on the expedition because I would be able to communicate with one of the smallest minority peoples we expected to encounter—in their own language.

After five or six days of driving along the dusty tracks in Land Rovers, at last we reached what was reported to be the territory of the Monchak people, a tiny minority of 1,200 in the western part of the country. The Monchak are not even officially recognized as one of Mongolia's minority people; they are so few as to escape official notice almost entirely. To find them, I had our impatient city guides make multiple stops at encampments along the way, where we asked the residents, "Where can we find the Monchak people?" Of course, the Monchak were migratory, like everyone else, but locals knew their movements, and eventually we arrived at an impoverished encampment with a straw stockade, a few dozen goats, and four cows.

This would be my home for the next week. I bade farewell to our caravan of Land Rovers and our city drivers with their bad manners, and I settled into the hospitable embrace of a local family, consisting of a 33-year-old man, Nedmit; his wife Nyaama; and their 12-year-old son, "Brave," and 10-year-old daughter, "Golden New Year." I knew I needed to spend time alone with a local family in order to build the kind of trust and communication that would lead to a deeper understanding of the language. As much as I appreciated the efficiency of our caravan and the ability to cook our own food, I also needed to experience daily life with the local people.

Hardly anyplace could be considered more completely off the grid than the far west provinces of Mongolia, or a people more steadily grounded in ancient lifeways than these nomads. Yes, they are aware of the outside world. Some of them have traveled to cities and seen airplanes and computers and cell phones. But they have many reasons for preferring their own traditional way of life, and strong feelings about the security and comfort they find in basing their living on yaks, sheep, and camels in the high mountain passes.

The first way Nedmit's family made me feel welcome was to slaughter a sheep. Few events in the life of the Monchak are so highly ritualized, so full of protocol and traditional meaning, as the slaughter of a goat or sheep. The entire life of the nomads is

Nedmit demonstrates for me how to make a horse hobble.

centered around the welfare of the sheep. It may seem odd to a western mind that people who cuddle a tiny lamb next to the stove in February can dispassionately slaughter the mother of that same lamb in September. Yet the killing of sheep is done with care, with honor, and with feeling. The sheep is the livelihood of the people. It dies to sustain them, and the Monchak show in their ritual of slaughter how they value and respect that sacrifice as they do life itself.

Nedmit performed the slaughter with a quiet intensity. No one joked, sang, or talked loudly during it. After all, this was a sheep they had raised by hand and cared for since birth and even bestowed a pet name upon. Preparations included filling a bucket with fresh water and sharpening a knife against stone, a rasping that sent the family dogs into a state of agitated expectation. The sheep seemed to know something was afoot as well, and they bolted into the security of their fenced enclosure.

One of the fatter sheep suddenly found itself detained, its hind leg grasped firmly and pulled upward. In vain, it dug in its other three legs to resist being pulled backward out of the pen. A clean spot on the ground was chosen, as usual quite close to the door of the yurt in order to be close to the stove.

Nedmit then flopped the sheep onto its back and bound its front legs with a short cord. He held a back leg under his left knee and had his son hold the head down by its horns. An experienced man can do the entire job solo, but teaching the skill to his son (for sheep can be slaughtered only by men among the Monchak) was part of the routine.

Parting the sheep's wool just to the left of the breastbone, Nedmit made a careful four-inch vertical incision through the hide, exposing the inner lining of fat that contains the internal organs. The whitish-pink fat bulged out slightly through the incision, but no blood spilled out. The sheep lay still, making no sound. Nedmit formed his right hand into a point by pressing the tips of his five fingers together and drove this point, spearlike, deep into the sheep's abdomen, not through the middle, but down along the inside of the rib cage to the spine, where he felt out the main artery with his forefinger and plucked it once, severing it. He removed his hand slowly, again taking care not to spill a single drop of blood. The sheep passed into a coma within seconds. Being both Buddhists and animists, the Monchak take great care not to inflict unnecessary suffering on any living being, and this was evident in the way they slaughtered the sheep. Before proceeding, they waited for the sheep to expire fully. Within a minute, the sheep's eyelids no longer twitched when Nedmit flicked his finger against them: the definitive sign of death.

The first stage of cutting up the carcass began. The legs were snapped off at the knee joints, making loud, snapping sounds. The legs would not be eaten, but set aside for the sheep's head soup.

Demdi, a Monchak Tuvan, slaughters a sheep in the traditional way.

Nedmit expanded the original incision in four directions, again cutting only the outer hide, not nicking the layer of fat and flesh beneath it and spilling not a drop of blood. He then stripped the hide back in four directions and weighted it down at the corners with rocks, creating a clean space on which the rest of the carving was performed. The sheep was now shed of its skin, lying belly up and glistening white and fatty. Only a tiny patch of wool remained on the sheep, a piece about three inches wide and eight inches long covering the sternum. The removal of this piece marks an important symbolic moment in the process and is done with the greatest reverence. It must not be touched with the hands. Instead Nedmit leaned carefully over the sheep and grasped the end of the strip of wooly hide with his teeth. He then rocked backward slowly, pulling the strip away from the carcass. Only then could he touch it with his hands, and he handed it carefully to Nyaama, his wife. She would either offer it to the fire or keep it inside the yurt in a neat little pile along with the head and feet until after the sheep was consumed.

Now the second stage of the carving could begin. Nedmit cut into the abdomen, making a larger opening in the center and two smaller slits along the bottom. Into these slits he inserted the ends of the sheep's lower leg stumps—which act as natural springs, stretching the abdominal opening wide so that there is sufficient space to work. With the internal organs fully exposed, a number of strategic cuts were made in a particular order. These allowed the various organs to be removed, again in a particular order and with surgical precision.

I grabbed my field notebook and began asking questions. I wanted to know the name for each internal organ and part, as well as the verbs that described the actions. I scribbled Monchak words in my notebook, learning their terms for liver, kidneys, gallbladder. The latter contains poisonous bile and must not contaminate the meat. It is a taboo object and must be hung up to dry inside the yurt near the ceiling, where it serves to propitiate the spirits. I felt a bit queasy at the smell of fresh sheep guts, but at the same time I was mesmerized by the ritual. By the end, I would collect more than 50 new words in my notebook. At the same time, I felt like an adopted son who had been taught one of the most important activities in Monchak life.

The stomach was carefully lifted out. It was full of rank-smelling half-digested grass, and I recoiled at the stench. A critical moment came when the stomach was severed; at that instant, it had to be handed over to Nyaama, and from then on could only be handled by women. Nyaama and Golden New Year took it to down the riverbank, where they emptied it, turned it inside out, and washed it thoroughly.

Next came the large and small intestines, carefully uncoiled and placed on a specific type of flat rectangular wooden tray.

They too had to be prepared by the women, methodically turned inside out, emptied of the little balls of dung they contained, and washed thoroughly.

The end result, about an hour later, was a large bubbling cauldron of what the Monchak call "hot blood," a stew of all the carefully prepared internal organs. The cleaned stomach became a bag into which blood was poured (it would congeal into a blood pudding). The meat was not eaten yet; it would be hung on the walls to dry and consumed over the next two weeks. The sheep's massive fatty tail, weighing at least five pounds, was the dish that would be consumed first—and it was offered to me, the guest of honor. I was given a knife and sliced off a small wedge of fat to present to each family member, in descending order of age, as protocol demands.

Afterward, as I lay in my sleeping bag in the yurt, my stomach full of sheep organs and fat, I was amazed at how much I had experienced in just one day. I'd been befriended by an entire extended family, participated in a sheep slaughter, helped collect dung for the fire, and helped herd, corral, and milk the goats. Above all, my brain was buzzing with information, new words for dozens of objects that only yesterday I had not known existed—for example, the sheep's bile sac or the chunk of fat on the sheep's tail. I had a new appreciation for the intricacies of naming objects in a culture where knowledge means survival. Collecting words during a sheep slaughter could not have been further from a dry academic discussion of how a grammar is constructed. Yet it revealed a richness and precision about the Monchak way of talking, indeed of how they apprehend the world.

THE LANGUAGE AND THOUGHT DEBATE

My time among the Tuvans, the Tofa, and the Monchak made me realize just how many important concepts they possess that have no exact counterpart in any other language. This reminded me of a long-standing debate among scientists about the relation between language and perceived reality. As biologist Brendon Larson has noted: "There are multiple challenges in examining this linguistic link between ourselves and the natural world because such reflection is akin to a fish reflecting on the water in which it has lived its entire life. We cannot escape language to look at it."[4]

Scientists and philosophers have long speculated: Does the language we speak impose certain categories, pathways of thought, or filters that affect the way we perceive the world? Or is the language we speak irrelevant, exerting no effect upon the way we think? This thesis was classically formulated in the Sapir-Whorf hypothesis, as described by Benjamin Lee Whorf:

> We dissect nature along lines laid down by our native languages. The categories and types we isolate from the world of phenomena we do not find there because they stare every observer in the face; on the contrary the world is presented in a kaleidoscopic flux of impressions which has to be organized by our minds—and this means largely by the linguistic system in our minds.[5]

Taken in its strong form, linguistic determinism effectively means that language determines reality—that it determines what we can think and therefore what we can say.

The strong form of the thesis has been largely discredited, though a weaker form—the theory of linguistic relativity, which holds that language *influences* our experience of reality—has been mostly accepted.[6] Another way to formulate this is that language doesn't tell us what we *can* say, rather it tells us what we *must* say.[7] Instead of thinking of language as a kind of blinder that prevents us from seeing or saying certain things, we can think of it as a magnifying glass that focuses our attention, requiring us to pay attention to certain details. So, for a Tuvan speaker, because he must know the direction of the river current in order to say "go," the language is forcing him to pay attention to river flow and to be aware of it at all times.

Languages may focus or channel our thoughts in particular ways. A speaker of the Carrier language must know the tactile properties of an object in order to say "give." What is being given? Is it small and granular? Fluffy? Mushy? Liquid? Each type of material requires a different verb form for "give." And so speakers must talk about tactile properties of objects. In many small ways, languages focus thought rather than limiting it.

No better example can be found than the controversial subject of how many words the Eskimo have for "snow." A Google search for "Eskimo snow words" yields more than 10,000 hits. Deriding this as an example of bad science run amok has become somewhat of a game among linguists. A leading academic in his book *The Great Eskimo Vocabulary Hoax* stated unequivocally that the Inuit people of Alaska do *not* have many words for snow, and in fact have only about a dozen basic ones. The debunkers rely on this count to show that Inuit snow words are neither prolific nor special. This stance feeds into a more general agenda of asserting that all languages are equal and equally interesting to science.

Proponents of this view became so intent on debunking it that they spawned a new term—"snow clones"—to mock all such statements that "The so-and-so people have *x* number of words for *y.*" Entire Web pages are devoted to listing mock Eskimo snow words that have imaginary meanings like "snow mixed with husky shit" or "snow burger." Even Steven Pinker took up the issue in his book *The Language Instinct,* stating: "Contrary to popular belief, the Eskimos do not have more words for snow than English. They do not have four hundred words for snow, as it has been claimed in print, or two hundred, or one hundred, or forty-eight, or even nine. One dictionary puts the figure at two. Counting generously, experts can come up with about a dozen, but by such standards English would not be far behind, with snow, sleet, slush, blizzard, avalanche, hail, hardpack, powder, flurry, dusting, and a coinage of Boston's WBZ-TV meteorologist Bruce Schwoegler, snizzling."[8]

Sadly, the snow-cloners have missed the point. They have grossly underestimated the number of words by relying on very limited modern accounts and thinking that just because the number was inflated in the past by people who should have known better, the true count must be unimpressively low. As we will see, the number of snow/ice/wind/weather terms in some Arctic languages is impressively vast, rich, and complex. Furthermore, they have missed the forest for the trees, failing to see the importance of how words encode knowledge. Beyond the sheer numbers of words for natural phenomena like snow and ice, these languages demonstrate the complex ways in which words package information efficiently.

The Yupik people have one of the most amazing survival technologies known to mankind, one that has allowed them to thrive in the world's harshest environment, the Arctic, for over 6,000 years. A tiny fraction of their knowledge of snow and ice is beautifully captured in a brilliant book called *Watching Ice and Weather Our Way,* one the snow naysayers should read. As Dr. Igor Krupnik, the Smithsonian Museum of Natural History's Arctic expert, notes in his book *The Earth Is Faster Now:* [9]

> The use of wind directions, . . . allows Yupik observers to collect and pass on information by highly meaningful environmental packages. . . . Hence, it is not the observation itself that makes an impression of Native knowledge being holistic, intuitive, and multifaceted, but rather the whole cultural "package" that is associated with each specific ice and weather term it uses.

Krupnik goes on to show how native knowledge is based on principles quite different from modern meteorological science:

Scientific . . . weather observation . . . is based on following the temperature and pressure curves, and on recording their current trends. Unlike scientific monitoring, the Yupik watch is focused upon specific signs that signal shifts from one phenomenon, condition, or weather and ice regime to a different one that can be defined by a different term.

So what makes a Yupik such a skilled weather forecaster? In Krupnik's view, "The more words (and combinations) one knows, the more precise one's observation and forecast can be." Now that Yupik is shifting and giving way to English, the environmental knowledge and ability to forecast weather are being degraded:

As the use of Yupik words for specific weather patterns of ice and weather by younger people declines and the Yupik terms are replaced by English words, with a different (and often much more simplistic) meaning, the hunter's overall awareness of his environment fades away. That is why the Yupik elders are very proud of, and so keen on passing on to younger people, their extended Native terminology of ice and weather conditions.

Nor does their complexity end with ice. As it turns out, the Yupik also know names for different winds. Chester Noong-wook, a Yupik elder, says: "We have several kinds of winds here in Savoonga. Aywaa (Aywaapik) is a direct north wind from the sea. Nakaghya is a northeasterly wind, it comes from Nome. Kenvaq is a northwesterly wind; this is the old name, and we now call this wind Naayghiinaq ("that from Siberia"). There is also another northerly wind, Quutfaq, that can come from anywhere between northwest and northeast. Asivaq is a direct east wind," and so on.

Besides winds, they have specialized names for many kinds of ocean currents, stars and constellations, and all manner of seasonal phenomena. All this information feeds into a sophisticated weather forecasting ability honed over a lifetime of careful observation. Its profound depth cannot be compared to what American snowboarders know about snow, not even in the slightest. And it should be of deep and urgent interest to all branches of science, not only linguistics but also biology, climatology, anthropology, and others. We are losing one of the finest, most sensitive systems ever devised to detect weather patterns and climate change. And the system can survive only in its original form, in the heads of local Yupik experts who apply it to local conditions.

Is it science? Is it systematic, falsifiable, and reliable in the way we expect the scientific method to be? Or is it just haphazard, unreliable cultural intuition that we can replace with our better science? I'll give Dr. Krupnik, the Smithsonian's Arctic expert, the last word:

> Native observers . . . have their own ways of memorizing and documenting such events. They look for certain and, often, very specific indicators that are meaningful to them, both culturally and individually. To a scientific observer, the resulting story may seem "intuitive" and even eclectic, but it is no less solid, since it is based on the very same practical indicators followed over many years. . . . Despite a popular perception that Native knowledge is generally intuitive and holistic, Yupik ice and weather watch is not scanning for every environmental signal possible. It is very well organized around a few key factors—such as wind, current or ice movement—and it focuses first and foremost upon

conditions for maritime hunting and the related behavior of critical game species. Therefore, Native experts usually have a very coherent—one may say, "fully scientific"— vision of the annual sequence of weather and ice regimes, the migration patterns of major maritime animals, and how these two cycles are related.[10]

To sum up, the Yupik elders are the premier Arctic observers and experts, and they possess a knowledge that is scientific in its attention to detail and ability to remember patterns, and a language that has encoded all this knowledge in complex ways in hundreds of specialized and highly descriptive words. The snow debunkers should observe the uses of these words in their native context, relying on the accounts of the Yupik elders, before blithely claiming that there is no such thing as complex snow and ice terminology, and that even if there is, it is of no interest to science. What the Yupik know about ice and snow is part of our common human patrimony. As an unparalleled repository of expertise on Arctic weather conditions, it may contain clues that could help us understand and adapt to the current radical patterns of global warming that disproportionately affect northern latitudes. We ignore Yupik snow and ice knowledge at our peril, and we stand to profit greatly from acknowledging its complexity and its antiquity.

Living in one of the harshest environments on Earth, with an acuity driven by survival, the Yupik identify and name at least 99 distinct sea ice formations. Here are a few ice descriptions from *Watching Ice and Weather Our Way:*

| *Qenu* | Newly forming slush ice. It forms when it first gets cold. |
| *Pequ* | Ice that was bubbled up by pressure ridging. [The] bulb cracks and falls down, and when it |

breaks, the water shows up. It is then covered
by new ice or snow and it is very dangerous
to walk on. So, when this happens, you better
detour it. . . .

Nutemtaq   Old ice floes that are thick and appear to have
had a snow bank on them for a long period of
time. Good to work on.

Nuyileq   Crushed ice beginning to spread out; dangerous to walk on. The ice is dissolving, but still
has not dispersed in water, although it is vulnerable for one to fall through and to sink.
Sometimes seals can even surface on this ice
because the water is starting to appear.[11]

Notice all the information encapsulated in these definitions:
the dynamic conditions that cause the ice to form; its appearance,
texture, solidity, and (in)suitability for walking on; the season or
time of year; the usefulness for hunting; and the possibility of
finding sustenance.

How many hours and days, in a lifetime of Arctic hunting and
foraging, would an elder have devoted to learning the smallest
nuances of ice and weather patterns? Igor Krupnik, who helped
collect the sea ice terms, describes how ice-watching is "a lifelong and twenty-four-hour passion, since there is always someone
checking weather, sea and ice at any given moment. In a critical
time—when men go out hunting, during the spring whaling season, or when the weather is shifting rapidly, several people spend
hours scanning the horizon and discussing signals (indicators)
related to the status of weather and ice."

The Yupik science of weather has a very different foundation
than modern meteorology. Our focus is on temperature and baro-
metric pressure, indicators that are little regarded by the Yupik.

Their science relies on "an extremely sophisticated system of wind terminology that identifies some ten or twelve (or more) types of winds by specific direction and other features." The system of information packaging that links wind types to weather outcomes has a payoff, Krupnik notes: "Each wind is known to bring a certain type of weather, snow, or ice movement. By identifying . . . its Yupik name, an observer can make a quick judgment and even make a basic forecast of upcoming conditions."[12]

This knowledge is of immense value, both cultural and cognitive. The Yupik cataloging of local conditions gives them a sophisticated understanding of a topic that modern science is still trying to codify. Such specific knowledge extends far beyond Arctic ice, though. If we are willing to explore the margins of the world's many peoples, we find many other bodies of knowledge that are of immense potential value to humanity, all rapidly vanishing. Among them is crucial knowledge of healing.

A PLANT FOR EVERY AILMENT

The Bolivian Altiplano (high plain) is one of the most desolate landscapes on the planet. It features mostly loose clay and rocks, with scrubby vegetation growing here and there. Being a lowlander, I found it very hard to breathe at 12,000 feet above sea level. Even climbing a short flight of steps left me winded. Despite the dryness and severity of the landscape, the Altiplano is rich in culture and in biodiversity, especially animals found nowhere else (alpacas, vicuñas) and a wealth of healing plants.

I went to Bolivia in 2007, along with my fellow linguist Greg Anderson and a crew of three filmmakers, drawn by the prospect of encountering one of the smallest and most unusual languages on Earth.

We landed in El Alto, at a dizzying elevation of 13,600 feet, then descended into the deep bowl that is La Paz. Taking Diamox to prevent altitude sickness, we needed several days to adapt. During that time, we met local scholars and a group of intrepid students at the University of La Paz who were translating Windows software into Aymara, the major indigenous language (with over four million speakers) of Bolivia.

As soon we could, we headed up and out of town, in a convoy of two Land Rovers. Our destination was the mountain redoubt of Chary, where we hoped to meet the mysterious Kallawaya medicine men *(los medicos)*. These famed healers of the Andes not only possessed unparalleled secret knowledge of medicinal plants but also had developed a secret language to protect that knowledge. Handed down for at least four centuries, since the collapse of the Inca empire, the knowledge has been fiercely guarded, in part, by allowing only young male initiates to learn the language.

After eight hours on the steep, winding passes, we arrived in the tiny hamlet of Chary. Asking around, we found a man who was a local healer and claimed to speak Kallawaya. We eagerly set up our cameras, microphones, and prepared to interview him. Disappointingly, he turned out to speak only Quechua, one of the most common indigenous tongues of the Andes, and Spanish. We thanked him for his time and pressed on.

On our way back to the decrepit hotel, we passed a man bearing an enormous cloth bundle on his back. He waved us to stop, asking for a ride into town. By sheer luck, he turned out to be Max Chura Mamani, a renowned medicine man, a speaker of Kallawaya, and just the kind of person we were seeking.

As guardian of an ancient knowledge base about healing plants, Max wielded considerable power and authority. People would come from miles away to consult with him, and he was used to being accommodated. Back at the hotel, we agreed to have him perform a ritual for us, and he cast coca leaves to determine a good time and place for it. He scolded us a bit for our

Antonio Condori (left), with his son Illarion Ramos Condori (center), both Kallawaya healers, talking with David Harrison (right) in Chary village, northern Bolivia, June 2007.

haste and eagerness. We gave Max money to make the necessary ritual preparations, and then settled in to wait and drink tea as the fog rolled in. More than a day would pass before Max resurfaced, as we impatiently paced the floor and wondered if we had been fleeced.

The Kallawaya have a sophisticated knowledge of pharmacology that they developed through trial and error, a method we can only consider to be scientific. Here are just two of the treasures from their pharmacopoeia that they have discovered and chosen to share with researchers:

Anis del Campo (wild anise). The Kallawaya use it as a *carminative* for indigestion, stomachaches and colic. It is given to nursing mothers to produce milk, and used with aspirin for colds and flu. For birth delivery, a *mate* of anise is given to the mother as an *oxytocic* to promote rapid labor and to help her expel the baby.

Amapola (opium poppy) is prepared in different ways (boiled in water, mixed with pig fat, etc.) to cure a variety of ailments from hemorrhoids to dysentery to insomnia, and boiled with milk to alleviate coughing and hoarseness.[13]

White poppy is reported by botanists to contain many different alkaloids, a basis for creating analgesics (painkillers). Codeine, one of the alkaloids extracted from the white poppy by pharmaceutical companies, is widely used in cough-suppressing medicines. The Kallawaya knew of beneficial poppy properties long before Western medicine did, using their own process of experimentation.

The Kallawaya healers anticipated the information age by half a millennium. They realized that, although they could not restrict access to the specimens (nor patent the knowledge) of the thousands of medicinal plants they had discovered, they could encode their specialized knowledge in a secret language to be transmitted only within practitioner families and between males (e.g., father to son).

Despite the 400-year-plus interlude since the fall of the Inca empire and the widespread use of the Quechua language in the community, the Kallawaya have preserved their secret language, maintained their elite position as healers that attract a national and international clientele, and achieved the (moral but not legal) protection of being recognized by UNESCO as part of Bolivia's (and the world's) intangible cultural heritage. In addition to knowing uses of native plants, they were quick to discover uses for plants introduced by European colonizers, such as the *borraja*, or "bee plant," used as a *sudorific* (a drug that induces sweating) to treat symptoms of measles and smallpox.

Kallawaya poses challenges to our Western notion of intellectual property and copyright. For small languages and the knowledge they contain, Western legal regimes have neglected to provide any protection, because they do not represent ideas that are individually attributable "eurekas," but rather bodies of collective knowledge worked out and passed down over millennia. Legally unprotected, such bodies of knowledge are vulnerable to "bio-prospecting." Pharmaceutical companies may swoop in and (legally) steal traditional medicinal knowledge possessed by indigenous peoples, profiting handsomely while paying them no royalties whatsoever. This scenario—which applies to indigenous groups around the world, each with a specialized knowledge base—may partly explain the Kallawaya obsession with secrecy.

Max did finally return to us, and he performed a spectacular, five-hour ritual of healing. It involved the spilling of alcohol, burning of many ritual objects (e.g., llama fetuses), and the blood sacrifice of a guinea pig. Throughout the entire ritual, he used secret Kallawaya words, further ensuring their secrecy by mumbling. We were perplexed how anyone could ever learn this cryptic tongue. Max uses the language, along with perhaps 100 other healers, to perform sacred healing rituals in a remote Andean village. No children learn it from birth; rather, it is taught to teenage males who are being initiated into the secret practice.

What we learned, and what had not previously been reported in the scientific literature, is that Kallawaya is also a plain everyday language that can be used to say things like "The llama is eating grass." In other words, though it is no one's native language and is passed on in secrecy, it approaches being a full-fledged language in which speakers can talk about almost anything. Although reportedly the exclusive province of men, Max may have secretly passed on the language to his daughter, who stood by his side and assisted during the entire ritual. Kallawaya is so tenaciously guarded, and provides so much of the healers' livelihood, that it may be perfectly secure, not endangered, despite having so few speakers.

WHO OWNS A LANGUAGE?

So far, we have considered how the theoretical conception of language needs to be expanded, and in turn, how the words of small languages can expand our knowledge of the world around us. Yet Kallawaya also shows that a language's dynamic function in a people's culture means they may not *want* to share its riches. Kallawaya is an excellent example of a language that could be patented for both its form and content, for the economic well-being of the community that invented it, and for protection against predatory pharmaceutical corporations that seek to exploit that knowledge without recompense.

They are not the first group to assert ownership of a language. On August 12, 2005, the leaders of the Mapuche tribe of Chile wrote a letter to Bill Gates accusing him of "intellectual piracy." Microsoft was creating a version of Windows in Mapudungun, the language of the Mapuche. Since the Windows user interface had already been translated into lesser-known languages like Quechua and Maori, Microsoft no doubt thought it was doing a good thing for the Mapuche.

Mapuche leaders, in an eloquently defiant letter to Bill Gates, took a very different position, however:

> From a human rights perspective, we would like to present to you our profound concerns regarding the scope of the agreement between Microsoft and the government of Chile. . . . Mapudungun represents a fundamental part of our culture and our cultural heritage. On the basis of our right to self-determination as indigenous people, the Mapuche People is the main custodian and interpreter of

THE POWER OF WORDS

its cultural heritage and only the Mapuche People must and can safeguard, maintain, manage, develop and recreate its cultural heritage.

The Mapuche authorities and their traditional institutions are of the firm conviction that our rights to our intangible heritage such as our language, Mapudungun, spirituality and religious beliefs are the last resources that we possess and constitute the essential and fundamental basis of our identity and our collective rights which reside in our minds and our collective consciousness. However, we have observed that these rights are the object of acts of intellectual piracy.

The fact that indigenous peoples have the right to own, control and manage their cultural heritage, deriving from their right to self-determination and to their lands and resources, implies that elements of their cultural heritage cannot be used, transmitted, displayed or managed by other persons without ensuring the free and prior informed consent of the relevant indigenous people. Therefore, the appropriation of our language as fundamental part of our culture by researchers, linguists and public officials constitutes a violation of our inherent and inalienable right to our cultural heritage.[14]

Word of Mapuche audacity in resisting one of the most powerful companies in the world raced through the blogging community. Most bloggers—despite having no stake in the outcome—expressed vitriolic disdain for the Mapuche leaders. One of the tamer, less blatantly racist comments read: "To those who filed suit: if you wish your language to die, by all means continue your death grip on it." Another added: "Someone should sue them for using English. What the hell is their problem?"

One blogger described the principle of exclusive linguistic owner-ship as incompatible with freedom of speech. "We can't dictate who speaks English, so why should the Mapuche be able to dictate who speaks their language? It would be one thing if this was some closely guarded tribal secret, but the fact is Mapuzugun [*sic*] is a living language."[15]

Few defended the Mapuche. Some sympathetic voices noted that the Mapudungun translation mangled the language and that Microsoft had never approached the Mapuche leaders to ask for collaboration. Some observed that a Windows version would introduce drastic changes, including a new orthography (a writing system that represented all the sounds). These commenters were generally dismissed or insulted outright.

While the blogosphere evinced no sympathy for the idea that a language could be owned, we readily accept the notion that a simple phrase like "Just do it" can be trademarked by Nike or that an author can copyright a work of fiction. For the Mapuche, as for many traditional societies, language *is* knowledge, and is indis-tinguishable from it. Therefore it follows that if knowledge can be owned, so can language. True, not all communities try to assert ownership or control, but some do so quite vigorously.

In my experiences with some of the world's smallest speech communities, I find a heightened sense of linguistic ownership in reverse proportion to the size of the community. But ownership has two distinct faces. For many communities, ownership means responsibility to share freely with all who may be interested, so that the language has every possible opportunity to be passed along in any form once the last speakers fall silent. The Tofa and Chulym of Siberia are excellent examples of *language sharing*. They value the fact that their words can be "immortalized" in video and audio recordings, so that even if the languages were not written down or published in books, they have enhanced survival odds by being recorded. Speakers who are language sharers feel a custodial responsibility to ensure that their last utterances are not the end of the line. By sharing their words, they widen the world's knowledge of lesser-known subjects, such as the characteristics of reindeer.

Another face of linguistic ownership, commonly found among some Native American groups, is *language secrecy.* Dr. Richard Grounds, one of the most eloquent activists working to revitalize the nearly extinct Euchee language of Oklahoma (also spelled Yuchi), has stated quite clearly that the only viable way his language can survive is to create new speakers, who will continue to own and use it. He believes that if the fate of Euchee were to end up existing only on dusty 3×5 cards in a museum or on audio recordings in an archive, then it would be better if the language did not exist at all. It would, he notes, be the "ultimate triumph of colonialism" for Euchee to exist only in an archive. Richard is right, of course. Only a spoken language is alive. How and where Euchee will survive must be decided by the owners of the language. Of course, many native speakers do actively pursue preservation technologies (e.g., databases, online dictionaries) as a means to use technology to save languages.

The Hopi of Arizona, who number just under 7,000, are also known for their very strong position on linguistic ownership. According to tribal policy and practice, the Hopi reportedly regard their language as strictly for the use of the Hopi people. In the 1990s, a Hopi day school located on the Hopi reservation began an initiative to create a Hopi language program. "The school board (composed entirely of Hopis) had reached the last hurdle of approval when someone pointed out there were four or five Navajo children attending the school. The possibility that some Navajo children might learn to speak Hopi was perceived as a worse threat than the fact that Hopi children otherwise would not learn it. The plans were scotched."[16]

While canceling a language program simply because some non-Hopi may learn it may seem extreme, this is an entirely logical position of exclusive linguistic ownership. The Hopi language is for Hopi only, and this may contribute to its survival if they continue to choose to speak it.

Technology should not be seen as a threat to language, but rather as an enabler. The lowly text message may lift obscure tongues to new levels of prestige; translated software may help them cross the digital divide. Fortunately, Microsoft was not discouraged by the Mapuche reaction and has continued to translate its software into local languages: Inuktitut, Irish, Maori, and more. With nearly 100 local language packs available, it's off to a good start. But with 6,900 yet to go, the technology has much room to grow. Many languages—even those not yet using writing—will someday soon be spoken, heard, and stored in innovative computer programs. They will be texted and blogged. They will have established a foothold in cyberspace.

From sheep guts to ice floes to medicinal plants, languages encode the infinite range of topics that humans care to talk about. Many of these topics, once relegated to "folklore," are now seen to have growing relevance in a world strained by human industry. As knowledge is valued, debates about who owns it, and who can share it, will surely continue. Above all, the value of the knowledge serves as an argument for sustaining language diversity. Because of the way knowledge is packaged into words, it resists direct translation. All of us benefit from maintaining the human knowledge base, and therefore we all benefit from a multitudinous Babel of tongues.

{ CHAPTER FOUR }

WHERE THE HOTSPOTS ARE

*In the end, we will conserve only what we love,
we will love only what we understand, and we will
understand only what we are taught.*

—Baba Dioum

SINCE I COINED THE TERM "language hotspot" in 2006, it has become a leading metaphor for understanding the worldwide distribution of language diversity and the global trend of language extinction. The hotspot concept itself is not original: we have biodiversity hotspots, wi-fi hotspots, volcano hotspots, and many others. But no one had previously applied the idea to languages.

In introducing the term, I had two goals in mind. First, it serves as a promotional metaphor by allowing us to visualize and understand a complex global trend. Second, I hoped and expected that it would be a predictive model. If correct, it could reveal previously unnoticed concentrations of diversity that is both highly fragile and threatened. This could lead to new additions to the linguistic map, by helping us locate "hidden languages" previously unknown to science. Using the analogy of heat (or perhaps fire) as destruction, we consider hotspots *warm* if the languages spoken there are safe and thriving, *hot* if threatened by extinction.

The hotspots model, though only a few years old, has been moderately successful already. The term "language hotspots," which yielded no Google hits when I first coined it, now gets more than 5,000. And the model itself has grown, from an original selection of 13 hotspots published in *National Geographic* magazine in 2007 to over two dozen now. We define language hotspots as those regions of the world having the greatest linguistic diversity, the greatest language endangerment, and the least-studied languages.

The lion's share of language hotspots research has been done by Greg Anderson, my close collaborator. Greg is a walking encyclopedia of linguistic facts and a skilled fieldworker. Together, we've been fortunate to be able to visit six of the hotspots, where we interviewed hundreds of speakers. We plan to visit them all.

I was inspired by the concept of a "biodiversity hotspot," defined by Conservation International as a concentrated zone that meets two criteria.[1] First, to be a biodiversity hotspot, a zone must have at least 1,500 vascular plant species native to it (more than 0.5 percent of the world's total). Second, a zone must have already lost 70 percent or more of its original vegetation and thus be severely degraded, like parts of Amazonia. Using this simple two-dimensional metric of diversity and degradation, ecologists have identified 25 hotspots. Added together, biodiversity hotspots cover just 1.4 percent of the Earth's surface. Yet they are vital to the planet's health, being home to fully 35 percent of our world's land-dwelling vertebrates and 44 percent of plants. The biodiversity hotspots model perfectly captures the extremely skewed distribution of species diversity across space and highlights its fragility. It illustrates how very small areas, if threatened, could yield disproportionately large losses of the planet's biodiversity.

The biodiversity hotspot, with its metaphor of concentrated heat as destruction, lent a new energy and perspective to the conservation movement. As evidence of its scientific influence, in 2003, just 15 years after the model was launched, 30 scientific papers devoted to the topic were published, with a further 200 citations of the original paper.[2] The model helped focus research and set priorities in conserving endangered species and in identifying the estimated 83 percent of plant and animal species that remain unidentified and unclassified by Western science.[3] By focusing on specific ecoregions with high levels of endemic species (i.e., those found nowhere else on Earth), high species diversity, and severe degradation, the biodiversity hotspots model illustrates the rich interrelatedness of species and ecosystems, rather than studying individual species in isolation. It has also advanced efforts to quantify and map distribution and density of biodiversity, allowing us to formulate a better picture of extinction rates and trajectories.

Languages, though not precisely analogous to species, also have an ecology.[4] "Ecology" derives from the Greek word *oikos,* meaning "home," and is used in English to indicate the total environment—organic and inorganic, whether helpful or hostile—that an organism faces in its struggle for survival. Languages, like species, have a home or habitat. They exist in a complex social and ecological matrix, they show uneven global distribution, they have unequal threat levels of extinction, and they can thrive or fail. Languages rely on both internal (social) and external (political) factors for their survival. Their natural habitat is the speech community. They are dynamic, constantly changing, interacting with and coming into contact with other languages. They can exist in a healthy or a degraded habitat, and their transmission from one generation to the next can be threatened, reduced, or even fully interrupted. Efforts at preservation must look at the entire habitat.

While we can preserve some of a language's information in dictionaries, grammars, and recordings, these are artificial environments, like a stuffed dodo bird in a museum, not a living being in its natural habitat. Languages must be spoken to thrive. Each tongue is unique, and smaller ones exist only in a single location or community on Earth, so they can never be replaced or reintroduced from elsewhere. If speakers—or anyone else, scientists, governments, societies—wish to maintain languages, the languages must be allowed to thrive, to evolve, to change in a natural setting. New kinds of discourse, new uses, new words, and new speakers must be allowed to emerge freely and organically. These are the hallmarks of a healthy language.

Unlike species, languages are not bounded entities, unable to intermingle. A traditional boundary line among species is that two animals of different species cannot interbreed and produce fertile offspring. Yet languages can and do constantly intermingle and change. What biologists call "horizontal transfer" of genes has an analogy in languages, which may freely borrow not only words but also grammatical structures from other languages that are unrelated to them. Creoles, and languages of mixed parentage like Kallawaya, can and do arise. There are really no limits on what elements of one language may mix with or be borrowed into another. But unlike the gene transfer experiments of laboratory geneticists that take, for example, a gene for florescence and add it to mice and monkeys, causing them to glow, the transfer of linguistic features is a wholly natural phenomenon and can give rise endlessly to new ways of building words and sentences.

Being separate but parallel domains, languages and species do have deep and still poorly understood interactions and effects upon each other. All landscapes that are inhabited by humans are modified by them, whether by hunting, foraging, path-making, or modern technologies we impose on the earth. Interactions between humans and ecosystems are mediated and shaped by language in both directions. For example, many language hotspots are populated by traditional hunter-gatherer or other subsistence societies and thus contain knowledge about intense human interaction with the environment. Hotspots by definition have a high level of language diversity, and they give a rich picture of the long-term coexistence and mutual influence of languages over long periods of time.

AUSTRALIA: WISDOM IN PLANTS

Aboriginal Australian cultures are among the world's most ancient, dating back perhaps 48,000 years, before humans inhabited Europe or the Americas.[5] Their unique languages and traditions are primarily oral, not written down or recorded, and in many cases they are still relatively poorly documented by scientists. At least a hundred indigenous languages of Australia are now in danger of extinction.

In 2007, as we launched the Enduring Voices project at National Geographic, we chose Australia as the destination for our first expedition.[6] Northern Australia comprises the top-ranked language hotspot, ranking very high on both the diversity and endangerment scales. Though they have been the focus of intense work by linguists for decades, the languages there still have much to reveal to science. It is also, we would learn, one of the leading places in the world for language revitalization. We went there to observe that work, and to especially take note of what the local indigenous communities were doing to preserve their languages.

The elders (and youngsters) we met generously shared with us some of their vast knowledge about language, mythology, plants, animals, climate, and human adaptation to a harsh environment. It was a rare privilege to have a glimpse into these amazingly complex and ancient cultures, as well as their efforts to ensure continuity of the traditions.

Our exercise in taking the pulse of languages was to observe the current state of language endangerment and revitalization in several remote communities and to interview elders and other local experts. And we got an earful! Elder William Brady of the Night Owl clan, a speaker of the Gugu-Yaway language and expert hunter, explained how his native tongue connected him to his outback countryside. A hunter must have skills in reading footprints and in using the spear and boomerang, he explained, but beyond that, must be able to communicate with animals. "Whistles and animal sounds," he insisted, "are a part of our language. If you can't speak the language to that animal, you're not a good hunter." He concluded, "If you can't speak the language of the bush, you'd better not go into it!" William believes that language can be taught only in its natural setting. "You can't learn language in a box like this," he noted, gesturing to the classroom where we were sitting. "Go out and feel, smell, touch, be *on country*."

At the Batchelor Institute of Indigenous Tertiary Education, a leading center for Aboriginal language revitalization efforts near Darwin, Northern Territory, we sat down with the experts. Jeannie Bell, who works on languages spoken on her homeland, Fraser Island, noted how difficult it was to get government funding for language revitalization. Nazareth Alfred, of the Masi Island Kolpa tribe, who studies the Kulkalgowya tongue, said her language "is deteriorating rapidly" as the youth prefer to speak Kriol. She pointed to some very practical social benefits of saving the language: "The youths who are taught traditional culture have more connectedness and are less angry and violent."

Lynette Cockatoo told how she is trying to "retrieve" the traditional Nigarakudi language, faced with very low retention rates of less than 10 percent of the population. Leonora Adidi, a speaker and activist for her native Kalaw Kawaw Ya tongue (also called "KKY"), spoke of the urgent need for more government support and more enlightened policies. Each of these experts expressed a desire and aspiration to help revitalize and document their language. It was impossible to walk out of that meeting and conclude that saving languages doesn't matter, or that the effort is a lost cause.

After a day at Batchelor Institute, we took William Brady's advice and headed out to be "on country." Our first stop—after several hours of driving along dusty roads—was Nauiyu Nambiyu, a tiny but neat village of single-story houses, surrounded by dense green woods. Aboriginal scholar Patricia McTaggart, a speaker and expert of the Nangikurrunggurr language, told us she had just completed a dictionary, coauthored with linguist Nick Reed, after many years of work. Nangikurrunggurr, she explained, may be literally interpreted as "language of the swamp people." Another language Patricia speaks, Ngengiwumerri, means "language of the sun and cloud people." She invited us to come along and meet some of the swamp, sun, and cloud people.

Sitting on their lawn, elders Molly Yawalminy and Kitty Kamarrama gave us our first formal "welcome to country" ceremony. They took us down to a nearby river and, standing on the sandy bank, anointed us with river water. Raising their voices in a song, they announced our presence so the local spirits would not harm us. The ceremony, which they allowed us to film, was performed in the Nangikurrunggurr language, with surprisingly loud singing, considering the frail appearance of the two elderly ladies.

The elders then sat down for an extended conversation about traditional ecological knowledge. They rely on "calendar plants" to tell the best time for food-gathering activities. When the bark peels easily from the gum tree, for example, sharks in the river are fat and may be hunted. When the kapok tree blooms, its seed pods disgorge fluff into the air, indicating the time to gather crocodile eggs along the riverbanks. The ladies' eyes sparkled at the mention of traditional delicacies like turtle and crocodile eggs, nowadays a rarity.

Elders Molly and Kitty, full of stories and laughter, were clearly more comfortable sitting outdoors on the bare ground than in their small bungalows. They represented a direct link between the human past of hunter-gatherers and the human present of global technologies. They were amused, and quite patient, to bestow their ancient wisdom upon our modern ignorance. An immense knowledge gap yawned between us. Our team had the latest in digital technology and an ability to upload our recorded conversation to a website to share it with people around the globe. Yet for all this technological reach, I felt unbelievably shallow. The elders were narrow, to be sure—they had never traveled more than 50 miles from their birthplace and had not met many nonlocal people in their lifetimes, nor mastered most modern technologies. Yet they were grounded in this place, Nauiyu Nambiyu, this obscure backwater, by the deepest possible intellectual and cultural roots, far surpassing any connection I had to anyplace I had ever lived. Their exhaustive knowledge of this one small place put to shame the superficial and scattered knowledge of the most peripatetic world traveler.

Our next stop was the western seaside enclave of Wadeye, which enjoyed a particularly bad reputation in the Australian press as a site of Aboriginal violence and unrest. Our guide, assigned to us by Tourism Australia, told us we would be living under heavy security and not allowed out after nightfall. On landing at the dusty airstrip, we saw a gaggle of smiling children and a stern hand-painted sign saying, "Don't bring ganja into our community." We found the people of Wadeye to be gracious and hospitable.

Accompanied by elders, including three ladies over 70 years of age,[7] we set off to visit several sacred sites. Walking along through the light underbrush and rustle of dead leaves, the ladies kept up a constant dialogue. They suddenly stopped at a spot that to our untrained eyes looked hardly any different, yet for them was a clearly marked sacred site. An oval of slightly raised ground, it had two rock "nests" containing "eggs" of a mythical duck. Sitting down on the leaves, they told the Dreaming story attached to that very place. It involved a deity that metamorphosed—first as a human, then as a duck—stopping along its journey to rest and deposit eggs at this site.

As the ladies sang, the children foraged, finding tasty termites in rotten logs nearby, procuring fat grubs, and finding the greatest outback delicacy, a twig oozing wild honey, called "sugarbag." They shared these with us, and we shared our much less exotic fare of sandwiches and boxed apple juice.

After lunch, we were guided by local Cyril Ninnal up onto a bright orange rock escarpment, covered with impressive rock art. He sat down beneath the most spectacular one, a rendering of a headless man, and began to tell us the story in the Murrinh-Patha language, which is spoken locally but not endangered. Trouble was, Cyril was bound by taboo not to mention the name of the main character in the story, because that name also belonged to a deceased relative. Cyril's sister Tess was present, however, and not bound by the same taboo, so he decided that every time he came to a place in the story where the hero's name appeared, he would pause and Tess would call out the name. But here we encountered one more taboo. Cyril and his sister, as adult opposite-sex siblings, were forbidden from speaking to each other at all, and Tess could not even look in his direction. So, the request was relayed to Tess via an unrelated person, and then she stood off to the side, not looking at Cyril, but calling out the taboo name each time he paused in his story.

One severely endangered language that we encountered near Wadeye was Magati Ke (or Marti Ke). Magati Ke is now reported by the community to be down to three elderly speakers.

Yolngu musicians near Darwin, Northern Territory, Australia

Accompanied by local linguists Maree Klesch and Mark Crocombe of the Wadeye Endangered Language project team, who have been working with this community for years with great results, we met with and spoke to three Magati Ke speakers, including "Old" Patrick Nunudjul.

Patrick (born 1930) and his wife, Mona (born 1942), live outside Wadeye village, on ancestral lands overlooking a sandy beach. Vast spaces surround their house, along with wide-open seaside vistas. Yet when we arrived, they were sitting huddled together, an entire extended family of nine, sitting so close as to be touching, as if for warmth, except that it was over 80 degrees outside. Mona sent the kids off, and soon they returned with turtle eggs for us to sample (gooey and runny, they slide down the throat). Patrick and Mona sat down near a burbling stream, and Patrick taught us some words of the nearly extinct Magati Ke tongue: *hoong-ge-ret,* "head"; *ning-e-ning,* "tongue"; and *der,* "teeth." Then he told us the "Teeth Dreaming" story, which the Wadeye project team told us they had not previously recorded. Listening along, and showing at least a partial understanding of the language, was Patrick's nephew Aloysius Kungul (born 1956) sitting with his own son Isaac Kungul (born 1992). Isaac watched intently, and though he did not repeat Patrick's Magati Ke words aloud, I watched him mouthing them silently, thus showing that he had taken it upon himself to learn fragments of the language. With the recordings we made and sent back to the community, perhaps Isaac, or someone of his generation, will be able to retell the Teeth Dreaming story long after the elders have made their exit back into the Dreamtime.

As we visit the hotspots and take the pulse of languages, we find some more robust than expected, but others more feeble. Many languages we record have never before been recorded, and for some, it may be the last time they are captured on video. In order to preserve language diversity and to create healthy habitats for small languages, we need to understand how they are adapted to both their social and natural environments. More important, we need to know *where* and in what state of vitality they exist, what kinds of knowledge systems they contain, and what that knowledge reveals about the natural world. We will need the entire sum of human knowledge as it is encoded in all the world's languages to truly understand and care for the planet we live on.

A LAST SPEAKER?

Sitting under a massive rock outcrop in a cave in Australia, we gazed up at the massive, fierce image of the Rainbow Serpent that adorned the rock. Aboriginal elder Charlie Mangulda, in the overpowering presence of the Rainbow Serpent, became positively solemn. "This is our ancient myth, how the Rainbow Serpent creates and destroys life," Charlie began, as we perched on boulders in the red-rock cave. Considered to be a "last speaker" of Amurdag, Charlie is at the best of times a reticent man, He told us he had not used the language conversationally in some years and remembered words with difficulty.[8]

Greg Anderson and I interviewed Charlie about his language and culture at this important dreaming site at Mount Borradaile, chosen carefully for its cultural significance to Charlie's people. Charlie was not a talkative man, and most of our questions got monosyllabic answers: yeah or no. But once he got to talking, Charlie also shared stories of this place—learned from his father— of the Turkey Dreaming and of the Rainbow Serpent (described later in chapter 7).[9]

We were very excited to be in the presence of a speaker of Amurdag. We pulled out a vocabulary list we had brought along and asked for words represented there. As Charlie shared with us names for animals in Amurdag, we were able to verify from the word list that we were indeed hearing the nearly extinct tongue. We dutifully recorded words like *malayiwar,* "wallaby"; *iraba,* "father"; and *malawuruj,* "dream."[10] Some of the longer or rarer words—such as *ingirijingiri,* "blue-faced honey eater," or *yal,* "hot sand under ashes of fire"—Charlie was not able to remember or confirm for us, attesting to possible attrition of knowledge through lack of use. Amurdag, even in the tiny sample we were able to glimpse, shows some wonderful metaphorical expressions, the word for "west" is simply the phrase "sun go down." And it can extend to accommodate modern life: *jura* reportedly refers to "paper," "book," and "office."

Charlie's difficulty in recalling a language he had known from birth, but now almost never used, is what linguists call "attrition."[11] Can a person forget his own language entirely? Immigrants who seek to assimilate to another culture may go decades without speaking their mother tongue. Later, if they try to retrieve it, they may find their knowledge rusty or deficient. As the neural pathways decay from lack of use, they cannot even string together simple phrases in a language they once commanded natively. Many of the last speakers I've met, like Charlie, show both of these effects. They can barely remember common words, and the locally dominant language, whether English, Spanish, or Russian, has thoroughly infected their mother tongue, leading them to make all kinds of ungrammatical (from a traditional point of view) utterances.

The image of Charlie speaking to us in the Rainbow Serpent cave, expertly photographed by National Geographic fellow Chris Rainier, was picked up and reproduced in press and Internet sites around the world a few months later, when we launched our language hotspots model. It brought unprecedented visibility to the plight of endangered languages, through the face of a single individual. But it also stirred up controversy and resentment among a few colleagues, who upon seeing the photograph and caption assumed that we had somehow claimed to discover Amurdag's last speaker, had rushed in with helicopters for a photo op, and had failed to acknowledge prior work. We were well aware of the decades-long efforts of linguists and speakers to document it and so many other rare Australian tongues, and in fact mentioned such efforts at every opportunity.

Our visit with Charlie was not for the purpose of documenting Amurdag, which would have been the task of a lifetime. Rather, we wanted to hear Charlie's own views on *why* his language is important and what it feels like to be the last reported speaker. We hoped to provide a global audience for Charlie's viewpoint, believing that the fate of last speakers would be of intense interest to people if they only knew about it, if they could put a face and name to the problem. A primary goal of our hotspots model is to shine a light on the efforts of Charlie and others to hold back the tide of extinction. Judging by the amount of press, radio, and TV reports, we did just that, not only for speakers like Charlie, or for Australian Aboriginal tongues, but for the hotspots generally and many last speakers.[12]

NEIL MACKENZIE GOES ON WALKABOUT

We continued our Australian expedition in Broome, a beautiful coastal town in Western Australia. The beach resort hotels and surfers contrasted with the sights only a few miles inland. The landscape that was sacred to the local people remained almost unchanged. Here we visited the Rubibi people, a tiny remnant of a community that once roamed these lands freely. Their language, which they call Yawuru, is now reportedly down to three fluent speakers, with perhaps a dozen speakers of other levels of fluency. We sat on the back patio with the elders as they told us about the great changes they had lived through. Thelma Sadler, age 97, remembered when her people had first contact with the white settlers, and in a few years changed over from a hunting and foraging lifestyle to living and working on a cattle station. When they tried to leave to go back to their homeland, they were not allowed and were maltreated by the station boss.

"I was born under a tamarind tree," Thelma began, and then taught us a few words of her ancient tongue. "We say *nyadi mingan* for 'Hello, how are you?' and you can say *galabu* or *galamabu ngangan* for 'I'm good.'" Laughing at our attempts to repeat the difficult words, she admonished that "language is best learned outdoors." Thelma's friend, Elsie Edgar, in her 70s, sat by her side reminiscing. "We used to build tree houses, called *waragai,* among the mangrove trees, and fish from them." Elsie's daughter Susan Edgar nodded approvingly. "Our grandmothers," she said, looking at Elsie and Thelma, "are ceremony singers.

They have specialized knowledge. People don't realize how strong language is. . . . When we say the names of places, we can see those places in our mind."

To understand the Rubibi world, we needed to venture beyond the pleasant beachside town of Broome, where Elsie and Susan live in typical suburban homes, and to see the traditional places. And so we spent three days walking around the outback with our Rubibi guide Neil Mackenzie. Elders like Neil rely on an intimate knowledge of plants and landscapes to help sustain the language. Although he is an authority on cultural knowledge and survival, he does not consider himself a fluent speaker of the language.

On a sandy plain overlooking the ocean, Neil stopped at a spot and began digging with his hands in the soft sand. Though the ground seemed completely dry underfoot, within two feet he struck water. "[This is] something we have been doing for thousands of years. People would never understand what the hell they're doing, nobody trying to preserve it, look after it, continue it, keep going. Teaching kids and teaching people about how precious, what we have here, in this country, in our environment, and protecting waterholes. Nobody would know, they would not think there would be water here."

"This is all songline country, this is where all the young people travel at the songlining age, because you find a lot of water. Small watering holes, like living water. This is what we call, what we relate to in our Dreamtime, *bogarigada*. And a lot of these waterholes, they exist here, and you can find them. But as you get closer to the township, a lot of the holes are buried up and have buildings on them, because they wanted to keep people, Aboriginal people, out of the town. And they kept them out here. This is the reserve they created for the Aboriginals, from the 1905 Act. We were regulated under the Flora and Fauna Act. We were part of the animals, native animal species. We weren't regarded as human, not even classified as citizens of Australia, until 1967. I was born an illegal alien in my own country. We didn't have the privileges of, what do they say, normal people. We weren't normal people, we were outcasts. Even today we are second-class citizens. We are still not recognized as or considered normal."[13]

Despite their outward appearance of complete acculturation (driving a pickup truck and talking on a cell phone), Australian Aboriginals like Neil have managed to hang onto at least some of their wealth of ancient knowledge. Knowledge of the medicinal properties of plants, he explained, was commonplace: "This is a vine. You can see it grow here, coming from the ground, so it's using this as a host. It's a parasitic vine. And it grows this little seed, or bead. Common name, they call it crab's eye bead."

As he pointed out more and more plants to us, we began to understand how sophisticated Rubibi survival technology was. What appeared to our eyes as a rough and inhospitable landscape was to Neil and his people more like a grocery store, pharmacy, and living room all in one.

"In the early days, when they were surviving in the bush, they moved around a lot, following food," Neil explained. "Because when they went to one waterhole, the animals would move to another waterhole, so they had to follow the animals from waterhole to waterhole. And sometimes, there's always droughts, and times are real lean, not a lot of food around. If they were carrying a baby, or a fetus, and they knew that they would not be able to get enough nourishment for themself or the baby, they would use this in a way where they would crush it up and make a concoction out of it. But only people who have an idea how to make this concoction of preventing the birth, we would abort the unborn fetus of the child. The mother would live on and be able to survive in drought. So this is like, um, an abortion pill.

And today, the colonists came and they made rosary beads out of them, the missionaries. Little did they know, 'cause they're Catholic, you know, they're against abortion, they were wearing these around their necks, with rosary beads. The powder in them, there's enough toxin in there, if it's not prepared properly, but the powder in this is the toxicity level, can kill a frog or a dog, from that one bead, or seed here."

As Neil chuckled at the irony of rosaries made of abortion pills, he told us one reason why the knowledge needed to be kept secret: "They don't use it anymore because a lot of the people that didn't know how to make a drink out of this, or a concoction to abort the unborn fetus, actually killed the mother, too. So they no longer use it anymore, because it was too, um, dangerous a method of doing things like that. But before that, in nomadic life, they used to use this to abort the unborn fetus."

A hundred yards away, within view of the pebbly beach, Neil stopped and pulled up by the roots a six-foot canelike plant. "You know we never fished?" he said. "We speared a lot of fish, with spears, but we never used the fishing line. We'd go out in the rocky pools, and the fish traps had so much water in the bottom there." He gestured to his knee to show the depth of water in a tidal pool, where fish would be trapped when the tide receded. "We'd take this plant out here, pull the bottom, get these roots and crush them up with a stone, and break it off, mash it up, mix it with the sand, walk in the pools. . . . A couple of minutes later, you see the fish come up, upside down." We marveled at the power of a plant root that could kill fish, and I asked if it was harmful to humans. "It's actually not a poison," he continued. "It gives off a little bit of a milky sap and it coats the gills and stops the oxygen coming in from the water into the gills so they float upside down and to the surface." He made a satisfied motion, as if scooping up fish. "Big fish, that big"—he spread his hands a foot apart—"and little ones. Yeah, you wouldn't starve, 'cause the tide comes in every six hours!"

Neil paused to pick and eat a snow pea–like pod he called "green bird." "When this tree dies, we know there's something at the bottom there that's eating the roots, 'cause it's killed the tree. And we look and see a burrow and you see a worm that's in there. And this worm is like a witchetty grub and tastes very much like macadamia nuts. And you can eat it. We call that one *bein*. I think it's a moth that lays eggs, a particular moth. That's what damaged those roots, back there."

A bit farther on, Neil pointed out Dreamtime's main waterhole. Standing over it, all we saw was sand in a shallow pit. Neil jumped down into the hole and began digging, and sure enough, within a foot he struck water. This waterhole is called *Bugarigara*, which means "the Making" or "Dreamtime."

"By making the waterhole, singing songs to the waterhole, our ancestral spiritual being caused that we came to exist in this country. We come from the ocean onto the land; some people come from waterholes, and the rivers. When they'd sing the song, to the waterhole, they'd use boomerangs, and they'd beat them together. The men are the dreamers, in this country. They're the story keepers. But because the women are more influential now, they seem to keep a lot of it themselves and pass it on. The men are more likely to be susceptible to alcohol than the women. They keep all the stories of their uncles and their grandfathers alive, if nobody else wants to take it on."

As Neil painted a picture of forgetting and cultural decline, he also revealed powerful connections that still kept everything in place. "The Dreamtime, it ties in with everything, the language and the culture here. You'll go back now, and you'll dream about all this. It'll come to you, take you off in another, sort of, dimension."

Despite the odds, Neil and the Rubibi people are actively working to revitalize their language. We were still shaking the outback dust from our boots when we were invited into a serene, air-conditioned classroom at the local primary school. Accompanied by Neil, we were allowed to observe and film a Yawuru language lesson conducted by an elder for students at Cable Beach Primary School. Doris Edgar, an elder of uncertain age in her 80s (births were not recorded when she was born), sat calm and dignified, holding forth to a circle of rapt fifth graders. Beside Doris was a table with dozens of plant specimens arranged into neat bundles, including many we had seen in our outback walk with Neil. The room was full of objects labeled in the language: a papier-mâché shark, for example, and a stuffed wallaby. Bright drawings of jellyfish illustrated Yawuru numbers: one, *waranyjarri;* two, *gujarra;* three, *gurdidi.* After three, the small numbers combined to make larger ones: *gujarra gujarra* ("two-two") meant "four," *gujarra gurdidi* ("two-three") was "five," and *gurdidi gurdidi* ("three-three") meant "six." After six, the number series ended with *manyja,* a borrowed form of the English "many."

The eagerness and determination on the students' faces gave the lie to arguments that small language death is a natural result of progress and that we should not lament the loss of these tongues. It flatly contradicted the notion that children will not learn an obscure language or cannot be motivated to do so. It was truly inspiring to see children understanding and speaking an ancient tongue. Why did they want to learn Yawuru, we queried, instead of a larger, more useful language? A chubby 10-year-old girl with braids piped up instantly. "It's a dying language," she said solemnly, "and we want to help it survive."[14]

Australia holds the top-ranked language hotspot, but we had many more we needed to visit. Poring over our maps, we selected

Paraguay as an urgent priority and began planning our expedition. It would turn out to have some parallels to Australia, including— among the Chamacoco tribe—elderly speakers who had known a hunter-gatherer lifestyle in their youth and now flew on airplanes and used cell phones.

A MEETING WITH GODS

I crouched in the underbrush, at the edge of a remote Paraguayan village, listening to odd muffled sounds and chants that echoed among the leaves. As usual, my fellow linguist Greg Anderson was just a few steps away. Two steps in front of us ran a small footpath that led to the sacred dancing grounds of this village, Puerto Diana. We wanted to simply observe, not disturb, so we remained camouflaged out of sight. All around, murmurs, chants, and an occasional whistle filtered through the thick underbrush, mingling with the whine of mosquitoes that buzzed in my ears. Suddenly three runners appeared, advancing swiftly in single file through the bushes. They looked like nothing I had ever seen. Their heads were completely covered with heavy sacks woven of fibrous vines and ringed with emu feathers. Their upper bodies were smudged black with charcoal, and their waists were adorned with thick skirts made of emu feathers and twigs. They made odd, chickenlike movements of their heads and uttered strange guttural sounds.

These were the shaman's soldiers, whose role was to appear fearsome while dancing in single file around the sacred tree. They assisted by carrying ritual objects such as bundled sticks and gourd rattles. Assembling first in the hidden men's grove, out of sight of the village's women and children, they adorned their bodies, smoked, and drank a hallucinogenic substance. Then for an hour they chanted, jumped up and down, and swayed side to side to work themselves into a trancelike state. As soon as they heard the shaman's summoning call, they made their running entrance onto the main dance grounds, where the people awaited. None of the hundreds of villagers would have been able to identify them, so well disguised were they. In the beliefs of the Chamacoco people— also called the Ybytoso Ishir—these dancing masked figures, shamans and soldiers, do not merely *represent* the gods, they *are* gods.

The dance site, located at one extreme end of the village, was a flat, round tract of grass with a single, enormous tree in the center. The dirt was packed down from years of use, and no grass grew, but it looked as if had been unused of late.

With the permission of local leader Kafote, our National Geographic team had come to observe a reenactment of a ceremony that had not been performed in half a generation, very nearly stamped out by the efforts of missionaries.[15] A ritual of vital importance to the Chamacoco people, this was just one small part of their complex religious beliefs, connecting sky to earth, past to present, and the sacred to the profane. The main dancers, believed to become gods during the ritual, maintained strict anonymity. They wore full face and body masks, some with only blackened feet protruding. The feet stomped ominously in a circular pattern. Chris Rainier, our intrepid photographer, was in the thick of it, jogging backward to keep up with the shamans' rapid circumambulations.

Surprisingly, even the small children who had not seen this ritual before did not seem alarmed. One boy about ten years old stepped boldly forward into the circle, offering his infant brother, who looked to be about a year old, to a masked figure. The god swooped toward them, reached out a hand, and for just a second lifted the infant in under his draped body shawl, bouncing him up and down, before thrusting him back into his brother's outstretched arms. Was this a blessing? An initiation? The infant, hefted by his older brother, kept calm throughout and did not flinch.

A young Chamacoco boy holds his brother up to be blessed by the masked shaman's assistant.

Agna Peralta, a lady of about 60, stood at the edge of the sacred circle, which women were not permitted to enter. Yet she was clearly a participant, supporting the chants with her own strong, deep voice and insistent rattling of her feather-decorated gourd. She had seen this ritual many times before in her younger years, but most of the bystanders, children and young people under age 16, had never seen it performed.

The entire Chamacoco religion, so brilliantly explored by Ticio Escobar in his book *The Curse of Nemur,* rests upon oppositions and rendings. Power is stolen from the heavens by men who dare to climb a sacred tree to copulate with a female goddess. Nourishment is stolen by men who clandestinely gather honey, the most prized food, then conceal it from the women. Images of bodily fluids pervade their mythology: sperm, saliva, and excrement all figure prominently as either hindering access to the gods or humbling poor wretched humans who live in the mud. The gods can be either beneficent or malevolent, but they must be appeased.

Back in the concealed grove, where only male participants of the ceremony could go, the shamans rested and conversed. The blind shaman Mario rocked back and forth on the ground in a trance, singing the same sounds over and over. Wearing a pair of yellow shorts adorned with feathers, and a high feather headdress, his entire body smudged with black coal dust, he had been in this state already for several hours. He held a gourd rattle and shook it persistently. No one paid him any special attention, yet everyone seemed to feed off his energy.

A few yards away, the two senior shamans sat huddled together. The first, painted black, began to retch and cough, a fit that lasted for at least ten minutes, until he suddenly reached two fingers deep into his throat and brought out a dangling worm. He "fed" the worm carefully into the mouth of the second shaman, who swallowed it. Moments later, emerging from their collective trance state, they smoked a cigarette and laughed at a joke someone was telling. Soon they would leave the grove to return to the ceremonial circle, where they would conclude the ritual.

Kafote, the young, dynamic leader of the community, sat down to talk to us about the future of his culture. What changes had he witnessed over the past 20 years? He turned immediately to the topic of the traditional religion: "The culture is weak now. Twenty years ago shamans were still curing; the culture was strong. Veneto is the last strong shaman with powers. He cures by biting the patient and drawing out the sickness in his hand, shows it to the people, then gets rid of it."

Though not a shaman himself, Kafote described different types of shamans: There are "big fish, rain, earth, and forest [shamans]. Some are more powerful than others. Some shamans live on earth and others live underground or in the sky. To be a shaman, one must dream of the invisible gods. When the shaman sleeps, he goes up to the god's world and obtains their powers. There are different types of gods and powers. When the shaman dreams and sings, the gods give him more power. The most powerful shaman lives in the area of Puerto Leda. We cannot talk to him because he is a god, and invisible."

Turning to the issue of subsistence, Kafote asked, "Why do we have to eat noodles now? Because we no longer have gods who help us. We have to work to get some kind of money and buy something. But before, the gods gave it all. You just had to sing, for example, to call a fish, and the fish would fall before you. Before, you could sing and call for the wild pigs, and they would come and we ate them. Now it's more difficult."

Thinking of all the fishermen we had seen on the river, we wondered if they still used songs to call fish, if they still practiced the religious rituals to ensure bounty. "Yes, people still use them, but we cannot get into Puerto Leda and visit the most powerful god, who would give power to our people. It is now prohibited to go on the land that was once ours. The government sold it to the Moonies. Now we can only work, so our way of life is degrading. In 20 more years, we will no longer have anything."

Concluding the interview, we asked Kafote what he would like the world to know about his people. Looking directly into the camera, he began an impassioned and tearful speech: "Our lands are so small," he began to weep as he said it, "*muy pequeñas,* and we are crowded in from all sides, with people taking our forests and poisoning our rivers. We have mercury in the fish, and a dry well in the village. We get nothing from the logging and mineral extracting companies. The toxins they use seep into our river and contaminate our water. We want to buy back some of our traditional lands, where there are still animals, but it's too expensive now."

LANGUAGES OF A SECRET LAND

The indigenous people of Paraguay remain a secret within an enigma. Many live in the inhospitable backcountry, the Chaco, accessible only by air, boat, or seasonally impassable dirt roads. In Asunción, the modern capital city, people expressed surprise at our destination: "There are languages out in the Chaco?"

While poor in some respects, Paraguay is indeed rich in languages, forming part of the central South America language hotspot. In addition to Spanish, Paraguayan peoples speak at least 18 languages, grouped into 6 distinct language families. To calculate the linguistic diversity index for Paraguay, we divide the number of families (6) by the number of languages (18), yielding an index of .33. This astonishing level of diversity triples that of Europe, which, with its 18 language families and around 164 languages, yields a diversity index of just .11. How did so many languages evolve in such a remote place, and among such a small (less than 200,000 total) population? Part of the answer lies in geography. The Chaco is burning hot and dust-filled in the summer, besieged by mosquitoes and impassible in the wet season, and filled with thorny plants and poisonous snakes. It defies even the barest level of subsistence living. And yet these small tribes have managed to thrive here.

Survival dictated mobility. No one place could support people year-round, and so the Chaco peoples fished at the riverbank for half the year, then trekked into the dry interior to forage for the other half. Conditions forced local tribes to continually fissure into smaller groups that could support themselves off the land and prevented the consolidation of peoples into larger settlements. Despite the ferocity of the land, richly imaginative cultures sprang up here, with fantastic mythologies, feather-dancing rituals, and discoveries about the medicinal uses of local plants. What remains of this knowledge in these survivor cultures?

Elders still alive today, like Baaso, who gave his age as 100, recall the precontact era. Baaso recounted to us how, during his early years, his people—the Ishir—wore no clothing besides animal skins, had no knowledge of metal, glass, or guns, and had no source of nutrition besides the fish they caught, small animals they shot with bow and arrow, and berries and honey they foraged from the forest. Dividing their time between temporary encampments along the river and foraging sites in the dry interior, Baaso's people had not at that time seen outsiders, airplanes, or any other modern technology. Once contact happened, the world came crashing in on the Chamacoco, and they were exposed to warfare, weapons, subjugation, and sedentarization. In Baaso's own centenarian lifetime, we can trace the arc of an isolated, precontact people from living as hunter-gatherers in a stone-age subsistence pattern to living in villages in sight of a mobile phone tower and an airstrip, granting interviews to visiting scientists, and sending out their stories and reminiscences to a global audience over the Internet.

Baaso's grandson, Alvin Paja, listened with a bemused expression as his grandfather talked about hunting with bow and arrow. Alvin likes to fish, but he uses motorboats and is conversant in text messaging and the latest Argentine telenovelas. He can only imagine the world his grandfather inhabited, and yet he is connected to it through the stories, the words, and the Chamacoco language.

Baaso, with grandson Alvin at his side, related all this with a sly sense of humor and a desire to tell his own story. He may have been pulling our leg just a bit, since an elder in another village insisted that Baaso was not 100, but only 85. Either way, his mind was clear, and his experiences, both pre- and postcontact, rang true. They are the Ishir people's collective fate. Having been plunged from the deep past into the dizzying present, fast-forwarding centuries of technology in the span of a single lifetime, Baaso's perspective is utterly unique and remarkable.

*Baaso, a Chamacoco elder, with his grandson, Alvin Paja Balbuena,
in Puerto Diana, Paraguay.*

Across the village from Baaso's place, elder Agna Peralta, wearing a bright red dress, took out her dried gourd rattle, stood purposefully in front of her house, and burst into song. The deep overtones coming from her small and seemingly frail body took us by surprise, a loud and potent mix of chant, rhythm, and incantation. The rhythm of the gourd shaker slowed down, then picked up speed again: *"Ekewo dashiyo lato ehuwo. . . ."* I jotted down syllables in my notebook, making a rough transcription but not comprehending. Agna later told us the lyrics were repeated variations on "Come, fish, come to my house." She learned this song from her father, a shaman, and its purpose was to beckon the river creatures to provide sustenance.

No fish were summoned by Agna's powerful voice on this occasion, but children from all over the village made a beeline to her house. They looked in bewilderment at us, the National

Geographic team with our cameras, recording devices, and notebooks, as we sat listening with rapt attention to Agna's song. The song itself was a rare occurrence, and the fact that a team of scientists had come from afar to hear it sung made quite an impression. I wondered if the children were paying attention to the lyrics, in a language they are increasingly filtering out in favor of Spanish. At last, Agna stopped singing and set down her rattle. "Maybe tomorrow I can sing again," she told us. "Now, I'm tired."

At the nearby school, a brother and sister aged eight and ten said, yes, of course, they still know songs in Chamacoco, and they dutifully sang a song at the prompting of their teacher, Señora Teresa. Though we saw joy in their faces, it seemed very much like an effort and a performance. Clearly they were more comfortable chatting among themselves in Spanish, and this schoolyard habit may have already determined the future fate of Chamacoco, at least in Puerto Diana. Señora Teresa said the children knew some Chamacoco, but it was "a language at risk of extinction." She showed us a first-grade textbook in the language, compiled by her and her fellow teachers. She asked her student, eight-year-old Pedro, to read from the book. Haltingly, he attempted to sound out the syllables. Señora Teresa corrected him and then translated for us into Spanish, from what sounded like a primer for cultural assimilation: "Here we are in the white people's school. They are teaching how to eat." "Eating on the ground is unclean." "On our desks we will do beautiful things."[16]

Departing Puerto Diana, we set off downstream in a couple of rickety canoes to visit one of the very smallest villages in all of Paraguay, tiny Karcha Bahlut, which in the Chamacoco tongue means "Big Shell, Little Shell." Fewer than 100 souls, plus a few itinerant fishermen, perch on a high escarpment that overlooks the river. The precipice is a midden composed of millions and millions of shells. Some archaeologists assume these were deposited by humans and are thus a sign of ancient habitation. An opposing view was explained to us by Jota Escobar, Paraguay's leading ornithologist, who thinks the shells were deposited by birds, and that humans happened along later to partake in the feast and add to the pile. Either way, the shell midden is massive and solid. Atop it stand rickety huts with hammocks and small fenced enclosures for pigs.

With some frustration, I shook my GPS, restarted it, and moved it to another spot so it could detect the satellites. It was hard to believe, but we appeared to be in a satellite black hole and could not get a fix on the location of the Chamacoco villages. I later confirmed with cartographers at National Geographic that there are indeed gaps in GPS satellite coverage, with its bias toward the Northern Hemisphere. The Chamacoco people exist in one of those gaps. Their lands can, however, be viewed from Google Earth or an airplane, where a sobering picture of rampant deforestation and river pollution emerges.

The only solid building in Karcha Bahlut is a brick school, said by locals to have been built by "Los Moons" (the Moonies) who originally came to proselytize but then left suddenly, apparently with no converts, leaving behind the gift of a schoolhouse. In it, we found young, energetic Alejo Barras shepherding his first- and second-grade students. As we watched the lesson, we realized how utterly foreign Spanish is to these kids. Just a few miles downriver from Puerto Diana, where the Chamacoco children chatter in Spanish all day, these village children laboriously repeated a few basic words: *casa, trabajo, mano*. It was a real joy to see that these children are basically monolingual speakers of Chamacoco, but their situation is unique and does not mirror that of most children in the other Chamacoco villages. They inhabit a linguistic island, the last and smallest place in all the once-vast traditional Chamacoco territory where Spanish has not totally dominated.

Inspired by Alejo's efforts, we asked what we could do to help out. Lacking a single clock or watch in the village, he said he had trouble rallying the children to school on time. I quickly took off my digital watch and handed it over to him. The value to me of a $100 sports watch was nothing compared to its value in this village. Then Alejo showed us an alphabet book designed to teach basic literacy in the Chamacoco language. It contained pages devoted to each letter and to objects that could be spelled with it. "We only have a few copies," he said. "Can you help us make more?" In moments, we set the textbook out on the ground in a sunny spot and carefully photographed each page. We would take these images back to Asunción and mass-produce a hundred textbooks for this village and for the school in Puerto Diana. This small gesture on our part, costing only a few thousand guaranis, could truly tip the balance in the effort to keep Chamacoco alive.

Fortunately, the Ishir do not lack for young, charismatic leaders, and we found such a person in Kafote. His Spanish name is Crispulo Martínez—like all Ishir, he gave his Spanish names first to outsiders, but his Ishir name remains his true, if somewhat secret, designation. Kafote represents the struggle of his people, as they cope with mercury poisoning in their river, clear-cutting of trees by Brazilian loggers, and cultural assaults by missionaries of all stripes. Their defense strategy is as simple as their basic needs: keep the land, fight for clean water and against deforestation, keep the culture, keep the language.

In so many ways, Paraguay remains off the map, an enigma. Guidebooks to South America give it the least coverage of any country, and it enjoys little tourism. It suffered for decades under a dictatorship that left it underdeveloped. Though Asunción is now a vibrant city, European in its tastes, the country as a whole remains largely unknown by outsiders. Perhaps it is meant to be kept secret. A local sculptor told us, "Thanks for coming to Paraguay . . . but don't tell anyone!" Most Paraguayan indigenous languages are quite poorly known and only minimally described in grammars, and those grammars are often produced in very small print runs and unavailable to scholars.

Happily, many of the Chaco tongues, though small, are still being spoken across all generations. Like the country itself, these ancient tongues hold many layers of secrets. We visited one such hidden community in Asunción. One moment we were whizzing along on an urban streetscape, with gas stations and shopping malls, and the next we turned down a deeply rutted, unmarked, and unpaved dirt road and found ourselves in "Communidad Maka." The Maka people, numbering 1,200, are known both for their elaborate feather costumes and for selling trinkets on the streets of the capital city. They survive by being insular. Though they live right in metropolitan Asunción, their women speak only Maka, no Spanish or Guaraní, and their children attend school only within the community. The men while away the time playing games of chance with sticks. They welcome outsiders, albeit with a great deal of dignified reserve, and are thoroughly proud to be different.

We sat down with Señor Tso Fai (he also has a Spanish name, we learned later) to investigate the enigma that was the Maka language. We did not get far, as he was pressed for time, though he was happy to provide many words and sentences and even read to us from a storybook. Like any first encounter with a "new" language, as linguists we found it thrilling, and we tried to absorb the unfamiliar sounds and rhythms.

Though small and spoken only in a single community, Maka shows remarkable resilience. We do not know why some languages persist against all odds, in situations where others would have long ago yielded to the dominant tongue. Maka attitudes—perhaps confidence in their cultural superiority, perhaps simply deep reverence for their history—sustain their tiny language. I predict it will be spoken for generations to come. The Maka are true linguistic survivors, on a continent where the twin bulldozers of Spanish and Portuguese, fueled by governments and schools, have already swept hundreds of larger tongues into oblivion.

A true hotspot—such as Paraguay—is one where high diversity, high endangerment, and low scientific knowledge all converge. These are the areas we must prioritize for research and revitalization. In our survey of the world's language hotspots, we find both alarming and hopeful signs. Often, we find the number of speakers is far less than what has been reported in the scientific literature, as we found in Australia and South America. Similarly, the level of endangerment may be higher than previously estimated, with few children learning it natively. Third, the degree of scientific documentation is often quite low. Though a few books, grammars, or even dictionaries may exist, for many tongues we encounter there are no known recordings. We are aware that the recordings we make are sometimes the first, and in some cases may be the last. Because the elders have shared knowledge with us, we feel a sense of responsibility to care for it, to disseminate if the community agrees, and to safeguard it for the future. In the years to come, there may be a shift in attitudes both within and beyond the community, and descendants may wish to reclaim lost knowledge. When they do, we will be able to provide it.

{ CHAPTER FIVE }

FINDING HIDDEN LANGUAGES

Indigenous peoples have the right to revitalize, use, develop, and transmit to future generations their histories, languages, oral traditions, philosophies, writing systems, and literatures, and to designate their own names for their communities, places, and persons.

—United Nations Declaration on the
Rights of Indigenous Peoples, Article 13

OUR FIRST ENCOUNTER with a hidden language took place in India.

What is a "hidden language," how do we become aware of it, and what happens when it comes to light? I use the term "hidden" because it's not appropriate to say "discover" in relation to languages. All language communities are aware of their own existence, so "discovery" represents an outsider's bias. However, some communities are known only locally and have managed by chance or design to avoid being identified in official records, censuses, and surveys and by scientists. I propose to refer to languages that have eluded prior notice by outsiders as "hidden languages." By focusing attention on the hotspots, the Enduring Voices project is working to fill in the blank areas on the linguistic map.

Language communities may intentionally hide. They may deny their own existence to maintain identity, to subvert it, or indeed to suppress it due to discriminatory pressures. Official government minority policy may be responsible for a hidden language being overlooked.

In the People's Republic of China, official government policy recognizes a maximum of 55 minorities—all ethnic groups must be subsumed under one of these 55 labels. Modern official ethnic minorities are defined in terms of how or to what degree they differ *culturally* (not linguistically) from the majority Han Chinese. In southern China, especially Yunnan province, a number of hidden languages have come to light lately, and others likely remain hidden and certainly are underdocumented in the interior Southeast Asia language hotspot. On the fringes of the Plateau of Tibet, from Yunnan down to India's Arunachal Pradesh (claimed by China) and westward into Bhutan and Nepal, many dozens of small communities inhabit a single valley, a small cluster of villages, or in the extreme case, only a portion of a single village. Some of these have been hidden by ethnic shame, difficult geography, government policy, or a combination of these factors. A thorough linguistic survey of the entire pan-Himalayan region should be a matter of urgent priority, especially since the locally dominant powers, China and India, continue to foster economic and cultural assimilation of minority peoples.

An example of official administrative undercounting occurs in northeastern India. Most of the region's ethnolinguistic groups numbering less than 10,000 are simply excluded or amalgamated into other groups for administrative convenience. The official census of India does not distinguish these groups. And some groups just above the 10,000-person threshold hide other even smaller groups, with shared cultural similarities but distinct languages.

Arunachal Pradesh state is a mysterious place that lies on the extreme edge of India. It borders China, Myanmar, Assam, and Bhutan. Arunachal is poorly known because outsiders, even Indian citizens, must have special "inner line" permits to travel there—permits that are only issued for short visits. Our Enduring Voices team determined to go to Arunachal because it is essentially a black hole on the linguistic map. Few linguists have worked there, and no one has drawn up a complete or reliable listing of the languages spoken there, their locations, or numbers of speakers. We did not know what we would find, but out hotspots model predicted extreme diversity with many small languages, some perhaps previously hidden to science.

We went searching in the far western part of Arunachal for two poorly known languages—Aka and Miji—known to be spoken in one small district. The Aka and Miji people share many cultural similarities: living in bamboo houses raised on stilts; raising pigs; cultivating rice and barley in terraced fields; and wearing distinctive and colorful woven shawls. The women also wear enormous colored beads and many silver bangles and earrings. The very oldest men maintain one of the world's most distinctive head ornaments: the hair is grown very long and bunched up into a topknot in front, held in place by wooden stakes, while an enormous bird's bill and feathers ornament the top and back of the head. The impression is that of a birdlike creature.

Both Miji and Aka are little-studied languages, and Aka in particular did not disappoint us, for it is a fabulously complex language full of wicked tongue twisters. The simple task of training our ears to decide on the correct phonetic symbols to transcribe it was exhausting and exhilarating. We worked late into the night by candlelight, marveling over forms we had recorded earlier in the day. Our team members amused the locals by attempting to say things like the number eight, pronounced "sgzhi," or the word for ginger, *tkshing* (each just a single, tongue-twisting syllable). Aka abounds in what linguists call "consonant clusters": it stacks up sequences of sounds that, at least for English speakers, are unutterable. Perhaps the most laughter was generated by our discovery

Katia Yame and his son Sunil Yame, speakers of the "hidden"
Koro language of India.

that the sentence "Three laughing fish drink rice wine" consists of words that all sound almost identical, something like *dzi* "three" and *tsi* "fish," with only very subtle differences. This was a formidable tongue twister even for native speakers, who could scarcely get through it without pausing and erupting in laughter. And so, day after day, we delved into Aka and marveled at its complexity.

Upon going door to door in the villages and talking to speakers of all ages, we were surprised to find not only Aka and Miji speakers but also, hidden among them, a *third* group, speaking a language called Koro. None of the scientific literature we'd studied reported the existence of a third and utterly distinct language in this region.[1]

UNCOVERING A HIDDEN LANGUAGE

This is the story of Koro, how it was hidden in plain sight, and how it came to light. There are still unknown numbers of hidden languages out there, and I believe that many of them, like Koro, lie within language hotspots. On a scientist's tally sheet, Koro adds just one entry to the list of nearly 7,000 world languages, increasing known diversity by just 1/7,000. But Koro's contribution is much greater than that tiny fraction would suggest. Koro brings an entirely different perspective, history, mythology, technology, and grammar to what was known before.

We've only just begun exploring Koro, so we have only the vaguest idea about its speakers' creation myth, their knowledge of forest ecology and rice growing, their calendar, their humor, or their songs. All these areas are potentially rich sources of useful knowledge. And many Koro people, once we asked them to speak, were not shy.

To reach the tiniest Koro village, we crossed a rushing mountain river, pulled across by a bamboo raft. Called Kichang, the village contains just four long bamboo houses set upon stilts. A notched log, an *ibi*, provides steps up to a shaded veranda, where you can glimpse the dark and cool interior of the house, with its small fire pit and cooking and sleeping areas. Despite the tiny demographic, the village was religiously segregated. Two houses were "Christian" and two were not. The Christian villagers refused to sit on their non-Christian neighbors' verandas, which were festooned with fertility shrines woven of rice stalks. But the non-Christians gladly agreed to sit on the Christian verandas, where a portrait of Mary and the infant Jesus (with markedly Indian-looking features) peered serenely out at the orange groves that surrounded the entire village.

As we munched on oranges on one family's veranda, we were treated to the life story of a young woman named Kachim, told entirely in Koro. This session was, as far as we know, the first time that anyone had recorded Koro as its own distinct language. Our team of linguists—myself, Greg Anderson, and Dr. Ganesh Murmu of Ranchi University—sat transfixed, even without understanding. We were mesmerized by Kachim's delivery and somber tone. Greg sat with his hand frozen in an outstretched position, holding the microphone, and I listened over my headphones and watched through the video camera viewfinder to faithfully record each gesture and expression. Many hours later and after multiple listenings and with translation help, we were able to piece together and partially translate the story—a young woman's sad tale of being sold unwilling as a child bride, overcoming hardships, and eventually making peace with her new life in an adopted village.

Ironically, our India-based film crew, as soon as they heard an unknown language (neither Hindi nor English) being spoken, switched off their camera to save batteries. After the story was finished, the crew switched on their camera and said to Kachim, "Can you tell it again in Hindi?" She obliged, and they recorded that version. We would have missed the Koro story entirely, but fortunately our own camera—which we used to record scientific video data—was rolling the entire time, so the story was recorded. On the way back to base camp, I sealed the videotape in plastic and stored the precious recording in an inner pocket. It would never leave my side until I arrived home and my lab processed it.

Who are the mysterious Koro? Can we avoid exoticizing them and simply understand them on their own terms, as they wish to describe themselves? The Koro are indeed a hidden people, perhaps by choice or by negligence. They are thoroughly mixed in with other local peoples and number perhaps no more than 800. The Koro do not dominate a single village or even an extended family. This leads to curious speech patterns not commonly found in a stable state elsewhere.

Many people who grow up in bilingual households know about "accommodation." If your grandmother speaks to you in Italian, you can answer her back in Italian (if you speak it) as a way to accommodate her. Or, if you feel less confident about speaking Italian, even though you understand what she asked, you can answer in English, without accommodating her choice of language but still successfully communicating. In most cases, this is not a stable situation, but one in which a language shift is occurring. Your grandmother may have grown up as a monolingual Italian girl in Italy. When she immigrated to the United States, she may have learned English, while her children spoke mainly English with only a limited command of Italian. Her grandchildren are more likely to be monolingual English speakers, leading to a complete shift. In the case of Italian, this is no great tragedy, since millions of speakers remain in the old country. But for a small language like Koro, language shift means the end of existence.

The Koro have strategically chosen to be bilingual, but to do so in a stable, long-term way. This means that sometimes they do not accommodate or at least they do not shift. So, among the Koro, along with intermarriage patterns, you find sons who speak it when their mothers do not, siblings who speak it when their older or younger siblings don't, spouses who marry a Koro speaker but never learn it, and other spouses who do learn it. None of this is surprising, but it's unusual to find this existing as a stable condition for such a small language over such a long time.

Nearly all Koro speakers live in mixed families and households where some members do not speak Koro but Aka or another tongue. This means Koro speakers must make a strategic effort in deciding with whom, when, where, and under what circumstances to speak Koro. They perform a constant, proactive exercise in linguistic choice, not simply choosing the laziest method of speaking the local majority tongue that everyone knows. This attitude may account for the vitality of Koro. Simply put, its speakers have linguistic pride; they value their ancestral tongue enough to make an effort to speak it.

The Koro are not recognized as a distinct ethnic group, since they are thoroughly intermixed with the Aka. As such, they were previously misidentified by missionaries, hobbyists, or travelers who encountered them. Until our National Geographic expedition in 2008, Koro was essentially undocumented, unrecorded, and unknown outside of local villages. It is not listed in the standard international registries, or indeed even in the *Linguistic Survey of India* commissioned by the Indian government itself, nor in the census of India. One obscure published source we found was written by a Colonel Grewal of the Indian Army, who had been stationed in the region and collected lists of local words as a hobby.[2] His book contains a grand total of 250 Koro words and five sentences (the longest containing just four words), but he did not recognize its status as a distinct tongue nor give the local name for it.

Even locals participate in hiding the language. Sursun, a village shopkeeper in Palizi, told us about another village: "In Bana," she remarked, "the other Aka people live. We can't understand them." Her comment suggests that while a linguistic difference is noticed, it does not correlate with an ethnic or cultural one. Local people consider the Koro people to be essentially the same, but speaking differently, and even that difference tends to be downplayed. This minimization of difference is shocking, because even to the untrained ear, Koro could hardly sound more different from Aka. They differ as much as, say, English and Japanese. Where Aka loves to cluster its consonants, Koro prefers minimal, easily pronounceable syllables as in *kapa,* meaning "good"; *ubu,* "stone"; and *sebe,* "goat."

Having confirmed that Koro was indeed unique, our next task was to map its current known locations and the number and identity of speakers. We would also try to assess its vitality and discover whether it was being used by young people. A local schoolboy, Sunil Yame, was our expert guide here. Though he was not shy about using the language, he often found himself at a loss for words, being more comfortable conversing in Aka, Hindi, or even English. Sunil was a living example of language shift. He invited us to accompany him to his village, located ten miles away along winding roads, where we could interview his father and village elders.

The village of Kadeyā was set on a high embankment over a river gorge, surrounded by steep slopes and elevated orange groves. Our arrival caused a sensation, and the youth of the village took a break from building a volleyball court to watch us work. On the veranda of Sunil's bamboo house, we interviewed one of the very oldest inhabitants, Nuklu. A diminutive, wiry man, he spoke fast and with gusto about techniques for hunting tigers and monkeys. Nuklu's stories were made believable by the fact that he was decked out with a fur-covered machete, an arrow-filled quiver, and a bow. At one point in his story, he jumped up and loaded a bamboo arrow, *ba,* into his bow, *le,* poised to shoot an invisible tiger.

Sunil's father, Katia Yame, spoke Koro fluently, but within the family, usage fell off dramatically. Sunil and his sister did not regularly speak the language with their parents, and never spoke it with their peers. Koro must be considered endangered because very few people under the age of 20 speak it. Speakers we interviewed admitted they tend to use it only in private, personal encounters with another person who speaks it, and never in the presence of nonspeakers. This behavior contributes to the somewhat hidden nature of Koro and maintains its secrecy within the community.

Having collected several thousand words and hundreds of sentences, our next task was to try to identify the language-family affiliations of Koro. Most languages have siblings, languages that descend from a common ancestor and are related. Italian and Catalan and Romanian are sister languages and daughters of Latin, for example. A few outlier languages, like Japanese and Basque, have no known relatives, and we call these "isolates." Languages are constantly changing, as populations disperse, and what once was a single ancestor language can split up into daughter languages. If this took place a very long time ago, say more than 5,000 years, the resemblances among the daughter languages are faint and hard to discern. If the split happened more recently, say 1,000 years ago, as with the Romance or Slavic languages, then the sibling resemblances are clear even to an untrained observer.

Whenever I give public lectures, a member of the audience always stands up and asks, "What's the difference between a language and a dialect?" I am surprised, not at the question itself, which is an old conundrum in my field, but by the degree to which members of the public seem vexed by this issue and want to know the answer. The answer I give them rarely satisfies, because I have to say, "Nothing," and then, "It depends." I say nothing because linguists believe that every language is simply a language; whatever comes out of a person's mouth and is understood, is language. We make no distinction between "proper" and "incorrect" speech. Most languages do have at least one variety that is abitrarily recognized as better, purer, or more sophisticated (for French, this is the 14th Arrondissement variety of French).

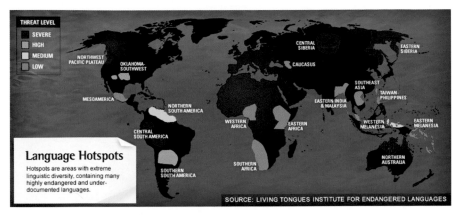

*The Language Hotspots map. Visit the interactive version at
www.languagehotspots.org*

*David Harrison and Greg Anderson with Charlie Mangulda,
the last known Amurdag speaker, in Mount Borradaile, Australia.*

Cyril Ninnal, of the Yek Nangu clan, relates the Murrinh-Patha dreaming story of the headless man depicted here in ancient rock art near Wadeye, Northern Territory, Australia.

Songe Nimasow and two other members of Aka tribal group in ceremonial dress, Palizi Village, Arunachal Pradesh, India.

Songe Nimasow, shown in his everyday dress.

Monchaks of western Mongolia sing to goats while milking them.

Nergu, a young man of the Monchak community in western Mongolia.

Kachim (left) and two other women of the Koro group,
Kichang Village, West Kameng, Arunachal Pradesh, India.

Greg Anderson (right) and Ganesh Murmu (center) interview Sange Degio,
a speaker of the "hidden" Koro language of India.

Illarion Ramos Condori, a Kallawaya healer, discussed medicinal plant knowledge with the author, Chary, Bolivia, 2007.

Críspulo Martínez (Kafote) a leader of the Ybytoso Ishir (Chamacoco) people of upper Paraguay, with his son in Puerto Diana, 2009.

Christina Yimasinant, of the Yimas people, a speaker of the endangered Karim language, Karawari region, Papua New Guinea.

Luis Kolisi, a Yokoim speaker of Kundiman village on the Karawari river, Papua New Guinea, shown here modeling traditional body paint for tourists.

Luis Kolisi, shown in his everyday dress.

But even this distinction is a fiction. Everyone has an accent; everyone's speech conforms to and differs from some imaginary standard. Even if we imagine that the correct way of speaking English is that of the Queen herself, we might be amused to learn that even Her Majesty Elizabeth II has abandoned her own queenly English in favor of an inflection distinctly more working class. Linguists analyzed the Queen's vowels by listening to recordings of her annual Christmas Day address delivered annually since she ascended the throne in 1952.[3] To their surprise, they found that the Queen's vowels had shifted from a royal cast to a more common variety. If even the Queen does not stick to one accent over her lifetime, then there can be no such thing as standard or "correct" pronunciation. We all have an accent, and it can change dynamically over our life span.

Koro—as we have analyzed it thus far—seems to have no close sister languages, nor does it seem to be a dialect of any other language. The larger family affiliation for Koro is Tibeto-Burman, a vast family that stretches from across a wide swath of Asia and has more than 400 known members belonging to many different sub-branches. We do not yet know exactly how Koro fits into the Tibeto-Burman family tree, or what tongues may turn out to be its cousins. This will require careful analysis, comparing as many words as we can from Koro to words from many other different potential siblings.

For example, let's take the Koro words for moon, star, cloud, and monkey. Comparing them to words from four nearby (and potentially related) languages, as shown in the accompanying table, we find that "moon" is shared (of course, they all have slightly different pronunciations, but we can recognize them as basically the same word). "Monkey," by contrast, is unique in Koro, not obviously related to any of the other five words (though some of those five do seem to be related among themselves).

English	Koro
moon	ala
star	dougrey
cloud	mugba
monkey	laasu

Taraon	Idu	Memba	Miji
haalo*	ela*	dagar	lu*
kaadeng*	adikru*	karem	do-tsung
aam	mato	tim-nu	meimiw
ta:min	ame	tu	shu-bo

In the table, an asterisk indicates a clear relationship to Koro. For "moon," four out of five candidate forms closely resemble the Koro word, with just minor changes. We call such words "cognates." For "star," the changes are more radical and require a trained eye to spot, but the identified cognates are still solid. "Cloud" represents more of a stretch, and there's no certainty any are related, though some could plausibly be. For "monkey," the Koro word stands alone, perhaps unrelated to all the others, possibly an ancient relic of an earlier state of the language, or a specific name that came to mean monkey in general.[4]

Expanding this comparative spreadsheet into a much larger one yields a matrix of relatedness that tells us a revealing fact about Koro's lineage. But for any set of words that look alike, we must also ask if cognate relationships are due to common ancestry or to borrowing. Languages borrow words promiscuously, but if a large percentage of words in two different languages sound similar, we reasonably assume that they spring from a common ancestor tongue.

As a small and struggling culture, what is the value of this recognition to the speech community itself? Does Koro *need* to be "discovered" by science? Will it benefit from being written about, publicized, and known to outsiders? There's no clear answer, but some thorny ethical dilemmas. Part of the uniqueness of very small languages is that their speakers may feel a sense of ownership over them. In the case of the Koro, even though they seem to be gradually giving up their language, it remains the most powerful trait that identifies them as a distinct people. Without it, they are merely part of a larger group, within India's population of a billion-plus.

In Gta', an endangered language of India, many words have specific meanings that cannot be expressed by a single word in English.

goteh	to bring something from an inaccessible place with the help of a long stick
buhno'	a ladder made from a single bamboo tree
nosore	to free someone from a tiger
poh	to kill lice by pressing them under your nails
ruhri'	to eat flesh from the bone

SILENT IN SIBERIA

While Koro was "hidden" by being overlooked and unnoticed, Chulym, or Ös, one of the smallest of Siberian tongues, must be considered a language that was intentionally hidden. Yet over the past few years, it has emerged from near invisibility to become one of the best known endangered languages in the world, thanks to the medium of film.

In 2003, five years before the Koro trip, documentary filmmakers Dan Miller and Seth Kramer called me and asked if they could accompany me on one of my field expeditions. They had been inspired—in part by the loss of Yiddish as a heritage language in their own families—to make a film about dying languages. In researching the topic and speaking to many linguists, including

Noam Chomsky, they realized that Yiddish was not alone (in fact, some varieties of Yiddish are now gaining new speakers, while others remain endangered). They came to me because I specialize in this work, and they thought I might be a potential documentary film subject. At the time, I had just finished up a five-year project in Siberia, along with working in Mongolia, and I wanted to go back to both places. I offered Dan and Seth the option of traveling to a field site where I had an established network of people, so that the filming would be easier. They declined, preferring a reality TV vibe in which everything would unfold spontaneously, and we might or might not find what we were looking for. In short, they wanted me to go somewhere I had never been and track down the last speakers of a language.

After consulting with my research partner Greg Anderson, who's an expert on Siberia, we settled on Chulym, one of the most obscure, smallest, and least known languages of Siberia. All we knew about Chulym was taken from a 1970s report that put the numbers at less than a few hundred speakers, and we anticipated that the number would be much smaller now. We also knew that little documentation had been done—only a few obscure publications in Russian, with no known recordings. Chulym seemed like a good bet for a language in the last stages of its existence. Fortunately, we also knew that native Siberian people are welcoming and fairly relaxed about being filmed.

With film crew in tow, Greg and I set off for a remote village that was not even shown on local maps. We had no idea at the time that this humble journey to hear last whispers would find a global audience in the celebrated documentary film *The Linguists,* which would bring this nearly extinct language to the ears of thousands of listeners around the world.

After many hours on dusty unpaved roads, our taxi driver deposited us in the sleepy village of Tegul'det. Poking around, we managed to rouse someone at the post office (it was "postal work-ers' day," and the post office ladies were enjoying a celebratory vodka lunch). They brought us to see the mayor, and that's when our adventure began.

A gruff, burly Russian, the mayor lost no time in telling us how worthless the local natives were. Those Chulym get drunk after just a couple of shots of vodka, he announced with a superior smirk. "The Russians are stronger, they don't get drunk as fast." He then summoned a Chulym to be our driver and guide. Vasya Gabov, an imposingly stout and affable man of 52, came along in his bright red Lada. We immediately felt we were in good com-pany, and he took us to his house, where his wife prepared tea and made us feel welcome.

The next day, we attended a special meeting of the Chulym tribal council. Many of the Chulym, due to intermarriage, are indistinguishable from Russians, though some tend to be slightly darker skinned and have dark hair. The tribal council had seven members, none of whom spoke Chulym. But they were very recep-tive to our proposal that we make recordings of the last speakers. They drew up a letter of permission and made just two requests: one, don't film any drunk people, and two, make a Chulym story-book for the community.

Now, if we could only locate some actual speakers, we could get to work! Vasya proved to be an ideal guide: he was warmly received everywhere and always had a laugh and a funny story to tell. One of the first speakers he took us to visit was, quite literally, incoherent. Varvara was about 70 years old, was possibly inebri-ated, and might have had Tourette's syndrome, as she was given to profane outbursts. Between swearing jags, she told us how glad she was we had come to visit her, and she sang a Chulym wool-spinning song. We had never heard the language sung before, and we strained to catch the words in her raspy voice.

Just up the path from Varvara's house, we met Max, who was nearly deaf. When we shouted into his ear, he managed to string together a few sentences of Chulym. I was born in "New Village," he told us, struggling to recall Chulym words he seldom used.

By the end of the day, we were discouraged, because neither Varvara nor Max was able to produce anything like coherent speech or a conversation. If we were to document the language, we would need speakers who could focus and answer questions, who were sober and thoughtful and patient.

Our run of poor luck continued when we met two of the oldest members of the Chulym nation, both ladies in their 90s. The first one, also named Varvara, was tiny and wizened, with a floral headscarf and large walking stick. Sitting down with us on a log, she warbled and gestured, clearly intending to say something, but neither we nor Vasya could grasp her meaning. The second, Anna, was almost completely deaf and could only nod and smile as her granddaughter shouted at her, "Say something in Chulym to them! Speak Chulym to them!"

At this point, having met four people who were unable to hear or speak Chulym coherently, we felt nearly defeated. I put away my notebook and shut off the video camera, and we prepared to say goodbye to our hosts. Just at that moment, Vasya cleared his throat and stood up. He leaned down and put his mouth next to Anna's ear. In perfect Chulym, he said, "What clan are you from? Whose daughter are you? Can you tell me in our Chulym language?"

We were floored, suddenly realizing that our reliable guide of the past several days was himself a fluent speaker, and a relatively young one at that.

Over tea, Vasya explained why he had not revealed himself earlier as a speaker. He and his peer group, now in their early 50s, had been made to feel ashamed of their skin color, language, and ethnicity. "From first through third grade, we felt ashamed to speak our language at school. The kids would tease us, call us 'black ass,' and so we felt ashamed." They had also, he told us, been made to feel ashamed of their language and forbidden to speak it. Under such pressures, he and his generation made the decision (one that they now regret) to avoid using Ös, as they call it, and to speak exclusively Russian. They made this decision at a very young age, not thinking that it would mean the loss of their ancestral language, thinking only about how to fit in, to avoid ridicule for being different.

Once the floodgates of Vasya's mind were opened, his mouth poured out a wealth of stories, songs, and words. We could barely keep up—it was like holding a teaspoon under a waterfall as we hurried to catch every word. Stories about bear hunting and moose hunting, about the first automobile that drove into the village and what a scary racket it made. Vasya was a "skipped-generation" speaker. He had learned the language largely from his grandmother, which explained why almost no one else his age knew it. He was the youngest speaker by 20 years, and if he lives out his expected life span, he will surely one day be the very last, with no one else to talk to.

If the Chulym people ever had an epic storytelling tradition, it is long forgotten. Only fragments of their folklore and oral tradition have survived. In two expeditions, linguist Greg Anderson and I managed to collect one aphorism, one wool-spinning song, and a few dozen stories about hunting moose and bears. We also collected plain old everyday speech, people talking about their lives, hunting and fishing, and their history. Already faded from the Chulym cultural landscape are ancestral hunting stories that once were verbally shared, retold, and embellished. Tales about bears, for example, never mentioned the word "bear" directly; instead they might say "furry one" or "brown animal." For the Chulym, the bear is a mystical animal to be both feared and respected.

The powerful creature demands special rituals be performed to assuage its spirit. These rituals formed part of an animistic belief system, which holds that spirits inhabit inanimate objects—rocks, trees, bodies of water—as well as living creatures.

But when these same tales are told in Russian, they are mere skeletons of the originals. As the Russian language absorbs Ös speakers, these stories are relegated to the recesses of the Chulym minds and culture, weakening their animistic religious beliefs. At one time, shamans, which the Chulym called *qam*, were prevalent in traditional society. They functioned as experts at interacting with the spirit world and were called upon in dire situations, such as serious illness or death.

During our visit, we met the only two Chulym old enough to have seen a shamanic ritual with their own eyes. One of them was the 90-year-old lady named Varvara. Though frail and largely incoherent when we met her, in 1972 Varvara had told the following story to visiting Russian researchers. The telling itself was a courageous act, for expressions of religion were severely frowned upon in Soviet society, and many shamans had been brutally repressed in the 1950s and 1960s. Even before the Soviets, shamans faded from Chulym society because native Siberians and Russians were converted to Orthodox Christianity, which forbade shamanic practices. After she told it and the researchers dutifully noted it in their notebook in phonetic transcription, it lay dormant for over three decades in the archives of the local university. Varvara's story is the last surviving eyewitness account of now-forgotten shamanic rites.

When the shaman shamanizes, there is a plate of meat and three liters of alcohol nearby.

Around her neck hang nineteen strings of beads, and a white scarf is on her head.

She holds twelve rings in her hand and beats them with
a wooden spoon.
Then she takes the spoon and shamanizes with it.
If the spoon lands right side up, it augurs good.
If the spoon lands upside down, it augurs bad.[5]

This fragment of a firsthand account is a glimpse backward
into prehistory—perhaps the only one we will ever have—of a lost
religious tradition. The Chulym get along relatively well without
their traditional religion, and some have converted to Orthodox
Christianity, but scholars of religions and culture worldwide are
impoverished. Given that so much of history is filled with the
eradication of belief systems and the colonial imposition of religions, we should be sensitive to the impending loss of any more.
As belief systems approach the vanishing point due to language
shift, the best we can do, perhaps, is to write down or record texts
or first-person accounts of what people once believed in.

Although Ös did not develop as a written language, we
learned that there was at least one example of written Ös. A born
outdoorsman, Vasya would spend weeks at a time out hunting.
During the day, he would patiently track bears and other animals,
and at night, sitting alone in his small cabin in the forest, he made
an audacious decision—he would keep a hunting journal in his
own native Ös language. He knew how to read and write in Russian, but Ös has at least four sounds not found in Russian. Since
Vasya was not a trained linguist, he decided that he would not
invent new letters for these sounds, but would use novel combinations of letters he already knew. After some time, he worked out
a system and began to make regular entries in his journal. He was
encouraged in his efforts by something his mother had told him
as a young boy: "My mother told me that it is necessary to speak
our Ös language. . . . Let the Russians speak Russian and let the

Ös speak Ös." This expression of linguistic pride inspired him to keep writing, and perhaps to even dare to think that Ös might be passed onto his children's generation. But his journal was ill-fated.

One day Vasya got up his courage and showed his journal— now containing several years' worth of entries painstakingly written—to a Russian friend. The reaction was catastrophic for him. "What are you writing there, in what language?" the friend demanded. "Why write Ös?" When Vasya heard these scornful words, he felt as if he had done something very wrong. All the shame of the schoolyard and stigma of being different came back to him. In a fit of anger, he threw his journal—the first and only book ever written in his native tongue—out into the forest to rot. "I might have wanted to show it to you," he told us, "but it's not here, it's there where I threw it away."

Despite this rocky start, Vasya agreed to demonstrate his writing system. He wrote a simple story and allowed us to film him talking about his writing system. He felt secure enough to express pride once more in his tongue. "I have always loved the Ös language and spoken it. . . . I will never throw away my language. I still speak it."

In the hope that we might encourage Vasya to let his writing system gain wider use in the community, we used it to produce the storybook that the tribal council had requested. We also commissioned local children—none of whom spoke the language—to draw illustrations for it. Their efforts, and Vasya's brilliant orthography, led to the very first published Ös book.

Though never written down, the Chulym people's history is a rich one. They were traditionally hunter-gatherers and fishers. Their livelihood, and also their name for themselves, derives from the Chulym River, which flows for over a thousand miles in a westerly direction and empties into the Ob River. At the time of their first contact with Europeans, in the mid-18th century, the

Chulym people lived in birch-bark tepees, wore fur clothing, and had no domesticated animals other than dogs.

The Chulym watershed is a low-lying, marshy ecosystem rich in plant, insect, bird, and mammal species and experiencing drastic seasonal fluctuations in temperature. Chulym culture, subsistence, and traditional knowledge center around river navigation and fishing, gathering of berries and roots, and hunting with snares and weapons. All Chulym knowledge systems are in decline. Use of medicinal plants has mostly been forgotten, as have the ecological (lunar) calendar systems, taxonomies of plants and fish, and techniques for making wooden dugout canoes, fur-covered skis, and fur clothing.

The Chulym people pose an interesting puzzle for genetics and the history of human migration. Descendants of an ancient local population, they are genetic and cultural kin to New World populations found in Alaska. At an unknown point in the past (possibly as late as the 18th century), they shifted from their ancient and unidentified language (likely belonging to Yeniseic, a now nearly extinct language family) and began speaking a Turkic language. They underwent a linguistic conversion of the same kind as their fellow Siberians, the Tofa, discussed in chapter 9. The Chulym did hold on to many ancient words, especially pertaining to rivers, fish, and traditional lifeways. Though they shifted languages, they kept many old place-names (especially river names) as well as vocabulary specific to animal, plant, navigation, and canoe-building technologies. By digging into the language of the Chulym, scientists can gain insights into ancient Siberian prehistory, as well as an understanding of human adaptation to some of the harshest living conditions known to mankind.

That work has become even more urgent today. Our work within the Enduring Voices project is to salvage, record, and analyze the fragmented knowledge that remains. In our field trips, we have collected, recorded, and translated a dozen new texts (stories, songs, and personal narratives), not only from Vasya but also from several others that we have discovered since. We met and recorded Maria Tolbanova (born 1931), previously unnoticed by us, and the oldest living fluent female speaker who is able to tell stories. In addition, we visited Anna and Aleksei Baydashev, the only remaining married couple who speak the language daily at home.

Nonetheless, the Ös-speaking population continues to decline sharply. Six speakers we interviewed in 2003 and 2005 have passed away. Only three speakers remain who are able to work with us. And only a single speaker, Maria, was able to tell an extended narrative about her life. What she chose to recall made her shake as she told it and brought tears to her eyes. It was a harrowing story of how, as a young girl, she nearly drowned. This is Maria's story:

I fell into the water. It was just about the time of the war. My mother sent me to live with her relatives in Beregayevo because she had gone blind. . . . So I went to live with my relatives, elder sister and aunt. One day when I was 12 years old, I went to fetch water. . . . I was naïve and young. It was during the wartime.

So I was going along and there was an ice rift, and the water along it was fairly shallow, and it wasn't far to the lake. I was going along with my pails and leather boots, but I didn't lace up the boots. Just as I got to the water I slipped and there I fell, my two pails fell in, and I fell in.

I flailed around in the ice, and I'm going down, then I looked and I was completely sinking. My leather boots fell off, and then I shouted out, "Mama I'm drowning." I looked up to the surface, but the water was already beginning to go white.

Then suddenly, it was as if my Mama pulled me out and made me stop crying. I was crying a lot, all cut up and all covered with blood. I ran back to the house, "Auntie, I fell in!"

My aunt said to me "How did you fall in? You let your boots fall in, you dropped your pails in."

I was shivering, my long hair was all iced. I shook and shivered as I warmed myself by the stove. Somehow I fell asleep.

Two days later all the ice melted and floated away downstream. Then my aunt Vera believed me.

My uncle came to fetch me back home. "Hey, let's go home," he said. But when I saw the ferry I was afraid. He had to blindfold me so I could get on the ferry.

The ferry sailed downstream until it stopped at our village. . . . My mama was waiting for me. "Daughter, daughter" she cried. . . . I was covered in scrapes and cuts, and I was ashamed. And when I think of it, I feel very bad.

We sat silent as Maria concluded her tale. The near-death experience had been so traumatic for her that it still brought a quaver to her voice more than 60 years later. Her own daughter, watching with us, had not heard this story before. Besides the privilege of hearing this heartfelt and deeply authentic life history, we were thrilled to have heard so much Ös spoken, and so passionately. The number of people who could tell such stories can be counted on one hand, and those who could understand, perhaps on two hands. Ös is dying of embarrassment and shame, hidden away, neglected, silenced.

"It would be very difficult to bring the language back now," opines Vasya. "But perhaps not impossible."

He has taken small steps, assisting me and other linguists in recording his stories, helping us locate speakers, and speaking the language to his wife and daughter. Coaxing an intentionally hidden language out of its hiding place is an arduous process. Ös was so effectively concealed that the few remaining speakers themselves, we found, were not aware of other speakers, who might have been living in the same village. Families were often unaware that their elders still spoke it, or they dismissed it as the rantings of the senile. It has lain deep in the recesses of memory, undisturbed for decades. And when it did come out, it stirred great emotion. The floodgates of memory opened, and stories from childhood and reminiscences of a lifetime spilled out.

With the permission of the Chulym tribal council and the support of elderly speakers, we decided to begin a bold social experiment with Ös. We created new social networks that we hoped would act as a powerful force in resurrecting this dormant language. Casting aside the idea that anthropologists should not actively intervene or affect the culture they are studying, we formed a partnership with the elders to help unlock their memories.

The Chulym council itself (with only one member out of seven admitting knowledge of Ös) affirmed that the language was at a critical stage. There were probably only two dozen speakers, if that, and it had fallen nearly completely silent because the elders who knew it still felt their old childhood shame and lacked opportunities to speak it. Even the presence of a single Russian speaker was enough to suppress their desire to speak it. And since Russian speakers dominated these Siberian villages, the pressures silencing Ös were always in force. This was the last best opportunity, the council believed, for scientists to document the language and to gain recognition for the community by bringing some of the most powerful stories to a wider audience.

We took extreme measures—driving from one village to the next, crossing rivers by ferry and reaching some locations by wooden canoe—to collect the elders. We brought them together for the sole purpose of having a conversation in their native tongue. Many of the elders we brought along had not visited the other villages, or even met the other speakers. They were unaware of the other elders who shared their fate of being silenced.

A commonplace that we take for granted—a conversation— was an utter novelty to these elders. We set up closed meetings in the villages and even posted bouncers at the doors of the houses to shoo away anybody who was a Russian speaker, whose very presence would have been enough to force the conversation to switch to Russian. The elders showed their joy at the opportunity by launching into long, laughter-filled dialogues in Ös.

The elders included Ivan, a diminutive elderly man about five feet tall, with a toothy smile and a hand-rolled stub of a cigarette between his lips. His face was deeply lined from a lifetime of hunting and fishing in the cold climate. And Anna, who looked older than her 65 years, a pensioner with a bright flowered headscarf and a boisterous laugh accompanied by waving hand gestures. They reminisced freely, regaling each other with tales of bear and moose hunting. They were so engrossed, they seemed to forget our presence, though they had granted us permission to film the session. We kept the cameras rolling, eager to catch every word.

Then the talk turned to cultural themes, as Vasya brought up the ancient lunar calendar system:

VASYA: How did we used to name our months? There was
   Fox month. . . . Ivan, you should know month names
   in our language!
ANNA: Ah yes, months!
IVAN: Well, there was Fox month, Chipmunk month, Green
   month, Riverbank month. . . .
ANNA: Green month, that's May, I said that! May is Green
   month!
VASYA: What else?

ANNA: I knew some of the months . . . my father he knew
them all. Oh, I've forgotten already. We've forgotten a lot
. . . of course.

Anna waved her hand across her eyes, a gesture of forgetting. Of
13 lunar months, the elders could name only four. So much had
faded from memory! They found it hard even to name plants that
grew in the yard—bilberry, whortleberry, dandelion, nettle—but
did not hesitate in naming animals such as mink, wolf, and moose.

Shifting the topic to hunting, Vasya entertained the elders with
a favorite story:

I got up in the morning before the sun rose, took my gun,
and set off to the lake. My boat was at the lake. I sat in my
boat and set off. Then I look: a moose is coming out of the
water! I landed the boat on the bank, took my gun, aimed
well, and made it go *boom!* The moose fell over. I smoked
one pipe of tobacco, then I took out my knife, skinned the
moose, put its meat in my boat, and returned home. My
wife and children were waiting for me at home.

Afterward, the elders were moved to laughter and tears simultaneously while watching the video playback on my laptop computer. For the first time ever, they saw themselves on video and
heard their own powerful, funny, archaic voices. While there is not
much that scientists can do to save a language, on that day, sitting
with the elders watching the playback, Greg and I felt empowered.
Our presence had awakened a slumbering culture, had created a
brand-new discourse, and had, however temporarily, breathed life
into a dying vernacular. "You've made us immortal," one of the
elders observed. Now people far removed in space and time from
these villages can hear the voices and listen to the stories.

*Anna and Aleksei Baydashev, the last remaining husband
and wife pair who speak Chulym at home.*

After returning from the village on what we knew would probably be our last visit to the Chulym, we were somewhat downcast.
We thought about the dramatic life stories that Maria Tolbanova
had told us. She had probably been waiting decades to retell that
story to an audience that could appreciate it in its original tongue.
We were awed and humbled to have been a part of that audience.
We knew that the story would likely never be told again, and so
we had a special responsibility to care for the recording, archive
it, translate it, and make it known to the world, as Maria had
instructed us. As we pored over our notes and replayed bits of the
sound recording to be sure we'd gotten it right, I had a sense of
finality. I was convinced no more stories like this one would ever
be told in this language.

But one more surprise awaited us. Back at the archives in
Tomsk, the city where we had originally begun our expedition,

we decided to examine once again a collection of dusty notebooks from 1971. Buried among the pages, we had uncovered all kinds of curiosities—a list of words for types of flowers and fish, instructions on how to bake bread on hot coals and how to fish with a net from a wooden dugout canoe. We had faithfully made copies of these texts. But we had overlooked one. To our amazement, on page 573 of the notebooks, we stumbled upon a truly epic story. As we flipped through the book, we realized that the story and its translation went on for a full 56 pages! Nothing of this magnitude in Ös had ever been published or even reported to exist. Not one of all the speakers we had talked to could tell a story of more than a few dozen lines. This was a truly astonishing find, and all the more so because it had lain hidden in the Tomsk University archives for nearly 40 years.

The story itself, "Three Brothers," is a bizarre mash-up of dozens of different folktale motifs. It has echoes of Ovid's *Metamorphoses,* the Brothers Grimm fairy tales, the *Arabian Nights,* and numerous other folktale traditions. It may be as old as or even older than any of these, representing an unbroken tradition of tale-telling from an ancient time. Handed down over centuries and passed through countless minds, it has been smoothed like a polished pebble by the process of hearing, memorizing, and retelling.

Because it had never been written down until 1971, it shows all the important qualities of oral tradition. Only what can easily remain in memory has been retained, and certain aspects have been dramatized, repeated, or embellished to make it easier to memorize. Some of the many memory hooks evident here are the repetitions, the heavy use of numbers (three, seven), archetypal animals (swan, deer, pike), and the scenes of violence (vampiric devils that stab with needles and drink blood). Like any good tale, it includes deception, doubt, betrayal, and revenge. No doubt this tale contains the threads of many ancient stories that have been woven together

146

into a single cord. It is the culmination and the end of an ancient tradition. No person alive can retell this story in the original tongue from memory, and only a few still living would comprehend it as told. It is ancient, and yet completely new to the world, a nearly forgotten monument to human creativity that expresses our most primal fears and some of our fondest longings. These can be seen here in portions of the translated story of the "Three Brothers."[6]

Once upon a time there were three brothers. They were out hunting.

Suddenly three swans came flying, honking to them.

The swans spent the night on the roof of their house.

The next morning, when the three brothers were out hunting, the three swans suddenly rose up and became three girls.

The three girls came into their house.

The eldest girl says, "I'll marry the big brother."

The middle girl says, "I'll marry the middle brother."

The youngest girl says, "I'll marry the small one."

Then eldest one washed the floor, the middle one washed shirts, and the youngest one cooked.

When the brothers returned from hunting, they said, "Who did all this for us so well?"

And so the three brothers married the three swan sisters, but things quickly went awry, as the story continues:

While the wives were living in their house, they grew thin and sickly.

The younger brother says, "Brothers, why have the wives gotten ill?"

The youngest brother told the oldest brother, "Lie in wait and watch!"

So the brother remained, lying in wait.

He saw ash rise up through the chimney pipe, and the chimney began wobbling wildly.

A devil flew out from the chimney.

He stabbed the wives with a needle. The wives cried out.

As their blood flowed out, the devil began drinking it.

He drank up, and then went back up into the chimney.

When the brother confronted the chimney-dwelling vampire, a cataclysm ensued, and the underground portion of the epic began:

As the youngest brother lay in wait, once again the devil came out.

His wife began to cry and scream.

The youngest brother started shooting with a gun.

Suddenly, the devil together with the house and the wife fell into a crevice in the earth.

He himself jumped out from the crack in the ground, then slaughtered some of his cows and tore and bound up their skins for ropes and lowered himself down into the earth.

He says to his brothers, "I will go underground to search for my wife."

Here the story shifts gears from a horror/vampire story to a what looks like a very typical quest tale. As the brother searches for his wife in the underworld, he encounters strange and fantastic creatures.

He comes to a large bird tied to an iron chain.

The bird says, "Free me now, and I will help you sometime!"

So he set him free and then went on.

Next he saw a large pike lying stuck in shallow water, who lacked the strength to go on.

"Free me now, [called the pike] and I will help you sometime!"

So he freed the pike.

At long last, the brother located his wife, but she had been imprisoned by an evil "Iron Khan." A wise old woman advised them that they must kill the Khan.

"How should I kill him?" the husband says.

"Make him drink a lot of vodka, and when he gets drunk on the vodka, he will tell you where his soul is," the old woman told him.

So then his wife went to the Khan and made him drink a lot.

She asks him, "Where is your soul?"

The drunk Khan told her about his soul, "You must go to a bog, to the steppe, and to a cave where you will find seven deer.

"You must kill all of those seven deer.

"Having killed the deer, split open their stomachs, and you'll find a small chest there."

So the husband did as the Khan said. When he opened the chest, there were seven eggs inside.

The husband took the Khan's eggs and dropped and broke five of them.

When he came back to the Khan with the two eggs, the Khan shouted, "Leave my soul alone!"

Her husband held on to the eggs with all his might, but one egg fell into the lake. Then the pike swam up.

"Young boy, what do you need?" he said.

The man says, "I dropped my egg into the lake."

So the pike went and got it and brought it back for him.

So the man held one of the eggs in his fist [threatening
to crush it],
    and he asked the Khan, "Where is your gold?"
    So the Khan told him about all of his gold.
    Then the man crushed the remaining egg and was able
to kill the Iron Khan.

Having killed the Khan and rescued his wife, the brother begins his
ascent from the underworld. He sends his wife first, but as soon as
she is safe above, his treacherous brothers cut the rope, stranding
him down below.

    The brother comes once again to the large bird, and he
says, "Large bird, I helped you before."
    The bird came to the boy: "What [do you] need, young
man?"
    The young man says, " I don't have the strength to get
up over the edge."
    "You go and shoot birds for me, forty birds," said the
great bird.
    So he shot some birds and brought them.
    The big bird approached the young man.
    "Get up on my back and give me a bird [to eat] each
time I call."
    So the young man gave one at each call of the bird.
    Flying up, they approached the edge.
    But at the next call of the big bird, the young man had
no more birds to feed him.
    So, he cut off a piece of his leg for him
    Again, and again (the big bird) called out for food, and
he cut the meat off his leg to feed the bird.
    When they reached the edge, he didn't have any legs left.

The big bird asked the young man, "What happened to you? You don't have any legs."

"I cut the meat off and gave it to you."

So the big bird spat up the meat and glued it back onto to the young man's legs.

The young man became better, and so he returned to his brothers.

But his brother had taken his wife and they had married.

His wife saw him and started to cry.

The young man asked his brothers, "Who cut my rope?"

His brothers didn't say anything.

So he said, "Let's all go outside. You two shoot arrows from your bows. Whoever is the person who cut the rope, the arrow will hit the mark in his body."

So they started shooting.

One arrow passed straight through the eldest brother, and he died immediately.

So the two younger brothers lived on, after they buried that other one.

The story ends abruptly, though on a happy note. It is a monument of oral literature, and we can only speculate how ancient it may be. It could easily be of the same antiquity as canons of Western literature like the *Odyssey*. It shows hallmarks of being stitched together from many different stories, indicating repeated retelling and reinterpretation. Alongside ancient motifs (vampires, an underworld quest), we see some modern touches, such as vodka and guns. It has been passed down only orally, always adapting, told around the campfires at evening. In the small birch-bark huts the Chulym once lived in, with blocks of ice for windows, stories like this would have provided the only entertainment during long winters.

How did these stories almost slip away? Why were they hidden? The Chulym shaman story was hidden out of fear, because native religion was banned. Vasya's writing was hidden out of shame, because he was made to feel inferior for his ethnicity and language. And the ancient underworld quest story of the "Three Brothers" was hidden partly by neglect—as new forms of entertainment like television replaced storytelling—and partly by politics, as the Chulym were never allowed to write their stories down in books or teach them in schools.

Whatever the reason for hiding a language, silencing a story, or subduing a song, on our linguistic expeditions we do the spadework that brings these hidden words back to light. At the very least, we can give them a continued existence in the pages of books or in digital archives. Beyond that, we hope to encourage a new generation to continue telling and singing them. Without our human stories, as diverse or as similar as they may be across time and space, we are not fully ourselves.

{ CHAPTER SIX }

SIX DEGREES OF LANGUAGE

*The entire world needs a diversity of ethnolinguistic entities
for its own salvation, for its greater creativity, for the more
certain solution of human problems . . . indeed, for arriving
at a higher state of human functioning.*

—Joshua A. Fishman

THE FAMOUS TRIVIA GAME "Six Degrees of Kevin Bacon" was
designed to show that all people on Earth can be connected by
just a few links. The odds are very good that you know someone who knows someone who knows someone . . . who knows
Kevin Bacon (or anyone else). Every person in the "human web"
is linked to every other person, if this principle holds true, by a
chain of no more than five people. What started out as an amusement has become a serious research effort at the heart of the
emerging science of social networks. We are all connected, and it
is language, not film, that plays the greatest role in spinning the
links between us.

Environments like Facebook provide an easily traceable map
of a person's social networks, the geography of their friendships.
If you "friend" me, I can look and see who all *your* friends are.
But the network exists, and governs all our lives, even if we do
not have Facebook to visualize it for us. Entire societies are built

upon the foundation of social networks, and we are all constantly kept busy with their construction, repair, and revision.
Social networks transmit information, allow us to feel we belong
to various communities, and, like language or ethnicity or social
class, help us to draw a firm (even if invisible) boundary between
"us" and "them." Humans are driven to separate themselves and
segregate into groups, and everyone belongs to multiple social
groups that inspire varying degrees of allegiance. Languages are
one of the most effective ways to signal group membership, and
we are hypersensitive to even minor differences in pronunciation
and vocabulary. If I say "pop" instead of "soda" in New York, I
instantly, with just that one word, signal my status as an outsider
to the local community.

Papua New Guinea, with its 800-plus languages, is the extreme
example of how languages signal group membership. For reasons
we don't fully understand, a relatively small population of seven
million people, belonging to small groups in constant contact with
other groups, has, instead of converging on a common language,
kept a massive number of distinct ones. This unique situation
sheds light on some mysteries about how languages function in
social networks.

If you use Facebook, currently the premier social networking
site, you may have drawn a "friend wheel," a visual representation of all your friends. You are at the center of the wheel, and
you (possibly) know all your friends personally. The more interesting question is which of your friends are connected to each other.
Clusters of friends appear together on the wheel, which is not
surprising, since, for example, everybody in my high school senior
class of 60 knew each other. More surprising are links between two
friends who happen to know each other and don't know anyone
else in common except me. We form a triad. And then, because we
live such mobile lives, there are always many friends on my wheel

who know absolutely no one else in my life and may never meet any of them. I am their one degree of separation.

I enjoyed periodically redrawing my friend wheel on Facebook, but at 600 friends, I reached the upper limit—the program cannot calculate more than that. I imagined what life would be like if 600 were the actual upper limit of friends one could have (of course, no one can have 600 really close friends, but I'm including casual friends, some colleagues, and my banker and barber here). Now imagine what would happen if we lifted my entire friend wheel, with all 600 people attached, and put us on a desert island. We would quickly form a society, with all the soap opera intimacies, *Lord of the Flies* rivalries, and *Survivor* politics. The wheel would grow many new spokes, as the 600 became more densely networked until eventually everybody knew everybody. At that point, the wheel would tell us nothing useful. We would be a maximally densely networked society, each member having zero degrees of separation. The thought is enough to make me claustrophobic. Since friendship is not transitive, I imagine many of my friends would end up hating each other (though some might fall in love, counterbalancing that). It would no longer be a friend wheel but simply a "people in my society" wheel.

While there's nothing magic about the number 600, or my imaginary dense network, that number approximates the total number of speakers of many of the languages in New Guinea and elsewhere. What happens when an entire language is spoken exclusively and constantly by 600 people who all know each other (they may not all talk to each other, but they all live in the same village where they *could* converse with, or overhear, everyone else's speech)? In 2009, our Enduring Voices research team arrived in Papua New Guinea, land of more than 800 languages, to delve into these questions.[1]

Panau (which means "give me"), a small language in Madang province, nearly fits the "friend wheel" profile. Spoken in just one small seaside village of 600-plus souls in Papua New Guinea, Panau has the densest possible network. Imagine what it must be like to speak such an exclusive language, with zero degrees of separation between every speaker. One direction such a language could take is that it could be very conservative, changing very little over time, thus having little or no variety (nobody from one end of the village to another has a different accent or dialect, and there are no "pop"-vs.-"soda" disputes).

On the other hand, we can imagine such a language changing very quickly, because it would be much easier to introduce new words. A Panau speaker could wake up one morning and notice a new (to him) object, say, an iPod that a neighbor brought home from the market town. With little effort, he could declare it a *"babala,"* and that new word might catch on and become the name everyone called it. Even if they decided to call it an "iPod," that would be a new loanword and could very quickly become known and used by every single speaker. In English, such innovations take much more time to ripple through the vast and dispersed population of speakers, even with the help of mass media. There are surely English speakers alive today who have not (yet) heard the word "iPod," though they must live fairly isolated lives. Many more will not yet have heard "Facebook" or "Napster." Yet a Panau speaker could stand in the center of his village and shout the new word, broadcasting with complete efficiency to nearly every single speaker at once.

So which is it? Do small, densely networked languages accelerate their evolution, or do they put the brakes on? Do they change rapidly or hardly at all? And what does the special character of very small languages tell us about human nature, social networks, and the future?

The author working in Matugar village, Madang province, Papua New Guinea, 2009, with Panau speakers Hickey Willie (right) and John Agid (left). Panau is spoken by about 600 people, making it an excellent example of a very small, densely networked language.

ALL FOR ONE AND ONE FOR ALL

As he hung the shell necklace around my neck, Peter Kosi told me, "Don't forget us." He looked at me piercingly with his right eye, turning his left eye, blinded and white, away from the camera. Peter was dressed in the full finery that the Karim people reserve nowadays for rare initiation dances, with a woven vine apron in the front, fronds of grass in the back. His elaborate shell necklace and a head ornament with pig tusks marked him as a man of high status, and when he spoke, it became clear why. Bare-chested to show off his powerful upper body, he boasted a physique honed not at the gym but in the jungle—by countless hours chopping bamboo, rowing canoes, digging soil with a wooden spade, and hefting logs.

Next to Peter stood George, a younger man with an even more impressive physique, and with a full pattern of ritual scars covering his back, chest, and upper arms. Intricate patterns of bumps, some protruding almost a half inch and several inches in length, formed what resembled a crocodile's skin superimposed upon his own flesh. It was as if a man had merged with a crocodile. Though he was a modest, soft-spoken man, George's scars signaled status and placed him among the most prominent members of his age group. He told me how he had been one of only two volunteers from his village who answered the call of distant clan brothers to be initiated into the crocodile clan.

In Papua New Guinea, people belong first and foremost to an ethnic group, identified strongly with a local place and languages, and so George was a Karim person. He also belonged to the nation as a whole, as a citizen of Papua New Guinea. But in between local and national identity, everyone also belongs to a clan. This requires special allegiance and bestows distinct privileges. A member of any clan—whether the pig, crocodile, cassowary, or eagle—has the right to travel to any distant village, perhaps even a place where he cannot communicate in the local tongue, and to be welcomed, housed, and fed by members of his same clan.

To prove his worth as an initiated crocodile clansman, George and one other village mate had traveled to a distant village for an arduous six-week initiation. He endured hundreds of cuts, using a technique that embedded dirt into the wounds to cause permanent bumps. His only anesthetic came from plants known to the local healers for their medicinal properties. His initiators stuffed large amounts of the leaf into his mouth both to alleviate pain and to keep him from screaming. While he had left Yimas village as a handsome young teenager on the brink of manhood, George returned a hardened veteran and initiated adult man of his clan, ready to marry, to father children, and to take on a leadership role in his village.

Wherever George goes, he is instantly recognized and taken care of by clan members. He has mutilated his flesh to show respect for his totem, the crocodile. This level of dedication far exceeds the tattooing of a loved one's name on your arm or devotion to a religious cult, and probably cannot be understood by outsiders who do not abide in the faith of the crocodile and do not share a worldview in which river spirits determine human destinies.

Karim religion is in decline, and important rituals are rarely performed these days. As we observed on the fringes, a powerful circle of dancers formed in the main square of the village known as Yimas 2. Wearing body paint, shell ornaments, and grass skirts, they formed two rings. Women took the outermost ring, men the inner. At the center, two figures enclosed completely in body masks wove their dance steps, swaying and plunging. Time was kept by a steady pounding on a large slit drum, echoed by small hand drums held by the male dancers.

This was an initiation ritual, performed out of time and place and entirely unfamiliar to the village's youngest residents. Originally this would have been performed inside a spirit house, with women dancing outside and men within, the teenage male initiate brought into the spirit house for his coming-of-age ceremony. But this village no longer had a spirit house. The village headman explained to us how the ritual had fallen into disuse and how glad he was to see it being performed, even if partly for show. The intensity of the dancers, as they sweated and chanted, and their obvious sense of cultural pride indicated this was no mere performance. Despite the infrequency of the initiation ritual and the fact that it took place at the initiative of our National Geographic team, the dance evidenced a certain resilience of belief. Even without a spirit house, the 40 participants had spent hours adorning and painting themselves, and they took great care to perform the ritual correctly.

Just upstream, in the sister village Yimas 1 (Google Earth location S 04° 40.871' E 143° 33.011'), a newly constructed spirit house presents a powerful visual icon of the crocodile. As you pass under the doorway into the spirit house—a place only men may enter—just over your head you see a carved wooden woman with her legs spread wide, giving birth to a crocodile. The crocodile has emerged halfway from the womb, its head and forelegs dangling downward. This painful imagery, perhaps grotesque to Western eyes, displays one of the most sacred totemic principles of the Karim people. Their creation myth begins with the birth of a crocodile. It introduces and sustains life and is to be worshipped and respected, as well as feared and imitated.

Just as the spirit house re-creates the totemic imagery, and the ritual dancing and drumming re-create the spirit narrative, the Karim language, now severely endangered, sustains the complex clan system and the mythology that underlies their religion. "Our children are starting to forget our language," Peter Kosi told me, explaining how the children—who attend school with children from a different tribe located just downstream—speak mostly Tok Pisin. "We need a linguist to come to our village and help us, before our language disappears." Indeed a linguist *had* worked among the Karim people, and even published a thick grammar book,[2] which they took great pride in. But that had been two decades ago, and the book itself was written for a scientific readership, in highly technical language, and was not available or useful for teaching the language to children.

Children are empowered decision-makers about whether to keep or abandon a language. When placed into a setting, such as a school, where their home language is not valued or encouraged, they may react by shifting away from it to speak the more dominant language. But it does not have to be so, as children can easily become bilingual. In the case of Karim children, school is the vector for language shift, specifically a school setting where they study with children from another tribe. One of the most powerful forces of ethnic identity—language—can vanish in a generation. It's certainly fair to ask: "Aren't kids better off shedding a small local language and becoming globally conversant citizens?" In response, wouldn't an even better scenario be kids who increase their brainpower by being bilingual and enjoy the benefits of both a close-knit ethnic community and a sense of national or global participation?

FEATHERS AND LOINCLOTHS

Standing on the riverbank just two miles downstream from Yimas 2 village, Luis Kolisi of the Yokoim tribe provided a perfect photo op. He wore a woven bark loincloth, red and white body paint, and an outlandish hat that sprouted chicken feathers. Watching him expertly split sago logs and hack away at the pulp with a stone ax, I realize what incredible stamina his life requires, and what ingenuity (and desperation) it took humans to perfect sago as a source of food.

Luis belongs to the "clever" Yokoim people, and much of Luis's demonstration is reimagined culture, like the body mask and carved crocodiles his village offers for sale, neither of which is part of their "traditional" culture. But what good is tradition without the freedom to constantly reinvent yourself? The Yokoim have reinvented themselves with gusto. Their tiny village, Kundiman, is home to nearly half of their entire ethnic group, the Yokoim people. It lies just a quarter mile downstream (ten minutes by boat) from the region's only tourist lodge, a location frequented by foreign tourists.

The Yokoim people have taken an utterly banal, everyday skill—the splitting open of sago logs, washing the pulp, and processing it into pancakes and porridge—into a marketable tourist attraction. Clever indeed. Tour boats bring tourists from the lodge. They may spend a few minutes in the village gawking at the naked children and bare-breasted women, who focus intently on their cooking tasks and avoid making eye contact. They may buy the wooden masks or woven baskets the village produces. The children often run around naked, to be sure, but there seems to be a bit more nudity and enthusiastic casting off of clothes when tourists arrive. In the women's body language, as they put on a cooking show for tourists, I detect a tinge of chagrin, perhaps a sense of doing work that is slightly embarrassing or demeaning, while at the same time utterly necessary and useful (feeding the children). I can only hope that this chagrin is shared by the tourists, who must realize that if the situation were reversed—for example, if busloads of Japanese tourists were delivered to their kitchen at 8 a.m. to observe and photograph them frying eggs in their bathrobe—they would feel utterly awkward and objectified.

Unfortunately, the Yokoim are paid only a pittance for these activities (though, in fairness to the tourist lodge, "locally appropriate wages"). They fear that if they ask for more, the work will be given to another group, and each village jealously guards its tourist prerogatives, specializing in drums, say, or masks, or one particular activity that it alone presents to outsiders. The Yokoim make minimal income from presenting these cultural displays. They also claim to receive no royalties of any kind for the use of the only local airstrip, on which the lodge depends and which was built on their land. Whatever the facts, clearly much progress could be made in how tourists, scientists, tour operators, and local indigenous communities interact, and one hopes for more balance and more economic fairness in these relationships.

What the tourists do not see, and what I was able to witness on repeated visits to Luis's village, is the congenial, close-knit, and arduous everyday life of a small village. Luis resides in a very large, elevated bamboo house belonging to his cousins. His own house had burned down (some local children were "pretend cooking" with real fire, he told me) and was under reconstruction. The house boasts a cozy, wide-open floor plan inhabited by multiple families, each of whom has their nook and their set of bed mats and mosquito nets. No one has any privacy—you can even walk under the house peering up and listening through the loose floor slats, which the neighbors did during our interview with Luis. This was in no way considered rude, and some interesting through-floor conversations and commentary ensued. Allowing someone to watch through the floor seems be a kind of halfway Yokoim hospitality, since the more select guests and residents were allowed up the ladder into the house to observe Luis's performance. What one would never suspect, watching Luis chop sago while wearing feathers and body paint, is that what he truly excels at is the role of a bluesy, folksy guitar singer, someone like Philadelphia singer Amos Lee or the Papuan artist Ben Hakalitz.

Dressed normally—that is to say, in old jeans and a T-shirt, sans feathers—Luis strummed haunting melodies of his own composition and, quite stunningly for me, with original lyrics written in Yokoim language. One, a love song, he explained, was a lament for a wife sung to her husband, a man named Kinjan Bunduwan, who appears to lie sleeping at her side, but has died in the night:

Aii, you better wake up
Ooooh, Kinjan Bunduwan,
Aaaay, you better wake up.
You had better get your penis to wake up.
You had better get your dangerous fellow to cheer up.

Aaaay, Kinjan Bunduwan,
Ooh, you better wake up, get up.
Why are you sleeping like that, sleeping so deeply?
Why are you like dead like a man sleeping?

This song will never be a *Billboard* Top 40 hit. Though the tune is catchy, the total number of people who could understand the lyrics without translation is a few hundred. Then there is the matter of the taboo word, which is censorable in English but a common everyday term in Yokoim.

Luis followed with another original composition, a song called "Imba Us" that at first seemed to be about poisonous snakes, but turned out to be a marriage proposal:

Your village, Singalan, is swampy and full of death adders.
I don't want to stay here, I'll come back, I'll come back to my own village.

Singalan is swampy and full of death adders.
I don't want to stay here, I'll come back, I'll come back to my village.

Come here, my dear, come to my home, come to my river.
My land doesn't have death adders.
My place doesn't have death adders.

Come here, my dear, come to my home, come to my river.
My land doesn't have any death adders.

My place doesn't have death adders.
My land doesn't have death adders.

That a language as small as Yokoim could have such an inspired songwriter as Luis may be one of the crucial intangible forces keeping it in existence. The importance of such influential individuals, whom I call "language activists," cannot be underestimated. Though they may not style themselves as activists, they have a deep conviction that their own tongue surpasses all others in its intimacy and power of expression. Based on this conviction, they make a strategic decision to use it with pride and creative force. No role model could be more powerful to the children listening under the floor than Luis's voice, a soft, nasally baritone, sounding out syllables of the mother tongue: *Imba us, imbaaa uuuuus.*

These same children go to school with the children of the Karim people of Yimas village, from a neighboring language group. Since it is a mixed-language classroom, a strict ideology of English and Tok Pisin is imposed. Since these two tongues are promoted as superior, the children make a rational choice of abandoning Yokoim to become subtractively bilingual in those two dominant languages. For want of a song or a shred of encouragement from an inspired speaker, the giggling children under the house may soon abandon the mother tongue. It would be fascinating to observe the language dynamics of the school playground—who speaks what to whom, and when. The children must constantly negotiate their status, identity, and schooling. In the classroom, we are told, no indigenous language use is tolerated by the teachers. And so an entire village is being "schooled away" from the mother tongue, and Luis's death adder love song will soon be incomprehensible. By comparison, schoolchildren from another Yokoim village farther upstream attend an all-Yokoim school. They, too, know Tok Pisin and English, but they are not abandoning Yokoim.

It seems indeed that a language is a dialect with an army and a school system.[3] Schools can be powerful incubators for language preservation and pride, or a strong force for abandonment.

WATER SPIRITS AND CROCODILES

In Luis's water world, the Karawari River basin, home to the Karim and Yokoim people, dugout wooden canoes provide the only means of travel. They are only about 18 inches wide, but can be 20 feet long. There are even mini-sized ones for children. Incredibly precarious and tippy, they are propelled by two punters. Luis demonstrated for us how he stands in the bow of the canoe, with one foot planted on the floor and one propped up on the side. He used a forked oar that both pushes water and can gain traction on the bottom. A woman or child can sit in the stern of the canoe, using an oval-shaped oar, and smaller children occupy the middle. Wisps of smoke behind the woman show she's carrying burning coals to light tobacco and a cooking fire once she reaches her garden site.

Since we were traveling by motorized boat, a rare sight in these waters, we had to constantly look out for canoes and slow to a crawl to avoid capsizing or flooding them. With this start-and-stop rhythm, we arrived upriver at Konmei village.

What we need is a "Masta talk place," declared Councilman Chris Nick. "The other languages upstream and downstream have their linguists and translators, but our language is alone. We want an expert to come and study it." Councilman Nick, along with his entire family, awaited us in full red body paint, a feather headdress, shell and boar's-tusk necklaces, and grass skirts. As we arrived at 9:30 a.m., we had the impression that they had all been sitting patiently for hours in the talking hut, even though we had not promised to arrive at any particular time that day. Their enthusiasm was contagious, and soon what seemed like the whole village (population precisely 396 souls, as the councilman informed us) turned out to watch.

We asked Councilman Nick to reprise the creation story he had told us two days prior. At the time, we felt it was an excellent oration, beautifully delivered, but had no idea what it was about. With the help of a translator from another village, we soon found out, and we were eager to hear it retold when we visited the second time.

The tale he told us recounts how his "clever" Yokoim learned from a mysterious water spirit everything they needed: hunting and architecture, planting and canoemaking, warfare and fire. Nick gestured off into the distance to indicate the mythical past.

It happened like this. . . . In the village, there lived a man named Waka. One day, his wife could not find him and she began calling his name loudly. Perhaps he was hiding from her, or busy, or just ignoring her, but as he did not respond, she called louder. Now it just so happened that in the river, this very Manjamai River, there also lived a powerful water spirit, who by sheer coincidence was the man's namesake, "Waka." The water spirit heard the woman calling "Waka" and thought she was summoning to him. Coming out of the river to answer her, he encountered the other Waka, her husband. He seized the husband, human Waka, and took him down under the waters.

I should mention here that the Yokoim people are avid swimmers, and children and adults alike take a daily plunge into the river. People often cross from one side of the village to another by swimming, as not everyone has a canoe. The river is not feared, but is part of the everyday environment that sustains life. It provides transport, news, security, recreation, and sustenance.

So being pulled under the river was not so much a dreadful as a magical experience.

Waka did not drown, but breathed water as if it were air, with the help of the water spirit. Still, his wife kept calling from the village, but she got no answer because the water spirit would not release his namesake. After some days, the wife—knowing nothing of the river sprit Waka—concluded that human Waka must have drowned. She painted her face white and began her period of mourning.

Meanwhile, the husband was having a lark underwater. River spirit Waka schooled human Waka in all manner of skills: canoe-making, hunting, and bow- and arrow-making. Day by day they hunted, waged warfare with stealthy raids on other villages, fished with traps, built bamboo houses, and perhaps even made *maley mamakey*, "bad water," a strong coconut liquor. We may think of it as impossible to build canoes, hunt fruit bats, and build fires underwater, but the tale insists that these all exist there. We may glimpse them on the water's surface, perhaps mistakenly taking them to be reflections of things in our world.

For almost a month, Waka inhabited this parallel underwater world that mirrored the world above the water. Finally the river spirit, having imparted all good and useful knowledge, released the man. He brought back to his people all the skills, techniques, and technologies they still use today. They use them so well, that they refer to themselves as the "clever Yokoim." "When we raid a village and shoot our arrow, we do not miss a man," boasts Councilman Nick. "We are the clever Yokoim, very clever men."

The legendary cleverness may be sorely tested as the Yokoim see their language slip away. "We need a Tok Pleis Masta," declared Nick. In his mind, that meant an outsider, typically a "white" person, who would come, live, and learn the local vernacular of that place, which locals call Tok Pleis, or "talk place." He had seen missionaries, linguists, and anthropologists come to other villages, but felt that his own people needed a dedicated scholar. "We want a book for the children."

The vitality of Yokoim could be greatly enhanced by a team of scientists showing an intense interest in the creation myth, or by a scholar helping the community to prepare their first book. Languages thrive or wither based on their prestige in the eyes of children, and prestige is a fragile quality that can spread as quickly as smoke, but also dissipate as easily. Clearly a substantial, long-term effort is needed, but to be effective that effort must be mostly in the local hearts and minds, not an outside intervention.

BODY COUNTING

Cleverness in the island nation is not limited to knowledge gained from water spirits. One of the most remarkable cultural innovations of Papua New Guinea is the wild profusion of body-counting systems. Nowhere in the world is such a wide variety of body math systems found, using points on the body like pegs on a cribbage board or beads on an abacus. These systems, far from being the primitive enumerations that scientists first labeled them, are highly sophisticated. Some permit addition and subtraction. counting ad infinitum, even multiplication. All ingeniously bootstrap and augment human memory by using the body as a short-term memory buffer. Using only bodies and body parts, some could count to infinity.[4]

We live in a world regulated by mathematics and numbers, and we are drilled in arithmetic from an early age. Skill in algebra is a gateway to high SAT scores and higher education, so we can be forgiven for thinking that math is a kind of anchoring rock that we depend on and that does not change. But viewed through the lens of other cultures, numbers look very different. Indeed, the whole premise of our counting system, based on units of ten, turns out to be a cultural whim, a mere preference.

Body counting is only the tip of the complexity iceberg, and New Guinea cultures hold many more mathematical surprises. We sat down in a small village on the Ambonwari River with the local schoolteacher, a man named Julius.[5] He spoke excellent English and had worked over the years with a visiting anthropologist, so he had the patience needed to teach foreigners things that should be perfectly obvious. Greg Anderson and I set up our camera and recording equipment and sat in the village's main house, with about a hundred people observing us. Much to their amusement, we were flummoxed by something they regard as utterly simple—counting to one!

Here's how our session unfolded. We started with a simple question, and learned that the word for the number one is *mban*—or so we thought. After a long detour through the number system, we found out that "mban" is just one manifestation of the chameleon-like word for "one" in this language. Like that colorful lizard, it changes its appearance continually, but unlike the chameleon, its changes are governed not just by the surroundings (e.g., what word it is modifying) but also by a complex system that divides all nouns up into special categories (e.g., living male things are different from living female things, which are different from inanimate objects that end in the letter *n*, and so on. Here's how the dialogue unfolded:

DAVID: And do you have a word for . . . one?
JULIUS: One. *Mban. Mban.*
DAVID: *Mban.*
JULIUS: *Mban* is one. We have only ten counting numbers in the language. One is *mban.* Two is *kripai,* three is *kriyen mau,* four is *samunung,* five is *suwam,* six is

170

sambaimbiyam, seven is *samba kripai,* eight is *samba kriyen mau,* nine is *samba usanam,* ten is *sumbri.*

Greg, with his astounding language aptitude and love of numbers, counted right back: "So, mban, kripai, kriyen mau, samunung, suwam, sambaimbiyam, samba kripai, samba kriyen mau, samba usanam, sumbri."

I was still struggling with one, and I thought I had heard something ever so slightly different, so I asked, "One is *mbang?*"

Julius replied, "*Mbang.*"

So it seemed we had two words for one, "mbam" and "mbang." Julius, patient as a schoolteacher, clarified: "All right, there is different ways in counting. *Mbang* we say for different things. *Mbam* also is the same as one. So, different items, we name them in different numbering systems."

Intrigued, we began trying to figure out when to say which form by asking him to count objects. "One banana" was *mambaing mbang* and "one coconut" was *wurang mbang.* This seemed clear: "one" is "mbang." But sometimes it is pronounced "mban": "one pig" is *imbiyan mban* and "one dog" is *wiya mban.*

Then we were confounded yet again: "one house" was translated as *yam mbo.*

Now it seemed like a simple three-way split. Words than end in *-ng* take the word "mbang," words that end in a vowel or *-n* take "mban," and some other set of words, which we hoped to identify, take "mbo."

We tested our hypothesis by finding another word that ended in *-ng—pambang,* "bow and arrow"—predicting that it would be modified by "mbang." But we were wrong. Being wrong with your initial hypothesis is just where things start to get complex and interesting. So we kept asking for more examples.

How about one man? Julius said: "*Yermasanar mban.*"

And one woman, we asked? *Yermasanma mbanma.*

So it seemed the word for woman had a special suffix -*ma*, to make it "mbanma." We confirmed this with other words denoting female persons: "One daughter" is *kiyawi mbanma,* and "one sister" is *mamiyang mbanma.*

I asked: "What else do you count with *mbo*? What about canoes?"

JULIUS: So, for canoe, I would say *kai mbai.* And for one song? *Siriya mbaiya.*

GREG: Okay, how about one crocodile?

JULIUS: *Manbo mban.*

GREG: Yeah, I'm catching that one. We're trying to find another word that we can get *mbo* with. What's the word for arrow, arrow you use on the bow?

JULIUS: Arrow. *Aring ganam mbam.*

GREG: Okay . . .

JULIUS: *Mbam.*

. . .

GREG: And so, can you say *mambaima mbanma*?

JULIUS: Yes, *mambaima mbanma* because it's a female crocodile.

GREG: Right, okay. Okay, I got some of the system here. So, you say, *yam mbo,* "one house."

JULIUS: *Yam mbo.*

GREG: Can you say anything else with *mbo*?

JULIUS: Yes, let me think first.

I exclaimed: "How to count to one in this language!" and Greg agreed, "Yes, we'll never get past one!"

JULIUS: Okay, for coconut. For coconut, I say *ip.* So one coconut palm is *ip mbo.*

DAVID: *Ip mbo.*

JULIUS: Yes.

GREG: And how about coconut fruit?

JULIUS: *Worung mbang.*

GREG: Okay, um, one tree?

JULIUS: *Iwan mbang.*

DAVID: We need another word that counts with *mbaiya*. . . . What else is counted with *mbaiya*?

JULIUS: *Mbaiya?*

GREG: How about river?

JULIUS: *Wangan mban, Kwonmei mbo,* because we have these two different river names, the Wangan River and the Konmei River.

DAVID: *Kwonmei mbo.*

GREG: All right, I'm utterly confounded now. It's partly phonological and partly not, as we thought, but . . .

DAVID: What else counts with *mbaiya? Saipa mbaiya?*

JULIUS: No, *saipa* will be *saipa mbo.*

DAVID: What's the word for a big meeting house like this?

JULIUS: *Iman.*

DAVID: One iman?

JULIUS: *Iman mbo.*

DAVID: There we go.

GREG: Yeah, we have four *mbo*'s now. We have river, belly, house, coconut palm. Yeah, I mean those are perhaps semantically connected, in some way that makes sense for them.

DAVID: Because its like a house.

GREG: Yeah. So we still need another *mbaiya.*

DAVID: Right, because we have *mbo.*

GREG: What else would use *mbaiya?*

JULIUS: All right, I would like to explain to you a little bit. So, like, we have planted something, but these things are

not plentiful. So we say *mbaiya*. Not plentiful is *mbaiya*.
If I say *yangri*, okay, "one hand" *yangri mbaiya,* and "one
leg or foot" *yamangos mbaiya.*

DAVID: It's like small numbered things . . . things that come
in pairs or small numbers?

JULIUS: Yes, things that come in small numbers.

GREG: We also have *mbai,* that's another one we need. We
have *kai mbai* ["one canoe"].

JULIUS: *Kai mbai.*

GREG: Is there another *mbai*? What other word can we use
mbai with?

JULIUS: Okay, let's say *sipi. Sipi mbai.* For sago, *sipi,* we say
for fried sago is *sipi.*

GREG: So one sago palm is *sipi mbai*?

JULIUS: Yes, *sipi mbai.*

GREG: We could sit here all day and do this, but we don't
want to take up all your time.

DAVID: Yes, thank you, schoolteacher.

Throughout this baffling dialogue, we had deduced several general principles of the counting system, without fully grasping its complexity. How do you choose which form of "one"? It depends partly on the sounds contained in the word; if a word ends in *-ng* or *-k,* you use "mbang," which matches it. If a word ends in *-n,* you use "mban." Some words that end in *-ai* take "mbai." But we uncovered multiple exceptions, where some special consideration overrides the expected choice. One special consideration has to do with the type of word—for example, whether it is a male or female person or animal. If it comes in small quantities or numbers, a body part for example, then it takes "mbaiya."

A system like this requires speakers to keep track of multiple different categories: what sounds make up a word, what does the word refer to? Is it male or female, numerous or scarce, and so on? Each piece of information might lead you to use a different form, but not all information is equal. Some facts are more important than others, so they override, and that is another factor that must be learned by speakers. They seem to do it all effortlessly, as attested by the villagers' delight and laughter in hearing us attempt to learn the system.

As we left the village, we marveled at all the many different ways to say "one." And we wondered how much of that complexity appears in the higher numbers, which might not only classify objects into different groups but also require the speaker to do mental mathematics.

If you survey the world's languages, you find radically different ways of counting, different ways of apprehending and framing mathematical relationships. Some of these, as discussed above, are based on using the human body as a living abacus. Others are more abstract and work with a number other than ten (which is our number base) to build larger numbers.

One of our favorite eureka moments was captured in India for the documentary film *The Linguists*.[6] A speaker of Sora, Oruncho Gamango, was teaching us the numbers: *A-boy* means one, *BA-goo* is two, and *YA-gee* is three. Each number had a unique name, all the way up past *GEL-jee,* ten. *GEL-moy* means 11, and 12 is *MEE-gel.*

We dutifully wrote down the names, which were all unique labels up to 12. English also has unique names for numbers up to 12, and then it begins to build numbers 13 and above using ten as a base, so "eighteen" can be thought of as "eight" plus "ten," and ten is a basic building block in English that builds the higher numbers.

By this point, we thought Sora would be a straightforward system, even a bit routine. But when Oruncho reached 13, he repeated the word for 12, followed by the word for 1: "Twelve is *MEE-gel,* and 13 is *MEE-gel BOY.*"

Greg and I burst into smiles at the discovery. Sora uses a base-12 system. This is unusual though not unique in the world, but we felt happy because we had not personally documented such a system before in the course of our fieldwork. Then, as the numbers became higher, another pattern emerged. Sora also uses 20 as a base to build numbers. In the higher numbers, you can combine 20, 12, and other numbers, so that the way to say 93 in Sora is actually "four twenty twelve one"! (This may remind some readers of French numbers.)

Each language potentially has a unique way of counting, and mathematicians tell us that there is nothing sacred about using ten as a base—it is merely a convenience. We could have a sophisticated mathematics using 4 or 6 or 12 as a base. Yet these alternative ways of counting are rapidly vanishing, as the standard base-ten counting system continues to spread. Numbers and quantities are a deep property of the physical universe, and mankind has contemplated them for ages. But smaller languages, with their sometimes radically different ways of conceptualizing numbers, may hold some unique insights—if we can learn them before they vanish.

Language is what makes society possible, by binding humans together into groups: village, tribe, *ethnos,* nation. It serves as a token of ethnic identity and belonging, as visible and obvious as ritual scarring. So potent is the need for identity that—as we saw in Papua New Guinea—one group may even claim their linguistic uniqueness to the exclusion of another group, even though that group understands everything they say. In each culture, language lays the foundation for the world as they (or we) may know it, whether by grouping and classifying items for counting or by providing a mythic ancestor to honor. Without it, people are adrift, unaccounted for, unnamed.

Because it is so powerful in shaping our worldview and our self-view, I cannot regard people being coerced—no matter how subtly—into abandoning their languages as anything other than a form of violence. It represents an erasure of history, of creativity, of intellectual heritage. Keeping one's heritage language is every person's right. Happily, we can each contribute to sustaining this right by effecting a shift in attitudes. By learning to appreciate and celebrate the diversity—not only in places like Papua New Guinea, but equally in Paraguay or Pennsylvania—we ensure its survival.

{CHAPTER SEVEN}

HOW DO STORIES SURVIVE?

Every story is us. That is who we are,
From the beginning to no-matter-how-it-comes-out.

—Rumi (trans. Coleman Barks)

STORIES are the most ancient and enduring of all human creations, older than the Great Wall of China, the pyramids of Giza, or even the prehistoric cave drawings at Lascaux, France. Yet stories survive as a living art only when they are verbally narrated, painstakingly passed from mouth to ear. They become memes, cultural creations that rely parasitically on humans to preserve and propagate them.

Many ancient stories are still in circulation in remote cultures. Stories like that of the three brothers of Siberia in chapter 5 provide a portal into the deep past. Peering through it, we get an inkling of how humans thought 5,000, 20,000, or even 40,000 years ago. These durable works may well outlast any of today's monuments built by human hands. But the life of a story is also fragile, and it can easily disintegrate under the weight of the technological forces now at work in our world.

I set out to learn the secrets of storytelling from some of the last practitioners of the art of memory. My travels have taken me to remote cultures in Siberia, India, Australia, and elsewhere. In each place, I met storytellers who still practice their art, recognizing the potent enchantment of the spoken word. They have made great sacrifices to protect their powerful stories from being forgotten, from intellectual theft, and from the din of global media.

These master tale-tellers are inheritors of a deep intellectual tradition. They have helped solve the greatest information challenge of our species: keeping all essential knowledge solely in human memory. They pass it on from generation to generation, mouth to ear, without ever writing it down. Writing is a wonderful (and fairly recent) technology, and it allows efficient transmission of a story to new audiences. But writing also ensures that a story will become fossilized, trapped on paper, no longer able to adapt, grow, or enchant listeners in the same way. If all our libraries disappeared today, it's doubtful we could find any living person who could recite from memory Shakespeare's plays, the *Iliad* and the *Odyssey*, and the Grimm brothers' folktales. All these are vulnerable, because they exist only in writing and could be lost.

We'll visit three storytellers in this chapter, each with a secret to share, a tradition to protect. Along the way, we'll encounter a rainbow serpent swallowing people in Australia, a hero frozen in the ice caves of Siberia, and a drunken god in India's jungles. These fierce creatures have survived the ages by the power of storytelling.

At the center of Siberia, among the nomads, I met Shoydak-ool Khovalyg, a master teller of nearly lost epic tales. He told me the story of Bora, a shape-changing heroine who disguised herself as a man to complete a magical quest.

In the remote Australian outback, Charlie Mangulda told a sacred Dreamtime story of the Rainbow Serpent, creator and devourer of life.

In India, among the tribal people who call themselves the Ho, master orator K. C. Naik told me a creation myth—wonderfully inverted—in which God tricked the first man and woman into having sex by getting them drunk.

These rich stories opened up worlds I had never imagined. As a scientist, I found they pointed to even greater mysteries. How had they survived and been retold and reshaped by countless minds and mouths across the eons? What secret patterns and rhythms had allowed these stories to be transferred from mind to mind? Did they have any use in our modern world? Would they survive the 21st century? And what could we learn from them before they vanished?

Prior to the invention of writing, all stories survived only in human memory and by being retold orally. Tended carefully by campfires at night, whispered by mothers to infants, recited by fathers to young men as they set out for the hunt, certain stories persisted, grew, and evolved. They became memes—powerful packages of cultural ideas that are passed by hearing, imitating, or other social contact. Over time, and as writing freed modern humans from the burden of memorizing, we've grown mentally lazy. Stories became locked in books, rarely remembered verbatim or recited by heart. Today we hear only the faintest echoes of that great oral tradition, in the world's smaller languages that have never yet been written down.

A WORLD BEFORE WRITING

In our literate age, we like to imagine that all useful information is written down somewhere, that we can find it in a book, a library, a database, or a Google search. Nothing could be further from the truth. In fact, we face an immense knowledge gap between what is recorded anywhere and what is known. Most of what humans know today, and nearly everything they have known throughout history, exists purely in memory and is transmitted orally, from speaker to listener. From the profound to the fanciful, from creation myths to apple pie recipes, we have relied on memory to keep the record straight.

Most of the world's languages make no or little use of writing. For millennia, indigenous cultures have been solving the problem of organizing, distributing, and transmitting vast bodies of knowledge, all without the aid of writing. How did they accomplish this? In order to find out, we need to focus on languages that are still purely oral, never written, and see what kinds of knowledge structure and strategies for transmission they may contain. Orally transmitted knowledge is robust and has served as the only means of knowledge transfer for most of human history. Yet in our digital age, when we increasingly rely on artificial technologies, it is also a fragile device, easily lost.

Writing is a new technology, and while it is incredibly useful, it has not been around all that long. Literacy allows us to rely on external sources like books to store much of the information we need. Once we come to rely on writing, we can stop remembering things—for example, I no longer memorize my friends' telephone numbers or my appointment calendar.

Today we face an information crisis as the bulk of human knowledge, never recorded or written down, begins to erode. As a scientist, I have spent the last decade on a quest to recover and record bits of the knowledge base before it vanishes. I've identified as an urgent conservation priority the knowledge contained in our planet's 3,500 vanishing languages, hoping to record a portion of it before the last speakers die.

Historian Barbara Tuchman once wrote: "Without books, history is silent, literature dumb, science crippled, thought and speculation at a standstill. Without books, the development of civilization would have been impossible."[1] I would revise Tuchman's statement, suspending for a moment the literacy bias we all share. Without books, humans remembered and passed on their histories and creation myths. They created vast poetic works like the *Manas*, the Kyrgyz epic tale comprising over a million lines. They performed sophisticated scientific experiments to discover the medical uses of thousands of plants and learned how to navigate the vast Pacific Ocean without instruments. They engaged in deep thought and composed fanciful songs. Without books, great civilizations such as the Inca and Aztec, Nuer and Mongol, arose and flourished. As Pablo Neruda observed, "On our earth, before writing was invented, before the printing press was invented, poetry flourished. That is why we know that poetry is like bread; it should be shared by all, by scholars and by peasants, by all our vast, incredible, extraordinary family of humanity."[2] We could substitute "knowledge" for Neruda's "poetry," and the statement would still hold true.

Humans have accomplished remarkable feats by force of memory alone, without the use of writing. As a civilization, we will never give up writing, but we can learn a lot from societies that have not yet adopted writing, or have done so only recently. What kinds of mental techniques do they use to remember and transmit vast bodies of knowledge? Do they think and organize information differently? Are they smarter than us? How have they solved the information bottleneck, the problem of finite minds containing potentially infinite knowledge?

From the Arctic to the high Andes, from the grasslands of Mongolia to the swamps of Oregon, and nearly everywhere in between, we can still see traces of the stunning intellectual accomplishments humans achieved without the aid of writing, through language and memory alone. How they did so remains mostly a mystery, and the window of opportunity for us to unravel that mystery is rapidly closing.

Dying languages are often hidden in plain sight, spoken in private or in whispers, concealed. The knowledge they possess is valuable to all of humanity, but is exclusively owned and safe-guarded by the speakers. For reasons they alone decide, many of these last speakers have chosen to share some of their wisdom before it vanishes. What do the "last speakers" want to tell us, the "last listeners"? And how can this simple act of knowledge transmission lead to a global rebirth of language diversity, a process we can all take part in?

RAINBOW SERPENTS AND LAST WHISPERERS

The Rainbow Serpent is described as a fierce creature that lived in the billabongs, small lakes that dot Australia's "top end." Perhaps a hundred feet long, it was multicolored, with gaping jaws and jagged teeth. This Dreamtime myth has many versions, and Charlie Mangulda's version was narrated to me and Greg Anderson, sitting in an ancient cave at Awunbarna—what maps call Mount Borradaile. This was Charlie's ancestral land, the place where his father grew up and heard this story.

As Charlie told it, the Rainbow Serpent was awakened one day by the crying of a child. The child was crying because he wanted a water lily. But when the flower was brought to him, he was unsatisfied and cried even louder. As the child cried day and night, the Rainbow Serpent, aroused from his slumber in the billabong, went out preying on people. As he crossed the outback, in his wake he created new billabongs, freshwater ponds, each full of life. Eventually the serpent came to Croker Island, a sliver of land where Charlie lives now, and there he devoured people. The serpent is thus a bringer of life and death simultaneously, a cosmic creator and destroyer, to be respected and feared. An ancient rock-art drawing of the serpent, with its jaws wide open and teeth protruding, dominates the sacred cave where Charlie told the story (see chapter 4). Its jaws gaped just overhead as he brought it to life in a reverential whisper.

Charlie clearly expended great effort to bring up from memory words he may not have spoken aloud in years: *un beriberi*, "crocodile"; *nyaru*, "rock wallaby"; and *wayo*, "child." The Rainbow Serpent story is sacred, and the version Charlie knows is the intellectual property of his people. To both protect and share this knowledge, Charlie decided not to tell us the story directly. Instead, he whispered it into the ear of our local guide, Charlie Bush, who belongs to another Aboriginal group. Freddie then retold it to us, while Charlie sat nearby nodding approval and making the occasional correction.

After the Rainbow Serpent tale, Charlie told us directly and in English a version of the Turkey Dreaming. In it, he identified the land we were sitting on as the very place where his people were created, marking it as sacred landscape. The story connects them to the Dreamtime, a complex web of beliefs, places, and myths. The Dreamtime—and the stories that weave it—has ancient origins in this place, dating back to a time perhaps as long as 40,000 years ago, long before humans inhabited Europe. What is truly ancient in Australia is not something you can see, not buildings or monuments, but something you can hear: stories whispered in a cave, syllables on the breeze, songs to the desert. Forty millennia or more of creative vision now hang by a thread, as these stories are assailed by the cacophony of the modern world.

MYSTERIES OF MEMORY

Human memory is at the same time our greatest intellectual accomplishment and our greatest weakness. Why does the brain insist on filing away millions of irrelevant facts (I remember that I wore a blue shirt to my first day of school at age six), yet forget crucial ones (like where I parked my car today at the supermarket)? And why is it so hard to memorize even a 14-line sonnet ("Shall I compare thee to a summer's day . . ."), yet so easy to recall gigabytes of useless sensory memories? Scientists are still very far from understanding how memory works or how we may enhance it or prevent its deterioration. But while the scientific study of human memory in laboratories is at best a few centuries old, humans have been experimenting with and perfecting the art of memory forever. Storytelling is the crucible in which human memory has undergone its most rigorous testing, and has reached its purest form.

Stories thus provide insights into how memory (and our brain) functions. In our so-called information age, knowledge tends to be shallow and diffuse. We no longer memorize long texts (except in the early grades of school, where we may have to recite poems), and we write down anything we really want remembered, from phone numbers to last wills. We possess massive tools and technologies that allow us to outsource work that our memory used to perform. Surrounded by a cocoon of memory aids, we rely on them as a kind of mechanical brain. Thus, we suffer from the illusion that any information we need is stored in some book or database. We imagine that anything can be Googled, retrieved, or transmitted on the Internet. The founder of Wikipedia, Jimmy Wales, asks us to "imagine a world in which every single person on the planet is given free access to the sum of all human knowledge."

With due respect to the mountain of knowledge that is Wikipedia, I view Wales's claim as exaggerated. With 10.7 million articles across 250 languages, Wikipedia samples a paltry 3.6 percent of the world's 7,000 languages.[3] The vast bulk of all human knowledge, our common intellectual legacy, has never been written down anywhere. So it is not captured in any blog, 'zine, or 'pedia. The true "sum of all human knowledge" resides in human memory, mostly in small languages, many of which are endangered. Up to 80 percent of the world's languages have not yet adopted writing at all or have done so only on a very limited scale. Most human knowledge thus exists solely in memory and is transmitted only verbally. This fact should give us a radically different perspective on information, knowledge, and culture. It ejects us out of our information cocoon, forcing us to contemplate our ignorance of the vast unknown.

The Internet is full of ads for mind tools that claim to improve memory. They promise enhanced ability to recite long numbers, connect names and faces, and do mentally onerous tasks. People work on sudoku puzzles for their touted cognitive benefits. Yet even with enhanced capacity and all the technologies to support us, we are flooded with information we cannot retain. Memory deteriorates across our life span, and we do not always manage to transmit crucial facts to the next generation.

Indigenous cultures, with their millennia of intense memorization, have successfully solved the information-to-memory problem many times over. They've managed to retain, transmit, and distribute vast bodies of knowledge—for example, the knowledge of thousands of medicinal plants possessed by the Kallawaya people. They've done so mentally, without the aid of writing or recording devices. What are their secrets? How do people in these societies distribute knowledge? How do they recruit entire social networks of people to act like a giant parallel processor, storing and sharing complementary bits of information? Some of the answers can be found in the ancient stories that people still tell in places like Siberia.

GIRL-HERO AND THE SIBERIAN BARD

I arrived in the dusty Siberian village of Aryg-Üzüü on a hot August day in 1998, looking for a splendidly talented Tuvan orator I'd heard rumors of. I found Shoydak-ool, a vigorous, cheerful man in his late 70s, living in a small log house with his wife and a dog and a milk cow out in the shed. Shoydak had retired from

Shoydak-ool Khovalyg, Tuvan epic storyteller

188

driving a combine on a collective farm to practice his avocation—storytelling. In recent years, opportunities had become scarce. "People are not interested in the old stories," he remarked. "Our kids just want to watch Jackie Chan movies nowadays." Not an inappropriate analogy, I thought to myself: heroes of Tuvan myths often represent the same archetypal character found so often in Hong Kong action flicks.

Shoydak-ool refused to tell his story without a proper audience, so we set out at seven o'clock the next morning to visit the nomadic summer camp of his relatives. He roused the family out of bed by announcing loudly: "I'm here to tell you a story."

Once morning chores were completed and some milky, salty tea boiled, Shoydak-ool donned a bright pink robe with a sash and a red, pointed, Santa Claus–like hat. Taking a wooden ceremonial spoon, he sprinkled tea as an offering to the spirits. Then he began his story, and it was a real cliff-hanger.

In Shoydak-ool's story, a girl-hero, Bora, lacks any obvious advantages or clear goal in life, but possesses wit, persistence, and strength of character. These traits are tested as she sets off on a quest to vanquish evil forces and revive her dead brother. Along the way, she suffers moments of self-doubt and receives sage advice from her clever talking horse. She must use magical powers, perform feats of strength, disguise her sex, and change her shape to become a rabbit. The horse advises her that she must win the hand of a magical princess in marriage. To do so, Bora disguises herself as a man. Her horse helps her perfect the disguise by gluing bear fur over her breasts and attaching a goose's head as a fake penis. Now passing as a (somewhat freakish) man, Bora dominates the archery, wrestling, and horse-racing competitions.

To give readers the flavor of this tale, here is the passage describing the wrestling match, when four fighters attack the heroine.

In a scene reminiscent of the World Wrestling Federation, Bora dispatches each opponent with animal-inspired agility and acrobatics.

A *fairly* strong wrestler came up, *flapping* his arms in an eagle dance.
Bora *knocked* him with the speed of a *kine*,
and *dropped* him upside down on *top* of his head.

Then another *super* strong wrestler *strutted* up to her.
Bora *gripped* his ankle with the courage of an *eagle*,
flipped him over her shoulder, and *flung* him down.

Then a *really* strong wrestler *ran* up to her.
Bora *flew* toward him with the agility of a *falcon*,
and laid him *flat* in a *flash*.

Another *fairly* strong wrestler *feinted*, to *frighten* her.
Bora *hopped* between his legs with the agility of a *hare*,
and *tackled* him painfully on his *tailbone* on bare ground.

In the end, Bora wins the hand of the princess, who uses magic to revive the dead brother. The princess marries the brother, Bora changes back into a girl and marries her own suitor, and they live happily on the high grassy plains herding sheep and camels.[4]

The memory secrets that I found in the Bora story were so deep that the storyteller himself was not aware of their existence. Even though he relied on complex sound structures to fix the lines in his memory, he had no ability to describe or explain them. A corollary would be the ancient Nazca lines in Peru. These gigantic drawings of animals were etched into vast expanses of the desert. The paradox is that these fanciful figures, hummingbirds and jaguars, can be viewed only from high up in the air, a vantage point never available to the lowly desert diggers. They created gargantuan works of art, without ever seeing them as a whole.

In the Bora tale, vast, extended patterns stretch across hundreds of lines. These mathematically exact repetitions of certain sounds are not perceptible to the individual storyteller. Unless he or she were to set the entire tale down on paper and then tabulate all the examples of certain vowels and consonants across the many pages, the storyteller would remain unaware that the pattern even existed. For example, in the wrestling passage above, the reader will have noticed that each line has some words in italics. In the original Tuvan, but not in English, all the words in italics within each stanza begin with the same sound. For example, in stanza 1, the words "fairly," "flapping," "knocked," "kine" (a type of bird), "dropped," and "top" all begin with a "d" sound in Tuvan. This creates a strong cluster of alliteration, making the passage more dramatic for listeners and more memorable for the tale-teller. The second, third, and fourth stanzas do the same, but with different sounds. For a full 12 lines, we get a barrage of alliterative gut punches to make the fight scene come alive. And this is just one small passage! Similar patterns play out across the entire epic. No one author composed the tale, and each teller was free to make his own changes. Yet the structure emerged over countless tellings as a solid, intricate framework, aiding memorization and shaping the tale into a grand work of verbal art.

As Shoydak-ool told his tale, the family greeted the ribald parts with laughter and the suspenseful parts with anticipation. This entire family of nomads, ages 7 to 75, and I, an American linguist, were together experiencing something quite rare. Most Tuvans have never heard a traditional epic performed live. What made this encounter even more poignant was a feeling that such stories could soon be lost to history. I was determined to wrest every bit of meaning from this story, and to bring it to a wide audience.

Coming back from the plains of Siberia to the ivory tower of Yale was quite a shock. I had a little basement office where I would spend hours poring over my field notes and transcribing my recordings. The Post-it note became my best friend, and I tabulated and cross-indexed my hundreds of pages of notes in a very low-tech way. While some linguists key all their data into a sophisticated relational database, I was a bit of a Luddite, preferring the serendipitous connections to the powered search queries. Bit by bit, in my basement corner, I put together the pieces of an immense puzzle of the sounds and structures of Tuvan, hoping that some sense, some pattern, would emerge. Writing a dissertation ("dissertating," as graduate students like to say) is a lonely business and puts a real crimp in your social life. The light at the end of the tunnel came in the form of careful comments on the margins contributed by the three professors on my thesis committee . . . and I was grateful for every little typo or large theoretical issue they pointed out. Many students get bogged down and never finish their thesis, and so I was particularly grateful for the advice: "There are two types of dissertations: brilliant ones and finished ones." I aimed for the latter type, and still managed to make a few discoveries along the way.

One element in the grammar of Tuvan really excited me, and I'll share it here in a nontechnical way. This was *vowel harmony,* a Zen-sounding phenomenon but actually a concept that might excite mathematicians more than Buddhists. Vowel harmony is a kind of statistical perfection, a strictly regulated pattern that shapes the way speakers speak in a language. Just as a sonnet must be precisely 14 lines and a haiku seven syllables (depending on who's counting), vowel harmony is a stringent template for an entire language, governing how sounds are arranged.

Tuvans have eight vowels to choose from (in English, we have between 12 and 14 vowels, depending on the dialect one speaks, even though we have just 5 symbols for writing vowels). From this set of eight vowels, they can use only half of them in any given word. Vowels "harmonize," meaning that certain vowels repel each other and thus can never ever appear in the same word, while other vowels attract each other. So a word as simple as *inu* or *emo* is simply impossible for a Tuvan to pronounce or perceive, given the filter imposed by vowel harmony, because *i* and *u* belong to different vowel classes, as do *e* and *o*. Meanwhile, words like *ona* or *edi* are perfectly harmonic—though they are not real words of Tuvan, they could be easily perceived and pronounced by a Tuvan speaker. A great deal of scientific study has been conducted on vowel harmony languages, such as Finnish, Hungarian, and Manchu, but Tuvan was a relatively little-studied example, and its system proved to be very complex and novel to science. So as I sat in my basement office, manipulating symbols on the page, I had a sense that a new discovery was being made. Just as when you examine snowflakes—though no two are identical, you may discern some basic patterns—I was delighted to pull tiny sound patterns out of an entire landscape of speech and display them in the pages of my dissertation.

Dissertations tend to go their way to a dusty death, and so I was amused recently when I opened a copy of my circa 2000 vintage writings and found them utterly obscure to me. Did I really write this? I wondered. And if I did, what possible contribution did it make if even I, the author, can scarcely interpret it ten years on? My wise professor had advised me that if I wanted my work to have a longer shelf life, I should stick to the descriptive facts. A certain amount of linguistic theory did have to be mixed in, because that is what the culture of science demands, but I viewed the theory part as the proverbial curl in the pig's tail. I do not value it much now, nor do I think it made any lasting impact. My factual descriptions of Tuvan sound structure, on the other hand, led to many practical projects such as the online talking dictionary of Tuvan, the iPhone Tuvan talking dictionary application, and a printed Tuvan–English dictionary that was distributed free to schools in Tuva to help Tuvan kids master English. All of this may seem like a long departure from Shoydak-ool, but I would like to think that my contributions will help maintain the ancient art of Tuvan storytelling for many speakers to come.

ALTERNATIVE CREATION MYTHS

In 2005, I began working in India with peoples known as "tribals," who reside below the bottom of India's socially rigid caste system. I was lucky that Greg Anderson, whom I had worked with for years in Siberia, persuaded me that a change of language and climate might inspire us. And so we set off to investigate what Greg had described as "some of the craziest" languages on Earth. Greg, being the scholar he is, had digested every bit of published literature that existed on these languages. For me, it was to be a sudden baptism into a whole new type of language, and a feast of complex words.

In Orissa state, on the Bay of Bengal, we met members of the Ho community, who have a distinct language and culture. Numbering perhaps as few as one million (small, in the context of the billion-plus Indian population), the Ho live as a scattered diaspora across portions of eastern India. Their ancestors settled here long before the arrival of the Aryan and Dravidian peoples who now dominate them. To this day, the Ho and other tribals are referred to as *adivasi,* India's first peoples.

While in India, I heard many stories that stuck in my mind. One self-taught scholar I met, K. C. Naik Biruli of the Ho people, did not fit the image popular in India's press of an uncivilized tribal. Neatly dressed and speaking fluent English, K. C. narrated for us an ancient Ho creation story in his own tongue, then expertly translated it into English. He also demonstrated the Ho alphabet, a spectacularly bizarre writing system that has not yet gained wide use among his people nor been accepted into world-wide technology for writing on computers.[5] Thus even when the Ho language is written down, it is written mostly by hand. Happily, this means Ho stories must be passed on almost solely by word of mouth, infusing them with vitality.

Few cultures I have encountered celebrate and revere the spoken word as deeply as the Ho people do. Their word *kaji* means "to say" or "to speak," but it also means "language" and "word," as well as "to scold." Kaji is wonderfully flexible, combining into more than 150 words describing what you can make happen through speech, or what linguists call "speech acts." The basic idea of speech acts is that words are not just ephemeral sounds conveying meaning. They can also perform actions in the real world, just like a hammer, a pen, or a hand. The classic example is the statement "I now pronounce you man and wife." The words themselves, apart from their meaning, actually make something happen in the world: Two people are married by the force of that particular speech act (provided, of course, that the person making the statement is authorized to do so).

The Ho language builds upon kaji to express more than 150 acts that you can perform by speaking. Peeking into the marvelous Ho dictionary written by Jesuit scholar Father John Deeney, we find many amusing examples, mostly describing unkind speech behaviors:

kaji-ker	to tell another's faults
kaji-boro	to scare or intimidate by verbal threats
kaji-giyu	to shame or embarrass someone by one's words
kaji-pē	to strengthen or encourage someone by one's words
kaji-rāsa	to bring joy by one's words

kaji-topa	to try to cover up one's mistakes or defects by one's words
kaji-ayer	to tell beforehand, to prophesy
kaji-koṭoṅ	to say something that obstructs, for example, an arrangement for a marriage or a preparation for a feast[6]

Clearly, the Ho are acutely aware of the power of words to discomfit and blame. The profusion of kaji expressions admonishes Ho speakers to choose words carefully so as not to inflict harm. Otherwise their hearers, by using kaji words, will be able to efficiently describe and report what they have done, thus assigning responsibility for many types of negative speech. These concepts can all be expressed in English, too, and it's fun to think of one-word equivalents in addition to the ones given above, so here goes: to bad-mouth, to harass, to shame, to hearten, to exhilarate, to foretell, to backpedal.

The Ho vocabulary, as sampled in Deeney's dictionary, is truly a bottomless well of knowledge about Earth, humans, the acoustic environment, social relations, hunting, plants, myth, history, and all manner of technologies. One choice entry found on the very first page—pertaining to silkworm cultivation—will suffice to show the expressive power and rich information capacity of a single Ho word:

> *aasar*—A bow and arrow; to make in the form of a bow, e.g., the rope stretched across the two ends of an arched stick of the *tiril* tree to which rope silkworm cocoons are attached when it is almost time for the moth to emerge; to attach silkworm cocoons to this.[7]

Readers are urged to browse Deeney's Ho dictionary, or any other well-written and ethnographically informed dictionary, to fully experience the efficiency of information packaging that can be found in vocabulary.

On a more positive note, the Ho celebrate the power of language to charm, regale, and entertain. They devote enormous efforts to telling, memorizing, and retelling their myths, many of which have never been written down, recorded, or translated. Over endless cups of cardamom tea, K. C. narrated a radical alternative creation myth. As the Ho like to tell it, drunkenness, sexuality, and shame are God's gift to the first man and woman. These behaviors, divinely instigated, led humans to reproduce and populate the Earth. It's an interesting twist on the biblical Adam and Eve tale, where God made shame and sin an eventual certainty.

The Bible relates that God placed the tree of the knowledge of good and evil in the Garden of Eden, where Adam and Eve could not resist Satan's temptation to eat its forbidden fruit. In an inversion of the biblical creation story, the Ho claim that temptation and original "sin" are not from Satan, but are gifts from God. And the original sin, as they tell it, led not to being cast out of the garden and condemned to hard labor, but to a golden age of universal peace, harmony, and fecundity on Earth.

Here is the Ho creation myth, "The Story of Past Times," as K. C. told it:

> Once there was old man Luku and old woman Lukumi.
> They two were alone on Earth.
> There were forests and mountains everywhere.
> There were beautiful springs, with fruits, flowers, leaves, trees and stones.
> Old man Luku and old woman Lukumi were very happy eating fruits in the trees.
> They two had no sinful thoughts in their minds.
> As for clothes, they didn't have any on their bodies.

God thought, "If they stay like this, there will be no more generations."

So God came down, and taught them how to make liquor from grass seeds.

They drank liquor in a cup made from leaves of the sar-fruit tree, and got drunk.

Then their minds felt another type of joyful thoughts;
About coming together as man and woman.

They started copulating, and felt shame and arousal.

So they covered each other up at the waist with tree bark.

Ten months later from Lukumi's body, a boy child was born.

In this manner, they bore seven boys and seven girls.

Thus they spread us humans on this Earth.

It was a Golden Age at that time.

There was no cheating, quarreling, cruelty, nothing bad.

There was no cold or starvation, fever or sadness.

The people remained in joy, happiness and peace.

This is called paradise.[8]

As K. C. narrated the story, a local group of Ho schoolchildren clustered around. Most of them could not read and write their Ho tongue, and they seldom heard it spoken at their boarding school. Raised to be modern citizens of India, speaking English and Hindi, they nonetheless listened eagerly to the ancient tongue. They felt proud of their Ho heritage, pleased to know that it could offer a tale racier than any Bollywood flick.

What is the value of such antiquated myths in the modern world? Every creation story is an attempt to make sense of the universe and mankind's place in it. We may be indifferent to the passing of the drunken Ho creation myth. But if it fades, we lose

K. C. Naik Biruli, a Ho orator, demonstrates the use of the Warang Chiti writing system, 2005.

as rich a world of possibilities as we ever could have inhabited, or even imagined.

A final twist in the story of Ho is the fractious debate over how it should be written. Alphabets are among the most politicized of human creations, and many small language communities find themselves locked into standoffs about how to write the sounds down on paper. For the Ho, their writing system, called Warang Chiti, invented by the revered pandit Lakho Bodra, has a mystical dimension. The first letter is the sacred symbol Om, chanted in meditation. It has no use whatsoever in the writing system, but bestows on the alphabet a sacred character. What follows Om is a collection of the most motley and odd-shaped symbols imaginable, including one that resembles a bolt of lightning and another that could be male genitalia. Those among the Ho who espouse this unique alphabet are fiercely proud of it. For them, each letter has its own mythology, signifying by its shape and sound the wailing of a newborn child, for example, and that same child when a bit older toddling and falling, or bodily functions such as vomiting. Others signify the sound of a tree falling, the shape of a plow, or a leaf cup from which to drink home-brewed liquor, as in the Ho creation myth. Each letter symbol tells a story, and together they relate an entire worldview. Some Ho thus consider writing sacred and believe that anyone using the letters should abstain from certain foods such as tamarind.

The world's oddest alphabet may turn out to be a barrier preventing Ho from entering the digital age. Or, with proper positioning, it could continue to provide a unique look and source of pride. Working with Greg Anderson and script specialist Michael Everson, we've petitioned the Unicode Consortium, the body that decides which scripts can be written on computers worldwide, to include Ho symbols. I imagine a day when the odd Ho letters will be as commonplace as Japanese *kanji* and will carry the most sacred and trivial of messages across the Internet.

A STORY MAP OF THE WORLD

As languages fall into forgetfulness, stories, songs, and epics approach extinction. We stand to lose entire worldviews, religious beliefs, creation myths, technologies for how to cultivate plants, histories of human migration, and collective wisdom. But it is not too late to record and sustain these rich traditions.

Imagine a story map of the world, one that identifies the hotspots where stories survive as a vital and wholly oral art form. Such a map would be a kind of inverse pattern to a world literacy map. In the places where literacy is most entrenched, memory has atrophied and almost no one memorizes or retells oral tales anymore. Yet at the fringes of the literate realm, deep pools of living memory remain. In the world's remaining oral cultures, unwritten stories still thrive. They change and evolve in an unbroken chain of narrative and memory.

Such story hotspots are as special as they are increasingly rare. Efforts to listen to and record small languages and their story traditions deserve our urgent attention. This must be accomplished while the elderly storytellers are still talking. If tales fall into disuse without being documented, we won't even know what we are losing.

Orality, the virtuosity of verbal art, is deeply disrespected and neglected in modern society. Any report on Third World development will trumpet high rates of illiteracy as a key indicator of stunted progress and will challenge policymakers to stamp out illiteracy. Policy and literature on human development routinely fail to recognize high percentages of orality, however, or to celebrate the verbal arts as an indicator of an intellectually and artistically accomplished society.

Acquiring literacy does open new doors for development, but what is the trade-off if ancient oral cultures are jettisoned, entire histories and moral codes wiped from memory? Why can't the two systems coexist? If we can overcome our bias toward literacy and appreciate the creativity and beauty of purely oral cultures, we will open a door to entire new vistas of the world and humankind's place in it. That door, still ajar in 2010, may soon close forever. Elderly storytellers around the world are eager to share their tales, generous with their wisdom, playful with their metaphors. Let's take the time to hear the stories, and be enriched.

{ CHAPTER EIGHT }

BREAKING OUT
IN SONG

*It has become evident that practicing one's cultural heritage
and speaking one's heritage language promotes
self-esteem in young people.*

—Harold Napoleon

SONGS MAY BE nearly endangered as stories, and though people
will never cease singing, local musical traditions often struggle to
survive. Global culture cuts two ways: it may stifle local creativity by bringing hugely admired genres that outpace older ones in
popularity, but it may also provide the seed for new creativity and
give little-heard singing styles a new, global audience. Ethnomu-
sicologists around the world are racing the clock, just as linguists
are, to record and help revitalize the numerous ways of singing
that may still be found. Many of the endangered language communities I describe in this book have song styles that are utterly
unique and equally endangered. Sometimes songs can outlast the
languages that spawned them; they may be all that remains of an
ancient culture.

Once my dissertation was defended and I earned my Ph.D., I
could hardly wait to begin traveling again. I was lucky enough to
get a generous research grant from the Volkswagen foundation,

based in Germany. Those funds gave me carte blanche to organize as many expeditions as I wished over five years to explore southern Siberia and Mongolia's smallest, most hidden tongues. Flush with grant money and a sense of discovery, I hastily assembled my dream team in the Siberian city of Krasnoyarsk.[1] Together in the dead of winter, we set off on what would be the craziest, scariest expedition I have ever had. Our destination, Tofalaria, one of the most remote, inaccessible, and godforsaken places on Earth. What I would witness there would change me forever.

The Trans-Siberian Railway wends for more than 5,700 miles across one of the most boring landscapes imaginable. If you spend three, four, or even six days riding the train, which slugs along gently at a speed of about 40 miles an hour, you can literally see nothing but birch trees and grass all day long. Most of Siberia is a vast water world, a swampy delta, the mushy ground interspersed between some of Earth's largest rivers, the Yenisei, the Ob, and others. Underneath, not so very far down, lies permafrost, which is now melting and will fill our atmosphere with more methane than any other polluting source on the planet. So potent is the methane from melting permafrost that in midwinter you can take an ax, walk out onto a lake that has a foot-thick cover of ice, chop a slit in ice, and light a match over it. You'll produce an enormous whoosh of flame that shoots out of the ice as the methane burns.[2] Siberia is both literally and figuratively Earth's coldest hotspot.

I landed in Krasnoyarsk, where I met the rest of my team—which included Greg Anderson, one of the leading experts on Siberian languages, and Sven Grawunder, an expert on phonetics and making recordings of obscure languages, along with a native Siberian guide and a driver. March was not the ideal time to trek into the backwoods of Siberia, and we waited three shivering days at the local hotel in Nizhneudinsk until the weather cleared. We whiled away the time playing cards, buying supplies, and drinking tea. While waiting at the airport, we noticed that our recording equipment was beginning to malfunction in the cold, so we cut up our thermal socks to sew little coats for our video cameras.

We finally made the bone-chilling, one-hour flight in a decrepit Soviet-era plane and landed on a meadow in Alygdzher, the largest of the three Tofa villages. No one was expecting us, of course, so we hitched a ride on a cart into town and ended up at the local clinic, which had a small guesthouse out back. We shared the space with a young Russian couple who had come to evangelize the natives. They were kind and generous and even put on a little celebration for my birthday.

News of our presence in the village spread so fast that we did not even have to seek out speakers. People began to point out to us who were the elders, and where they lived. Not all of them would speak to us, though. One fled from his house as we approached, one shut the door in our faces, and another was so painfully shy that she simply stared down at the floor.

At last, two elderly sisters, Galina and Varvara Adamova, welcomed us into their tiny log house, bare except for two beds and a small wooden chest containing some crusts of bread. I had seen Siberian poverty before, but this was true deprivation. There was no warmth or food, no blankets or pillows, nothing but two beds with dirty mattresses and a single wooden bench in the kitchen. Next to the stove, on the floor, lay a Russian New Testament, a gift from the missionaries. Varvara had put it to good use, carefully tearing out pages one by one to roll homemade cigarettes with *mahorka,* the cheap tobacco that elderly ladies in Russia like to smoke. Galina, the younger of the two, could barely stand upright, and leaned on a walking stick. Neighbors told us that in the 1950s she spent five years in a Stalinist labor camp for some minor infraction—no one could remember what. Somehow she

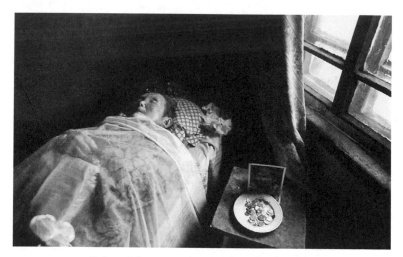

*Galina Adamova, a last speaker of Tofa, on her
funeral bier, Russia, 2001.*

survived that horror, and though she returned home with ruined
health, she became a promoter of Tofa cultural identity. She and
her sister were photographed in the 1980s sitting on the backs of
reindeer dressed in traditional costumes they had sewn themselves.
That photo became iconic, reprinted in books and calendars about
native Siberians.

Galina and Varvara loved to sing. They broke into song at any
opportunity. The problem was, there only seemed to be one song,
or rather just one melody for every Tofa song. Our team musicologist, Sven Grawunder, had traveled all over Siberia and many other
places documenting special vocal techniques and ancient song traditions, but even he was stymied by this impossibly small repertoire. Each time we asked for a different song, we were treated
to what sounded to us like exactly the same song with different
words. It was really a single couplet, with only five distinct notes.
We would later record four other singers who all seemed to be
doing the same thing, even though singers in the other village

insisted they were singing a different song. It again sounded exactly the same, the simplest possible pattern of five notes, repeated in two lines. It was as if every single song the culture possessed was as minimal as the first two lines of "Twinkle Twinkle Little Star," with no further variation possible.

Another odd thing they did with the songs was to cleverly disguise the words, interrupting every syllable with a kind of yodel, so that even other Tofa speakers could not repeat or understand most of the words. So, a sentence like "I'm riding my reindeer" would come out as I-*oho*-m ri-*oho*-ding my-*oho* rei-*ehe*-ndeer. It was like a speech-disguise game, pig latin or *ubbi dubbi,* scrambling syllables to keep the meaning secret.

Our initial hypothesis was that in past times the Tofa must have had a rich song tradition, as did all the native people around them, but that due to cultural decline they had forgotten all their songs apart from one basic melody. But after hearing dozens of variations on the theme and finding half a dozen people in two villages who eagerly performed songs for us, we realized this was not the tail end of some tradition. Rather, it was a truly ancient, basic, primordial song tradition that had persisted, resisting outside influences, special and insular unto itself. It was the original song for the Tofa people, perhaps the only one they had ever sung or cared to sing, even though they had been exposed to many other types of songs and melodies over the centuries of contact with outsiders. Nor was their musical ability limited. Like other Siberians, they had a heightened attunement to forest sounds and animal calls and, using their mouths, birch-bark horns, or birch-bark whistles, could imitate many different kinds of animal sounds. And their language boasted a large number of words describing different types of sounds.

We were excited to be sitting in the presence of two distinguished elders, but getting anything useful out of them proved difficult. Drunken relatives and neighbors frequently barged into the house and wanted to "help" us, rambling incoherently. The sisters, though eager to talk, were missing teeth and spoke nearly incoherently, whether in Tofa or Russian. And after recording several songs and deciding there was really just one song, we figured we'd gotten what we could. We sighed at the fact that, of the elders we'd met so far, several were too shy or too incapacitated to talk, while the sisters clearly wanted to talk but were incomprehensible. If this was all that remained of Tofa, we were in trouble.

One of the most animated moments we captured was when we managed to ask in the Tofa language about shamans. We knew from historical accounts that the Tofa were animists, believing in a profusion of local spirits, and that they had practicing shamans as recently as the 1950s. We had even seen a shaman's costume in the local museum in Nizhneudinsk. We figured the sisters would have witnessed shamanic rituals themselves. Though it had been a forbidden topic for many years under communism, we hoped they might be willing to talk about it.

No sooner did I utter the word "shaman" than Galina spryly jumped up from where she had been sitting on her bed. She began a little dance around the room. She waved her stick in the air—it suddenly was no longer a walking stick, but a shaman's staff, a *dayak*. She pretended to hold an invisible drum in one hand and beat it with her staff. "Dang, dang, dang," she sang, making drumlike sounds. "The shamans danced like this," she said. "If it's a good shaman, you will get well," she added, attesting to the healing powers once exercised by shamans.

I sucked in my breath and looked over at Sven, who was steadily aiming our camera at Galina. We had captured a truly special moment on film. This was a woman whose very culture had nearly been driven out of existence and who had personally been exiled to a labor camp. Any kind of cultural pride had been downright dangerous in her lifetime. Yet here she was, singing and dancing and celebrating the shamanic past, putting it on display for visiting foreigners.

As we left, she hugged us and said, "Come back soon!" Little did we suspect how soon we would be saying goodbye to Galina, and even though most of what she said was cryptic, we faithfully recorded every word. A few months later, on a return visit, we followed Galina's funeral procession and paid our respects as the village bid yet another elder farewell. The day after Galina was buried, her elder sister Varvara knocked on our door. "I've come to sing for you," she declared, breaking into the familiar five-note melody.

SINGING THE FLOCK BACK HOME

I crouched in the snow and waited quietly, deep in the woods on a northern slope of the Altai Mountains in Mongolia. My friend Mergen of the Tsengel people, an expert guide and hunter, sat next to me, waiting with his rifle and binoculars. He seemed to be hearing and seeing things I could not. His senses had been sharpened by thousands of hours spent observing this forest ecosystem, attending to bird calls, insect chirps, and details as minute as which side of a tree moss grows on and how deep an imprint a deer hoof makes in the moss underfoot. Mergen, at the relatively young age of 30, was already renowned for his hunting prowess: he bagged marmots in the fall, elk in the spring, wolves and foxes in winter, and squirrels in the summer. He knew the behavior patterns of each animal, its characteristic habits, resting places, and sounds. Stripping away a patch of birch bark about the width of two fingers, Mergen could make a birch-bark hunting whistle, called an *etiski*, in just minutes. Its squealing call resembled that of a small wild pig and could lure bears to come out in search of a meal. With more birch bark, carefully peeled away and soaked in a stream to make it pliable, he could make a *murgu*, an elk hunting horn that simulated a mating call.

Mergen's language, a minor dialect of Tuvan with only about 1,200 speakers, has a remarkably rich system of sound mimesis, words that mimic natural sounds. His people, in part because of the landscape where they live and the hunting and herding activities they engage in, have both a heightened sensitivity to the soundscape and an enhanced ability to mimic and stylize sounds. The language has many more words than does, for example, English to describe different types and qualities of sounds. It also has a "productive" system, which means that speakers can make up *new* sound-symbolic words on the fly, and other speakers can understand them.

The system uses high vowels (pronounced with the tongue high in the mouth, such a *ee, oo*) to describe high-pitched sounds, such as a tin can clattering down a cliff. And it uses low vowels *aa* and *oh* to describe low-pitched sounds, such as a large wooden barrel rolling over rocks. It also uses consonants to express particular types of sounds, so that fricatives (sounds like *s, sh, f,* and *z*) express friction sounds (such as scraping the soles of your feet across shards of broken glass) and plosives (sounds that involve a burst of released air, such as *p, b, t,* and *k*) describe impact sounds, such as a boot being thrown against a wall. By combining these innovative uses of vowels and consonants, a speaker can imagine and make up an entirely new word to describe, say, the squeaking sound made by new leather boots (such a word would contain high vowels and fricative consonants). Or the sound made by dropping a boulder into a lake, which would use low vowels and plosives. Or a bear scratching its back against tree bark.

New words made up according to the above principles can be understood instantly by others, which makes the system uniquely productive. And productivity is one of the key elements linguists look for to give us insight into how human cognition is organized. Some systems are not productive, like the irregular verbs of

English; they must be merely memorized as a list, with their various idiosyncrasies. A productive system is one in which small building blocks, phonemes or morphemes, can be combined according to some general rules or principles shared by all speakers to form new words that are understood by other speakers. Linguists have long theorized that the smallest meaningful unit or building block is the morpheme; for example, the suffix –*able,* as in "fixable," adds the meaning "able to do or be" to any verb.

Sound symbolism, the use of words that somehow represent sounds, like "blam" or "crunch," is hard to explain because it seems to be using even smaller units—individual sounds or what linguists call "phonemes"—to carry meaning. While linguists have had to acknowledge that some sound symbolism does seem to exist even in English—words like *hiss, gurgle, burble*—they typically dismiss this as a marginal aspect of language, highly idiosyncratic, and not a category that can actually be as widespread and productive as I witnessed among the Tuvans of Mongolia.

I had first visited the country in 2000, as a member of a National Geographic expedition, the one in which I learned the intricate Monchak sheep ritual described in chapter 3. The expedition leader then was renowned musicologist Theodore (Ted) Levin of Dartmouth College. Ted's mission was to explore the soundscapes of the Altai region. By "soundscapes," he meant both the naturally emitted sounds produced by rivers, rocks, animals, and winds and the ways that people who live in Mongolia and the surrounding Altai region interpret, perceive, and make music with these sounds. His exploration of these topics in his book *Where Rivers and Mountains Sing* paints a fascinating and very different picture of what people can do with sound.[3] As I tagged along on the expedition, I was lucky to hear a number of Mongolia's greatest virtuoso performers, some world famous, some known only locally.

A typical day on the expedition involved breaking camp at dawn, driving five to seven hours across the roadless, dusty plains of Mongolia, or crossing a mountain pass and pausing at the top to place spirit offerings on a stone cairn. By late afternoon, we would arrive at a campsite and have the same daily argument with our drivers. The drivers were urban Mongolians, and they viewed the countryside nomads with utter disdain. "They'll steal from you." "You'll get sick if you drink their tea," they scolded us. But we stubbornly insisted that we were here in Mongolia precisely for the purpose of meeting people, and so eventually we would win the argument and camp near the locals.

We were always received with the customary salty milk tea and hospitality, and the word would go out, on foot and on horseback, that we had come to hear music. Within the hour, like magic, musically talented people would begin arriving: an old man with a wooden nose flute, a young man with a birch-bark hunting whistle, a young mother nursing her child and willing to sing lullabies for us, a local teacher who was a virtuoso Jew's harp player. Almost always, someone would show up who could produce the striking overtones of the famed Mongolian throat singing. We were always provided with more music in any one location than we could listen to or record, and our sessions lasted well into the night. Though I am not musically inclined, I listened with appreciation to the orchestra of sounds that were produced by human voices and with such humble materials as horsehair, wood, home-forged metal, and goat-hoof rattles.

The most spectacular use of song that I witnessed in Mongolia was never intended for human ears at all. Herders not only herd, corral, milk, and look after their herds of shy, furry yaks, but they also *sing* to them. Not merely a form of bovine entertainment, songs sung to yaks, camels, goats, and sheep provide nomads with a *technology* to manage scarce resources. Songs are also a part of their adaptive ability, developed over many generations, to interact with the ambient sound environment by using sounds to decode, manipulate, and manage the natural world. Each animal and each desired behavior requires a different song. At first, the herders were shy about singing animal domestication songs because we asked them to do so in front of the camera, which was not a natural setting. But as soon as we went out with them to visit the herds, they sang eagerly to their animals.

Domestication songs represent yet another type of indigenous knowledge embedded within a linguistic system. The songs themselves have no meaning; they do not contain words, simply vocables, similar to the jazz tradition of scat singing, but they follow a precise pattern and melody, just like a composition written down in a musical score.

In my field studies of languages from Siberia to India, I've found, perhaps by coincidence, several languages that have incredibly rich systems of sound symbolism, suggesting that it must be given a more central role in our understanding of grammar. While English has a limited repertoire—words like *clang, sizzle, blam!* and *ka-pow!*—many languages have dozens or hundreds of phonaesthetic words and also allow their speakers to make up new ones and be understood. Sound symbolism is usually considered to be a fringe area of language, since most words do not actually imitate the things they refer to, but we do not yet know how far a language can travel down the path of having many such words, of inventing a large and very useful vocabulary to mimic sounds, shapes, or qualities of experience.

NOMADS AND SINGING CAMELS

Unless I had seen it with my own eyes, I would not have believed that you could control a surly, spitting camel by singing to it. I stood on the high crest of a windswept mountain in western

Mongolia, looking down into China to the south. We were on the move, on the second day of a trek that would take the nomadic family from spring to summer pasture. The trek had begun the previous morning, as the family packed up its belongings (two collapsible felt houses called *ög*, or in Mongolian *ger*) and all their contents (beds, saddles, lassos, wooden chests full of clothing, a stove, and cooking pots). All of this had been loaded onto an antiquated Russian truck that was on loan from relatives in town. In the cab of the truck sat the grandparents, too old to walk, and I sat up on the heap of belongings on the back, which also included dried dung for cooking. Most of the rest of the family, with the two dogs, went on foot and horseback, herding the 200 goats, 6 horses, and 40 yaks. Though I would have preferred to follow the herd, I was not an adept enough rider or animal herder, so the family packed me onto the truck, cradling two newborn goat kids that were too small to walk.

The plan was that the truck would arrive at the new campsite by evening, and the herds would catch up the next day after an overnight stop. Little did they know that we would reverse roles! No more than five miles along some of the worst roads imaginable, the truck broke down. Grandpa and Grandma were immediately put onto two borrowed horses and sent to a nearby neighbor to rest. After two hours, the truck driver decided we should unload all the gear, and he managed to restart the truck by rolling it down the hill. He told us, however, that it would never make it over the pass, and so he went on his way and returned to town. The rest of us—the mother, two young boys, and myself—were left to figure out how to transport two houses, a large load of manure, clothing, wooden chests, and goat kids across a mountain pass.

In front of me stood tiny Eres (his name means "brave"), who was about 12 years old and weighed 80 pounds. He held the lead camel by its nose rope. This was clearly unpleasant for the camel, and he pulled and brayed loudly. Eres was not intimidated, however. He put his face right up to within inches of the camel's snapping teeth and let loose a loud, melodic series of riffs. A kind of musical command, it could be heard clearly even above the howling wind, and it had an immediate effect on the poor camel, which promptly sat back on its haunches and perhaps resigned itself to carrying its heavy load.

What Eres was demonstrating was one of the most remarkable skills that his nomadic people have developed. They can read the moods of animals and manipulate and control them using little more than song. Of course, they also have other techniques, like piercing the nose of a camel with a stick and tying a rope to it, and binding the rear legs so they can milk them, but the physical manipulation of the animals is considered crude and a last resort. The primary tool is psychological, and is expressed through music. It's paralinguistic in that, while not a part of language proper, it does use the human vocal tract, has expressive capacity, and seems to communicate information, perhaps in a similar way that many animal calls do. It is also mimetic, meaning that it imitates and stylizes vocalizations that already exist in nature and are made by animals. By mimicking and turning the calls back at the animals, a specific psychological effect is achieved.

This technology allowed for one of the greatest advancements in human cultural evolution: the domestication and control of animals. While some animals, notably the wolf, which eventually evolved into the dog, were thought to be self-domesticating (e.g., they began following humans and eventually adapted to living with them), large animals like the horse, yak, and camel were tamed only by dint of very hard, persistent work and effort, coupled with a very sophisticated understanding of how they think, behave, and react.

A whole range of domestication technologies had to be tried, tested, and improved in order to fully make the animals come under human control and serve human nutritional needs. We have no idea how this was accomplished, since it predates the invention of writing and no records remain. The only record we have is cultures like the Tsengel people, who represent an unbroken continuity of knowledge, going all the way back to the first instance of animal domestication and practiced in more or less the exact same form up to the present day.

Eres's expertise, and that of his family, did not stop with camels. They sang to their yaks to make them calm for milking, to their goats to prod them along, to their sheep to render them passive for shearing, and to their horses to teach them to take a bit and bridle. Each song was as intricate and melodic as a lullaby sung to an infant, and each magically produced the desired effect. Yet they could be sung only when needed, as I discovered—much to my chagrin—when I asked Oyumaa, the 65-year-old grandmother, to sit in front of my camera and sing the songs. She giggled, blushed, and glanced around nervously. How could she possible sing a goat song, a camel lullaby, or a mare melody while sitting inside of her yurt with no animals present? It was like asking a mechanic to demonstrate an oil change with no car present—completely silly!

THE POWER OF THE SHAMAN

Many of the indigenous peoples I discuss in this book are still practitioners of an ancient religion, animism. Though the oldest and most widespread body of beliefs in existence, animism is still understudied and misunderstood. Many modern scholars refer to it simply as shamanism, which is in itself a misnomer. Though shamans exist in these societies, they are not essential to the practice of animism. In other words, the shaman is not to animism what the priest is to Catholicism. But early European explorers who encountered animistic societies tended to fixate on the person of the shaman, because he or she was the most visible, most exotic practitioner. Viewed through a European religious lens, this person became the focal point for what they then called shamanism. What I learned among the Siberian and other peoples is that animism is still widely practiced, even though no shamans may be present. Animism at its core requires a belief in spirits that reside in the local landscape (trees, rocks, streams) and that must be appeased lest they cause harm. Most people who practice animism have never seen a shaman or consulted with one. Nonetheless, they devoutly make offerings to the local spirits, fully engaged in their faith.

When we do find shamans, however, they can play a crucial role in preserving ancient aspects of their language and belief system. They do so by their healing practices, songs and chants, blessings, curses, and the other forms of verbal art they deploy. One of the most impressive shamans of many I have met was a woman you would never have suspected.

We met Kara-Kys (whose name means "black girl") in a high mountain camp in western Mongolia. She was a weary-looking, poorly dressed woman about 30 years old, though she looked older. She held in her arms a sickly child, pale and underweight. But when Kara-Kys sat down to talk with us, a dramatic transformation ensued. First, she handed the child over to a daughter for care, then straightened up her back, cleared her throat, and began chanting. Her voice and manner changed completely, and as I rushed to adjust my camera, I noticed that she had morphed from a shy, bedraggled woman to a commanding presence. Everyone present leaned in closer to pay rapt attention to her words. She began singing *aaaay-aaay-aaay-aaaay* in a deep voice, fixed her eyes on the sky, and seemed to enter a trance. She intoned a powerful blessing song, calling upon Kurbustug, a sky deity, for health and protection from evil spirits.

Masters of Kurbustug's world, come here, come here!
Masters of skies, let us be as equals and friends!
I am a woman of pure ancestry, not like you,
I want to be useful to the devils and demons.
Boys and girls, people of my time and place, friends,
come together, welcome, come closer, come near!
Mother of Kurbustug's skies,
be merciful to your children who have seen hard times.
Accept their presents of gold and silver.
I ask you to give back to my children.
Let kind and brave gods endow us with power they've
created.
Kuray! Kuray!
A spirit who has a name will respond when called.
A spirit who has something to say will utter it.
You rogues, don't bother or disturb the creatures of God.
This prayer is for thinking of good things and avoiding
bad things,
For getting rid of sinful misfortune and sickness,
For my relatives, my children, and me myself to be
healthy.
Let joy and happiness spread across the yurts, the
livestock, and the land.
Let our faith be effective, let changes for the better get
stronger.

As she finished her invocation to the gods, a lady placed a bowl
of milk and a wooden spoon into her hands. Exiting the yurt,
Kara-Kys sprinkled milk into the air in four directions as an offering. Then she came back into the yurt and lit on fire a small branch
of juniper. As the scented smoke filled the yurt, I looked around
at the intent looks on people's faces. They had clearly witnessed

something more than a performance of words, more than song or poetry. This unassuming woman had transcended herself, had, in the minds of all present, communicated with the spirit world, and had made specific demands and requests on behalf of all present. This ability of intercession made her powerful, influential, and essential in the eyes of the community. She was their protector, their enchanted poetess.

We spent another hour that day with Kara-Kys as she recited songs she had composed or learned from her grandmother, also a shamaness. The songs, not previously recorded or witnessed by outsiders, represented an unbroken chain of spiritual communication passed down for generations, intended to amplify weak human cries to the ears of the gods. Descending the mountain later that day to return to our campsite, I felt both blessed and exhausted.

Whether addressed to camels, lakes, or deities, songs project power. Not merely entertainment, songs are a way of making things happen in the world. We know of no culture that lacks them. Some suppose that poetry or song effects no real change, and in support, they may quote W. H. Auden's famous line that "poetry makes nothing happen":

> For poetry makes nothing happen: it survives
> In the valley of its making where executives
> Would never want to tamper; flows on south
> From ranches of isolation and the busy griefs,
> . . . it survives,
> A way of happening, a mouth.[4]

But Auden did not stop with "nothing." He went on to say that poetry (and I include sung poetry) is in itself "a way of happening." What could be more effective than calming the camels to produce more milk, summoning the sky god to endow blessings, or reenacting the now-extinct antics of a healing shaman? All the songs I've recorded from last speakers, the "last singers," make something happen. They pass on essential cultural beliefs, they elevate us, they use the unseen to move the invisible.

In the same way I have urged far more attention to the plight of endangered languages, I urge people to consider the rich diversity of vocal arts, songs, sounds, whistles, and overtones—all the things humans do creatively with their vocal tracts. Many of these traditions are now reduced to a few elderly practitioners, often living in poverty, unappreciated by their local communities. If we can persuade them to sing anew, we may hear entirely new—yet truly ancient—ways of singing.

CHAPTER NINE

WHEN A WORLD IS RUNNING DOWN

Language is the most massive and inclusive art we know,
a mountainous and unconscious work of anonymous generations.

—Edward Sapir

NIZHNEUDINSK is a place you'd miss if you blinked your eyes while traveling the Trans-Siberian Railway. The rickety town has potholed streets, cows wandering loose, and old planks for sidewalks. Drunkenness is rampant, and the only hotel is a crumbling hovel with room doors that don't lock. I was in town with my field team of linguists on the aforementioned expedition funded by the Volkswagen Foundation.

Nizhneudinsk was our jumping-off point for Tofalaria, a region that can be reached only by air or, in the dead of winter, by driving an all-terrain vehicle three days along the frozen river. We opted for a plane, but to secure one required lots of cash and vodka.

Our first stop was the town hall, where a surly, barrel-chested, and bearded mayor let us know he was in charge. First, he scolded us for being two days late—having mistaken us for a delegation from the Russian parliament. When he realized we were foreign scientists headed for Tofalaria, he practically spat out the word.

"Tofalaria is a bone in my throat!" he barked. Indeed, from his point of view, the poor, indigenous population had to be allotted resources far beyond their importance, including mail service and emergency hospital airlifts when someone fell ill. Never mind that the commerce monopoly was held entirely by Russians and that they squeezed every kopeck they could out of the subsidies intended for the native people.

Our next stop was the police bureau, where, according to old-time Soviet custom, every visitor who came into town had to be "registered." Natasha, the official, glared at us from behind her desk and then deigned to peer at our visas. "You can't be here. You'll have to leave as soon as possible," she declared. Indeed, we did not have the town Nizhneudinsk written on our visas, and so—according to a law that had been repealed a decade prior—we could not be there. We nodded and promised to skedaddle out of town, secured the all-important round stamp on our visas, and left her with a $20 bribe so she could feel she had done her part to keep the town safe.

At the airport, we spent two hours haggling over a charter flight, and 1,200 dollars later, we were issued tickets and promised a flight of our own on the following day, one of only two flights a week into the hinterlands.

Back at the hotel, the Tofalaria horror show continued to unfold. I was beset in the lobby by a weeping 40-year-old mother, Alina, and her daughter. I knew immediately that they were Tofa, because of their facial features and downcast look, and I also knew something was very, very wrong by the tears in their eyes.

"My baby died three days ago and the corpse is beginning to rot," the daughter said. "Can you take us with you on your flight tomorrow so we can bury the baby at home?" the mother implored me.

Trying to keep my composure, I bit my lip so hard that I tasted blood. Yes, yes, of course, I said, you'll be on the flight with us. We'll fly you back home tomorrow without fail.

Unfortunately, the next day was heavily overcast, and the pilots refused to take off, fearing a crash. The poor mother and grandmother sat it out another day, commiserating over tea. The girl's story was not unusual: She'd given birth at age 17 to a sickly baby that did not survive past its fifth month. The hospital staff, not to mention the airport crew, were hostile and indifferent. They viewed these native women and their dead baby as encumbrances.

The following day, we had to pitch a heated argument to get permission to bring the women on the plane, even though we had chartered the flight and paid for the fuel and pilots. More important to the local Russians was the shipment of vodka and flour for the village store, run by Russians, that enjoyed an absolute monopoly on trade in the region. Funds that were paid out to the native peoples as salaries or pensions effectively were spent back to support Russian-run stores. The enslavement and humiliation of the Tofa was nearly complete, and the only thing lacking was to deny them the opportunity to bury a dead child.

Though I have great fondness for Russian culture and for many Russians I have befriended, I can unequivocally say that their treatment of the native peoples of Siberia is as remorseless and inhumane as any I have seen anywhere.

At last, our entire team, along with the women and baby, boarded the plane, and we began the hair-raising one-hour flight through mountain passes and up into the Sayan Basin. This corner of the world lies virtually untouched, inhabited by only about 800 souls, most of them native Tofa hunters and reindeer herders, along with a few Russians who have migrated or married into the community.

We had come to Tofalaria because we had identified the language, Tofa, as one of the least documented, most endangered of

Siberia's languages. Another fascinating trait for me personally was that the Tofa were still herding reindeer, and many of them had grown up as reindeer herders and hunter-gatherers. Totally self-reliant, they migrated with their deer, drank deer's milk, hunted squirrels, collected roots and berries, and lived completely off the forest's bounty.

The Tofa people are a classic example of civilizational collapse, when a small indigenous people who had formerly been isolated and self-sufficient are invaded and colonized by a powerful civilization, in this case the Russian Empire. Secure in their mountain redoubt, the Tofa had probably never numbered more than 600 people in their history. They occupied themselves with the trapping and hunting of animals and developed a sophisticated knowledge of domesticated reindeer. A reindeer is very hard to ride; unlike a horse it does not have a flat back that is easy to sit on, but a steeply pointed one. A rider must balance carefully, and the Tofa were experts at this, using their reindeer to roam and manage an area the size of Rhode Island.

At some unknown point in their unrecorded past, they came into contact with one or more neighboring peoples who, though they lived a similar lifestyle, spoke an entirely unrelated language. The Tofa fell under the powerful influence of that other language and switched, en masse, to speaking it. This language would have been a relative newcomer to their Siberian forests. It belonged to the large Turkic family of languages that today stretches many thousands of miles to the west, reaching all the way to Istanbul and beyond. You can think of this shift as a kind of linguistic conversion. Here they were, the tiny Tofa nation, thriving in their mountain forests, speaking their own unique tongue. The Tofa would have learned the new language out of necessity, perhaps initially to trade resources, to socialize, or even to intermarry. Being few, they were easily outnumbered, and the linguistic conversion, when it happened, was probably quite rapid, in just a couple of generations.

We see this happening again to the Tofa in the 21st century, with Russian. But their conversion to Turkic was marked by one crucial difference. Rather than a wholesale abandonment of their prior language, the Tofa brought along many useful words into the newly adopted language. They may have retained them because they had a particular sentimental attachment to them, or because the new tongue provided no exact counterpart, or because the words were culturally important. For whatever reason, the Tofa crossed the threshold of linguistic conversion with considerable baggage, consisting of several thousand ancient words. Their neighbors must have marveled at the oddness of their speech, sounding superficially Turkic but peppered with archaisms. For me and my colleagues, these words were instant attention getters. Like the very odd Tofa word for bear, "ee-re-ZANG," we sometimes could simply not resist repeating them aloud, so odd sounding they were in contrast to the rest of the language. We delighted in them, made long lists in our notebooks, asked our speakers to repeat them, and made many recordings.

The differences are most striking when we focused on vocabulary related to hunting and gathering, the traditional core of their life. Many basic nouns and verbs not related to hunting and gathering look almost identical to other Turkic languages. For example, words like "sleep," "eat," "go," and "take." More culturally embedded words remain unique, such as the verb "say." Some animal names—for fox, pig, and even reindeer—have been imported from Turkic, the latter perhaps indicating that reindeer herding as a way of life was adopted later, perhaps around the time of the linguistic conversion. But when we zero in on culturally significant nouns, especially animal names, the language is full of ancient, non-Turkic forms for words like "bear," "bird," "chipmunk," and "partridge" that resemble no known words from any other language.

Not only that, but there are some domains of meaning where the vocabulary is so elaborate that it signals something that is both ancient and sacred. Sacred domains of knowledge are often signaled by extensive use of euphemisms, taboos, or both, and the bear, for the Tofa, clearly resides near the pinnacle of beings that are sacred, feared, revered, and respected. Witness the following list of special terms that apply exclusively to bears. Tofa has more than 40 such terms, many utterly unique, found in no other known language. Some are euphemisms, describing the bear without naming it directly, so as not to violate a taboo.[1]

grandfather animal
smelly thing
black furry animal
thing that has ears
thing that has a coat of fat
animal that makes tracks

How many names can a bear have? Ask the Tofa! Bear words represent an ancient and very deep layer of vocabulary that has remained stable despite the massive upheaval caused by their linguistic conversion. We don't even know what ancient language these Tofa bear words came from. We only know that they have resisted—like pinnacles of rock that defy erosion—all possible outside influences. They've left their mark, both on the landscape itself, in the form of place-names, and on the human consciousness, in the form of primal fears, beliefs, myths, and legends.

The Tofa had a rich mythological tradition with many gods and local spirits. They believed that water spirits could be benevolent or harmful, and they made regular offerings to them. A legend

*Marta Kongarayeva (born 1930), an expert hunter and skilled
Tofa storyteller.*

explains two rock escarpments that hover over the village on opposite sides as quarreling sisters. Angry, they spit back and forth,
causing gusts of wind and inclement weather. The landscape is
possessed and animated by countless spirits, whether good, ill, or
simply mischievous.

After we arrived in Tofalaria, our team of linguists traipsed
door to door in the village, seeking out people who knew even
a shred of the language. Finally, we met Aunt Marta, hale and
raspy-voiced. Marta greeted us on her back porch, from which
she surveyed her potato patch, a cigarette dangling from her lips.
We felt ourselves instantly in the presence of a warm, protective
person. Born in 1930, Marta had been a lifelong hunter, expertly
tracking and trapping squirrels, sables (in her language, "beautiful animal"), wild pigs, and moose. We would spend much of the
next ten days in her presence, soaking up stories, moved to laughter and tears by her incomparable backwoods life story.

"One day when I was just five years old, a great iron bird flew into town," she reminisced. "It made a terrible noise. I was so frightened I hid under the bed. Then later I would see that people could ride in it, but I was afraid to. My mother told me, 'Don't be afraid, it's an airplane!' But we always called it 'iron bird.'"

I went out walking with Aunt Marta in the forest one day, hoping to interview her about the plants, animals, streams, and things we'd see along the way. The "walk in the woods" is a classic technique in anthropology used to jog a person's memory and elicit environmental knowledge. I was in awe, knowing that virtually no one for hundreds of miles had a more intimate knowledge of the forest ecology than Marta. Honed by a lifetime of squirrel hunting, trekking on foot, riding on reindeer-back, and foraging, Marta's senses, even if now a bit dulled by age, were incomparably sharper than mine. She attended to the tiniest detail of moss, birdsong, texture of tree sap, pattern of animal footprint, and smell of budding flower. The forest was for her a calendar, an almanac, a weather forecast, an encyclopedia, a bible, and a menu.

As we walked, Marta pointed out animal tracks and sang me a little ditty, a celebration of the hunter-gatherer lifeways of which she was a lifelong and expert practitioner:

I'll take a shortcut and pick some cedar nuts to eat,
take a shortcut and catch a wood grouse,
take another shortcut and catch a quail.

Along the way, we met Marta's son Sergei and his wife, laden with shovels and pails. They were collecting *saranki,* a tiny purple lily-like flower. The Tofa gather the flower's edible bulb—mild and oniony— and eat it to ward off colds, winter malaise, and other illnesses. "You know, we used to call June 'edible lily bulb' month," Marta explained, "but now we call it *iyun* [June] just like the Russians do."

Intrigued at the idea of naming a month "Lily Bulb," I asked Marta if other months had similar names in Tofa. She'd forgotten most of them, and while other Tofa elders I spoke to were aware of the old lunar calendar, none could recite it from memory, and they disputed the details. Marta, an experienced hunter, insisted October was "rounding up male reindeer" month, while her cousin knew it as "migrate to autumn campsite" month. It turned out that they were both right, because the two villages, only four days' journey apart on reindeer, had different ecological calendars. A mere generation or two ago, this calendar would have been an important mechanism linking the Tofa to their endless cycle of hunting, lily bulb gathering, birch bark collecting, rope braiding, and the long, dark days of winter. Important activities that defined their life were spelled out plainly in their calendar. Now it existed only in a few scribblings in my notebook and in fragmentary memories of the elders.

In switching over to speaking exclusively Russian, Marta's grandchildren have shut themselves off from much of the knowledge of nature, plants, animals, weather, and geography that their grandmother would have been able to pass on to them. This knowledge is not easily expressed in Marta's less-than-fluent Russian. We might go a step further and say that the knowledge Marta has cannot be expressed in as intact or efficient a way in the Russian language. Russian lacks unique words for Tofa concepts like "smelling of reindeer milk" or "a three-year-old male uncastrated rideable reindeer."

Though the basic ideas can be expressed in any language (as I just expressed them in English), the concepts are packaged in such a way that much is lost when people shift from speaking one language to another. Newcomers to an ecological niche, speaking a language that has not yet developed specialized terms for its plants and animals, can quickly invent or borrow names as needed.

But much of this is done by metaphorical extension, and it often obscures or overlooks important connections that people previously living there had forged over time. Anybody can make up new names for newly encountered creatures (or imaginary ones, like Dr. Seuss's "sneetches" or A. A. Milne's "heffalump"). But discerning the subtle connections, similarities, and behavioral traits linking animals, plants, and humans demands careful observation over generations. This process of observation and testing is what we, in our culture, would call science. It is this science, encoded in languages like Tofa, that is now eroding.

LOST IN THE LANDSCAPE

After trekking 12 hours in deep Siberian forests, I felt certain we were lost. We had set out, our party of three linguists—myself, Greg, and Sven—plus a native Tofa guide, early that morning on foot from the tiny village of Nersa. We had been brought to Nersa by helicopter and were now attempting to return to Alygdzher, the village where we had begun our work.

Set high in the Sayan Mountains, Nersa is the smallest of three Tofa villages and is accessible only by helicopter, on reindeer-back, or on foot. The Tofa we met there subsisted on small vegetable plots, hunting, gathering berries and other forest edibles, and a few supplies (flour, sugar, vodka) flown in biweekly on rickety Russian helicopters. Their domestic reindeer herds, they told us, had long since turned wild and run off. As herding ceased to be a viable livelihood, many villagers sank into despair and drunkenness. Despite the bleak circumstances, our party was warmly welcomed, and we found people eager to share their stories. Perhaps this was because no one else ever asked to hear stories in the Tofa language. Indeed, no one under age 55 spoke Tofa anymore. "We were all sent away to boarding school," explained 35-year-old Valentina, "and that's why we don't know our language."

Two houses down, Constantine, a hale and deep-voiced 56-year-old, told us a Tofa story of three brothers turned into mountains as punishment after a quarrel over land inheritance. Pointing toward the Sayan range, he indicated the exact three peaks that had formerly been the three brothers. He also told us how he had been punished as a child for speaking his language, beaten with a switch and held back in the first grade for five years because he could not answer his teacher in Russian. His story of shame and abandonment of the ancestral language turned out to be a typical Tofa tale.

Just across the way, we found Svetlana, a cheery lady of 62 and former elementary school teacher, tending her potato garden. She, too, was of the generation that had been pressured to become Russian. "I lived in the boarding school dormitory for ten years," she told us. "During that time . . . I never even heard Tofa and wasn't aware that I knew the language. I guess it was forbidden to talk Tofa then—everybody spoke Russian. Such a beautiful, difficult language! Now it's all been forgotten. Everyone's become Russian."

You can only live in a place like this if you embrace solitude, and the themes of isolation and wandering come up again and again in the stories the elders tell. Svetlana told us a poignant tale of a man and woman so isolated in the forest that they came to believe themselves to be only people left in the world. One day, their dog's barking attracted a wandering hunter, who offered to guide them back to a human settlement. But the hunter needed to depart at once, and the husband was too ill to ride on reindeer-back. He sent his wife on to live with people and stayed behind alone to die. Svetlana framed this for us as a story of true love. Reading between the lines, though, we gathered that her story was also about her double solitude. Not only did she live in a tiny village far from everywhere, but increasingly she found no one to talk to in her native language.

Saddened, we departed Nersa, village of mostly forgotten stories. Loaded down with gifts of bread and berries, and our precious videotapes of Tofa stories, we set out with a native guide to return to Alygdzher, situated just 15 miles upstream as the crow flies. The villagers assured us it was a five-hour trek. Our guide, a young man of 25, led us on foot into the mountain forest at 8 a.m. Eight hours later, as dusk fell, our guide seemed confused. We grew impatient, but our guide seemed unsure as we crossed yet another river. Balancing our clothing on our heads, we formed a human chain to wade across in the frigid chest-high currents. We did finally reach the main village—at 2 a.m., shivering and dehydrated.

We found ourselves the object of sympathy and considerable village gossip. "How could you hire such a guide?" people marveled. Elders shook their heads in dismay. "Our young people don't know their own forests nowadays," Aunt Marta opined. She had spent decades hunting squirrels in the forests and herding reindeer and knew by name every tributary and ridge, cave and hollow. The very idea that a local could get lost in the woods meant that her world had turned upside-down. For her, this was not only a mental but a spiritual decay.

There is a misconception, dating all the way back to early encounters between Native Americans and the Pilgrims arriving on American shores, that hunter-gatherers do not *own* land, but merely *use* it freely. The Tofa, with their detailed geographic knowledge, are proof that this is not always the case. In Marta's younger years, the entire Tofa territory was divided into ancestral hunting grounds for exclusive use by individual clans. Boundaries existed solely in memory, passed down from father to daughter and son, and were strictly observed. Though one could roam freely anywhere, every important stream, rock outcropping, or distinctive landscape feature had a name, a legend, a resident local spirit, and a human owner. Territory was strictly enforced, and no Tofa hunter would think of poaching on the territory of another clan, out of fear both of angering that clan and of arousing local spirits who might do harm. When hunting on their own clan territory, the Tofa offered tea, meat, and reindeer milk to local gods to repay them for success in hunting and the use of the land. The land was to be venerated, and it bestowed blessings in return.

Once our guide sobered up, fully three days after our trek, I forced him to admit that he had never traveled between the two villages on his own and had last made the journey four years earlier. Trails between these two villages—the only two human habitations for hundreds of miles—had become overgrown from lack of use. Marta and the elders had once trodden these paths regularly. They knew every spring and mountain ridge intimately and remembered a time when success in hunting and reindeer herding, indeed survival itself, depended on applying such knowledge. As their language vanishes, so the mental map they once possessed is fading away, and they are detached from the land that once nourished their people.[2]

A FOOT IN BOTH WORLDS

The problem of knowledge erosion gained more attention in November 2007, when I was invited to appear on the comedy show *The Colbert Report*. Stephen Colbert wanted to discuss my book *When Languages Die*. I agreed, though I wondered how I was going to cram a decade of research into a four-minute spoof interview. Stephen began the segment by saying, "Friends, I have some good news for you, English is winning!" Then he began talking pig latin and challenged me to study his unusual idiolect. He followed with a few zingers about the word for reindeer in Tofa, and I was pleased to see an actual bit of data from my fieldwork displayed to millions of viewers.

Stephen then asked what the weirdest word I knew was, so I pulled out a word from Sora, one that I have often used to illustrate a process called "noun incorporation." The verb *poo-pung-kun-tam*, in Sora, translates as "I will stab you in the gut with a knife," which in Sora is a single verb that, vacuum-cleaner-like, has swallowed up all the nouns in the sentence—"I," "you," "gut," and "knife"—and glommed them all together into single weighty verb.

Finally, the "gotcha" moment arrived, a question I'd never anticipated. Stephen asked if I was planning to translate my own book into a dying language.

I had not anticipated the aftermath of appearing on a nationally televised show. Our website, www.livingtongues.org, got so many hits it crashed, and I received a flurry of emails, calls, and letters as well. While most were encouraging and laudatory, I was most impressed by some of the extreme points of view, ranging from cranky to downright farcical.

One day, a typewritten letter arrived in my mailbox with the mysterious return address "Latin Department, NYU, New York, NY." I pictured an elderly professor laboring away on an old-fashioned typewriter. I read it aloud to my research assistant:

> dear dr. harrison;
> i read your article on dying languages with the worry that they are not dying fast enough. what the hell does it matter if thousands die? . . . untold numbers probably have died without a trace . . . if thousands more die unrecorded would it matter? . . . there is no point in worrying what doesn't exist. language arose ad infinitum by illiteratess in our midst even now . . . with the appearance of jamaican english, with creole french etc. . . . and there are deliberate inventions such as esperanto, ido, etc . . . and klingon, elfish etc among writers who have nothing better to do.

so your lament over the imagination of illiterates, uncivilized is a waste of time by people like you who got nothing
better to study than unrecorded tribal languages. let them
all died, including all those with books cluttering the libraries of the world. . . . i am trying to sweep away almost all
languages except the few classical ones. if i am successful
i will be joyous, you will lament. such is life. yours, yama

In the closing lines, I envisioned a curmudgeonly old academic, with a rumpled tweed coat and a pipe, rising up from his
cluttered desk and typewriter to pick up a broom and sweep away
all languages except the chosen few, English and Latin. Even his
own (presumably native) tongue (which I presumed Bulgarian or
the like, based on some of his grammatical quirks) might get swept
away in the furor.

Though easy to dismiss as a crank, Yama's "let them all die"
manifesto makes some intriguing arguments. Many are ones I
hear raised by audiences when I give public lectures, though often
more cogently expressed. For example, people often ask, "Isn't
Latin a more logical [or regular] language than English?" (Not
knowing Latin, I will defer to the experts, but all living languages
have regularities and irregularities, and if Latin were still spoken
on a daily basis by children, it might look very different than it
looks in classical texts and textbooks.) Yama asserts that the problem of Babel (e.g., multilingualism) was "solved" with the classical
languages and presumably would like to see everyone convert to
speaking Latin.

It's not surprising that a Latinist would equate real language
with literacy, and indeed we see the literacy bias clearly displayed
in his comments about "ignorant tribalism" vs. "civilization" and
reference to "illiteratess [*sic*] in our midst." I like to remind people
that writing is a very useful technology, but also a very recent one,

having emerged just around 6,000 years ago, and that for most of human history languages and people thrived without it.

Regarding "untold numbers," I am often asked by people if we know, or even have any inkling of how many languages existed in the past, both cumulatively in the history of mankind up to the present day, or in any one historical period. Of course we do not. We lack even an accurate count for how many exist today, so extrapolating backward into the past is impossible. Only a select few languages left any trace in the archaeological record (clay tablets, papyrus, runes, etchings in stone), and the vast majority left no trace whatsoever. What we do know is that the distribution of language *diversity* is very uneven. By "diversity," I mean the number of distinct language *families* that are found in an area. There are very large areas (e.g., Europe) that have relatively low diversity (18 families), and quite small areas like Paraguay or the Caucasus that have multiple families and many languages.

People often ask me about Esperanto, or to a lesser extent other known "conlangs" (constructed languages), such as Klingon, designed by Mark Okrand for *Star Trek,* or J. R. R. Tolkien's Elvish languages in *Lord of the Rings.* Though Wikipedia reports, "A small number of people, mostly dedicated *Star Trek* fans or language aficionados, can converse in Klingon," Esperanto is perhaps the granddaddy among conlangs in that it has made the leap from artifice to mother tongue. This came about by the efforts of parents who, due to lack of another common tongue or by strategy, raised their children as native Esperanto speakers from birth.

My critic Yama notes that we should not lament the loss of languages because new ones continually arise—for example, creoles (such as Jamaican Creole). This, too, echoes a frequent question I get from public audiences, who want to know how new languages emerge and whether this process can offset or keep pace with language extinction. The answer is that, while languages continue to diverge, creoles arise only under special circumstances, and we no longer have in place on Earth the conditions for many new languages to emerge. This could only happen if many small populations diverged and lived in relative isolation. In our crowded, urbanized world, the pressures tend in the opposite direction, and so the pace of new language emergence cannot offset the pace of extinction.

The contrarian ranks have been joined by several prominent public intellectuals. Recently Dr. John McWhorter, a linguist who has written well-regarded books about language history, including *The Power of Babel,* has jumped on the "let them die" bandwagon. In a stunningly obtuse article he published in *World Affairs,* he dismisses polylingualism as so much nuisance, and the efforts of people trying to save languages as frivolous and ill-conceived.[3] McWhorter's article bears quoting at length, to point out some of the fallacies, but also to underscore that legitimate questions about the value of languages can be asked and should be answered.

McWhorter argues that differences among languages are simply the result of random drift, of chance and minor differences in meaning and pronunciation that emerge over time. As accent and dialect features accumulate over time, the two tongues may eventually be considered two distinct languages. Such differences, McWhorter argues, reveal nothing interestingly different about our "souls." He claims that "a language itself does not correspond to the particulars of a culture but to a faceless process that creates new languages as the result of geographical separation."

If so, then Stonehenge and Machu Picchu differ only because of different randomly evolved building methods, but tell us nothing interesting about the ancient Neolithic and 14th-century Inca cultures. It's hard to imagine a lesser regard for the products of human genius and their great diversity that arises differently under different conditions. As people have spread out and populated the planet, they have continually adapted, applying their ingenuity to solve unique survival problems in each location, and inventing unique ways of conceptualizing ideas. Geographic isolation and the struggle for survival have been the catalyst for immense creativity. All cultures encode their genius in their spoken languages, while many fewer do so in writing or in built monuments. They encode this knowledge in a way that is complex, not easily translated, and certainly not equivalent across time and space. We might as well say the study of human history has no value to our survival.

Going even further, McWhorter suggests that some languages are not suited for the modern world because of their complexity, citing the difficult counting system of Russian and the oddity of Berik, a language of Papua New Guinea in which anytime you use a verb, you must choose a form that specifies the sex of the person you are affecting, the size of the object, and whether it is daylight or dark outside. A similar example from Ket, a nearly extinct Siberian language, was shown in chapter 2, where the verb "stand" has four different forms depending on what is standing.

Such forms may indeed seem perverse, hard to learn, and maladapted to the computer age—from the point of view of English. Since they are so arcane and complex, we might think them unnecessary and worthy of being swept into the dustbin of history. Once again, however, this undervalues the wonder of human cognition. Languages are the way they are because brains are wondrously complex. Each language reveals different pathways of information, different packagings of knowledge that have arisen from the interactions of human brains through the medium of talk. Losing them, we will never have a full picture of what kinds of complexity the brain can produce.

A final argument is that people would all be better off (and might prefer) being monolingual, since language learning seems hard, especially as an adult, and bilingualism a burden. This viewpoint is likely widely held in our largely monolingual society where we have to laboriously learn language in classrooms. But our modern monolingualism should be seen as a historical anomaly, not the normal order of human affairs.

Let's get some perspective on what the human brain is capable of and the fact that humans may have been multilingual for most of their history. Anyone interested in this question should take the effort to visit a truly polylingual society and to ask anyone who lives there if they perceive any benefits or detriments of such a state. (I'll leave aside the examples of Switzerland or Belgium, where most people are comfortably trilingual.) I once saw a news clip of then senator Joe Biden saying he had never seen a country "that was successful that used more than one official language" (perhaps he hasn't been to Switzerland). To educate themselves on polylingualism, such doubters might visit Nauiyu Nambiyu, Australia, where Mayor Patricia McTaggert told me, somewhat apologetically, "Only nine languages are spoken in our town," and proceeded to say how this enriches them all intellectually and culturally.

Or they might talk with Aboriginal Australian elder Charlie Mangulda, who speaks at least 12 languages (English is number 12 or 13), and thus has access to multiple domains of knowledge, not just 12 different ways of saying the same thing. Or visit Papua New Guinea, where I met dozens of men and women who casually speak six or eight languages. None of these people have giant distended crania from too much information, nor do they appear to be mentally impaired by languages crowding out other knowledge. I would suggest they are smarter, more mentally acute, and more aware of different perspectives on the world than most of us.

Daily use of two languages helps build up what scientists call the "cognitive reserve," brainpower and mental agility, which gives tangible health benefits. Bilingual people are found to be better at what psychologists call "conflict tasks"—when a person is required to filter out irrelevant information to make a correct choice—and this benefit was found to be strongest for children and the elderly.[4] A study on nearly 200 Canadian subjects showed that active bilingualism sustained over the life span delayed the onset of Alzheimer's and other types of dementia by an average of four years.[5] Just as sudoku and other brain exercises keep the brain sharp, so does the use of multiple languages. And if it's true for the most elderly, it must also be true for people of all ages. This may explain Jared Diamond's assertion, in *Guns, Germs, and Steel,* that New Guinea highlanders are smarter than us.[6] He makes the point that they absorb, process, and retain information much as we do, but more of the information is relevant to the natural world around them and to their survival. Papuan peoples' practice of polylingualism might also contribute to their enhanced intelligence.

Benefits aside, we still live in a largely monolingual society, in which bilingualism is viewed as a social deficit, not a cognitive advantage. These ideologies give rise to conflicting sentiments found in blog comments all across the Internet. In reaction to a recent BBC feature, "The Death of Language?"[7] one Web posting opined:

> Not only is the death of languages a natural thing, it's also a good thing. "Whereof one cannot speak, thereof one must be silent," wrote Wittgenstein. By that he meant if you can't describe an object or a concept in a language, then you can't think about it or engage with it. Concepts of parliamentary democracy, the liberal economy or multicultural societies cannot be expressed in Mayan or Navajo or even Latin. It's one of the reasons they're dead while English-speaking societies thrive and prosper around from the world.[8]

This comment is exactly the kind of cultural triumphalism (believing we are the apex of civilization) that will lead to the demise of global language diversity. The very next commenter offered a sensible reply: "I grew up speaking a German dialect, and didn't speak English until I went to school. My father always asked us if we were richer having two dollars or one dollar. He said the same was true of language."

A further argument, stemming directly from the biblical Babel tale, is that multilingualism divides humanity: "The utility of a single global language, spoken by everyone as their mother tongue, would surely outweigh any loss of cultural heritage. Let languages die their natural deaths—there are plenty left."

One blogger wrote: "I think that the reduction in the number of languages spoken is also a great way to help unify the world and the human race in general. How can we expect cultures to keep peace between each other when they cannot understand each other? Having one, or a few global languages will make things much more convenient and seamless."

An even more extreme view followed: "Most of the problems in the world stem from a lack of communications. If we all spoke English then these problems might disappear. It may be sad to lose other languages, but we must strive for one universal language."

It seems easy for speakers of major world languages to proffer arguments about why small languages must be swept into the dustbin of history, about how this represents progress, modernity, and is not to be lamented. But in listening to the last speakers themselves, I find an entirely different set of viewpoints. They value their languages and the deep knowledge these contain. They do not willingly give them up, and do not wish to be coerced or shamed into doing so. They are perfectly willing to become multilingual in order to access the global economy, and they are generous in sharing their knowledge with others.

Working on endangered languages can be a depressing business, especially because last speakers are often elderly, downtrodden, oppressed, and in poor health. In this chapter, we have witnessed a world in decline. But many of the last speakers also possess a calm self-confidence that comes from being connected to their own ancient traditions. It is not inevitable, nor is it any kind of progress for these traditions to vanish. We have much to learn from them, if we are still willing to listen.

{ CHAPTER TEN }

SAVING LANGUAGES

Our native languages must be saved, as they define
who we are as a nation, embody unique world views,
carry on ancient wisdom and traditions.

—Wes Studi

MANY PEOPLE have compared languages to species in terms of the extinction threat. I think of these as parallel processes, yet interlinked in several ways. First, languages are more endangered than species, vanishing at a much faster rate. Second, we are at a similar state of scientific knowledge for both species and languages. According to the eminent Harvard biologist E. O. Wilson, over 80 percent of plant and animal species are not yet known to science or identified within a Western scientific paradigm. Similarly, at least 80 percent of languages are not yet adequately documented for scientific purposes, so we don't even know exactly what it is we are losing.

Third, many species and their habitats not yet identified in science are well known to local people, who have a sophisticated understanding of them. Much of what science does not yet know about the environment is known by speakers of endangered languages. Much (if not most) of humankind's accumulated knowledge of the

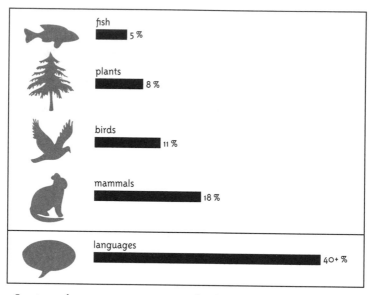

fish 5 %

plants 8 %

birds 11 %

mammals 18 %

languages 40+ %

Species endangerment rates compared to language endangerment rates

natural world is encoded solely in languages that have never been written down or documented and are now facing extinction.

With language extinction, we lose human knowledge about the natural world. As we have seen, languages uniquely encode in their grammars and lexicons specific information about topography, endemic species, and other environmental factors such as weather patterns and vegetation cycles. What the Kallawaya know about plants, how the Yupik describe sea ice and weather, how the Tofa name reindeer—all these domains of knowledge, only scantily documented, are eroding. Linguistic encoding allows for efficient transfer not only of names for things but also of complex and hierarchal taxonomic relations among species and other ecosystem elements. Most of this information is packaged such that it cannot be directly translated. Such knowledge erodes or dissipates when a community shifts over to speaking a global language, whether Russian, English, or Spanish.

TOWARD A DEEP ECOLOGY OF LANGUAGE

We borrow many metaphors from ecology and biology to talk about languages—for example, "healthy habitat," "sustainability," "extinction," or "endangerment." We could even extend this to include metaphors like "invasive species," and so forth, applied to big colonial languages.

Borrowing metaphors is useful, since they provide fundamental building blocks for how we visualize and imagine and understand the world. Biological metaphors for language are common, in scholarly and popular usage. Nevertheless, the term "endangerment," typically applied to biological species under threat of extinction, may, when applied to languages, suggest a false analogy or similarity between species on the one hand and cultures and languages on the other.

Linguist Nora England suggests that use of such metaphors can contribute to a sense of marginalization or "otherness" on the part of a small speech community, and that some people may find it demeaning to be "analogously linked to plants and insects and lower-order animals." Though "endangered languages" is now a widely used and efficiently descriptive term, and one that some small language communities have also embraced, England advocates further reflection about a "way of speaking about disappearing, shrinking or threatened languages that avoids a false biological analogy, and . . . places the discussion in a readily understood context of universal human social action and existence, both individual and collective."[1]

I believe there can be no right or wrong metaphor. I prefer to rely on what last speakers themselves tell me and the metaphors they choose to talk about the process of language death. They often express sadness, nostalgia, regret, and hopelessness. The mood can feel like being at a funeral. Common metaphors that speakers themselves use include death, erasure, forgetting, neglect, abandonment, and extinction. A 20-year-old speaker of Aka in India told me, "In 50 years, I think our language will be removed."

Aunt Marta, the 70-year-old last speaker of Tofa, told me, "Soon I'll go berry-picking, and when I do, I'll take the language with me." With "berry-picking," a Tofa metaphor for death, Marta directly linked her own mortality to the demise of her language. While she supported our efforts to study it, she admonished us: "You've come too late to learn our language. Nowadays we are a people whose days are numbered."

Speakers often express hope the situation could improve, that a language could be reclaimed or revived. Yet in many cases this is not realistic, so there is a sense of resignation. "Of course it would be difficult," Vasya Gabov remarked about the potential for revitalizing his native Ös/Chulym tongue, "but I think it could be doable." Within a single community, and even within a single person, I've found wildly divergent attitudes toward the fate of a language: shame, rejection, denial, sadness, hope, optimism, resignation. Speakers' own attitudes are the intangible forces that exert the most influence—more than scholars or governments—over that fate.

DO LAST SPEAKERS EXIST?

Is it possible to identify an ultimate, final speaker of a language? The answer depends partly on where you think language resides. If it is primarily a set of words and rules encoded in the brain (or a brain), then we can think of a language as still existing even if only one speaker knows it. It might even be able exist without humans, perhaps in an artificial brain, digital archive, or computer program. If, on the other hand, language is primarily a set of social interactions, made possible by shared and socially distributed knowledge, then it requires at least two to talk. The question of where language resides will not be solved here, but it will allow us to be more precise about what we mean by "extinction."

Consider some famous "last speakers" who have captured the popular imagination. In 2010, the death of Boa Sr, the last speaker of the Bo language of India's Andaman Islands, caused a flurry of press reports. Boa had been identified as the very last of her people for decades, and she had worked patiently with linguists to record her knowledge. Having lived in obscurity, the scion of an ancient lineage, Boa's haunting voice and a photo of her face suddenly reached millions through news websites and Facebook postings when she passed.

Another famous last speaker was Marie Smith Jones of the Eyak tribe of Alaska. Marie was widely heralded as the very last to speak this ancient tongue, which she learned as a little girl from her parents. After the death of an older sister in the 1990s, Marie had no one left to talk to. A renowned linguist, Dr. Michael Krauss, who was one of the first scholars to call attention to the global language extinction crisis, had begun working with Marie back in the 1960s. Their decades of joint effort left behind a rich archive of Eyak songs, stories, words, and sentences. These live on, in a kind of twilight existence, in the archives of the Alaska Native Languages Center in Anchorage, and portions of the language have been published. But that is a far cry from a living community of speakers. Language is not just a body of knowledge, but a form of social interaction. So when only a single speaker is left, it in one sense no longer exists, since there can be no conversation.

It has been my privilege to get to know a true last speaker of a language, Johnny Hill Jr. of the Chemehuevi tribe of Arizona. Johnny is a big, imposing man, but he has a gentleness and humility that instantly win people over. Johnny is regarded by many as the definitive "last speaker" of Chemehuevi, but even here the picture is a bit more complicated. As Johnny explains, there are in fact a few other elderly individuals who at one point in their life were fluent speakers, and would certainly be expected to know the language. The problem is, according to Johnny, that they no longer use it, because they either live at a distance from other speakers or choose not to speak it—or even if they wanted to, may not be on good speaking terms with the others. So, of the tiny set of all possible speakers, Johnny is the only one who actively uses the language. He has worked with linguists, including Dr. Susan Penfield, to make recordings of the language, patiently translating sentences into English. He does this in his free time when he is not working construction (his day job for many years) or serving on the tribal council (his current elected position in the tribe, now that he's retired).

More recently, since his cameo appearance in the film *The Linguists,* Johnny has become a celebrity. Although he had never traveled far from his reservation in Arizona or flown on an airplane, when the film was premiered, Johnny traveled to the Sundance Film Festival in Utah. He also opened the All Roads Film Festivals in Los Angeles and Washington, D.C. Johnny mesmerized audiences there with his life story, his account of the feeling of despair and helplessness, and the burden that comes with being a last speaker. Johnny also provided fascinating details of his biography, such as how he was taken from his parents, when they weren't getting along too well, and raised by a grandmother who spoke no English, only Chemehuevi. This makes Johnny a skipped-generation speaker, decades younger than anyone else who knows the language. He told how when he was first sent off to school, he spoke no English, and he sat in the back of the classroom and uttered not a sound. He noticed that some of the other little boys were pointing and talking about him, so when recess time came, he had to beat up on them a bit. Later, he reports, they all became friends, and with the boys' help, he learned English. Learning

English was Johnny's exodus from isolation; no longer did he have to be the only child in school who spoke just Chemehuevi.

At the other end of his life span, as all the elders have died off, Johnny finds himself linguistically isolated once again. "I have to talk to myself," he explains. "There's nobody left for me to talk to. All the elders have passed on, so I talk to myself. . . . That's just how it is." Johnny brought tears to the eyes of the Sundance audiences with his story, and he has become a highly visible and eloquent spokesman for dying Native American languages. "Sometimes I cry," he says. "It's not just the language that's dying, it's the Chemehuevi people themselves." Johnny has made efforts to pass the language on to his own children and others in the tribe. "Trouble is," he explains, "they say they want to learn it, but when it comes time to do the work, nobody comes around."

FROM FIRST CONTACT TO WAL-MART

The Washoe people of Nevada live just a short drive from heavily touristed Lake Tahoe, a body of water they consider sacred, called in their language *Da ow a ga*, "Giver of Life." Washoe ancestors cared for these lands for millennia in a sustainable manner, harvesting acorns and elderberries, cutting willow shoots to weave baskets, using controlled burning techniques to refresh grazing lands for animals, setting willow-branch fish traps in the streams. In a Washoe origin myth, cattails turned into people: some became Miwok, others Paiute, and still others Washoe. The myth reveals a belief in relations not only among kindred tribes but also between plants and people.[2]

I visited the Washoe in 2007, invited by linguist Dr. Alan Yu, who has devoted years to cultivating a close collaboration with the Washoe elders and documenting their language. In a double-wide trailer that served as the Washoe cultural center, we sat down with tribal elder Ramona Dick.[3] With the camera rolling,

Ramona enthralled us with the story of her grandmother, who witnessed the arrival of the first white people in Nevada, coming over the mountains. She reminisced about a childhood when Lake Tahoe was pristine, and when the local monster "Tahoe Tessie" was seen to trouble the waters. She explained why pine nuts are sacred to her people, and how they have become commodified and ruined, now sold at the local Wal-Mart but lacking in flavor. Tribal youngster Danny, a younger speaker in his 20s, joined the dialogue to talk about his efforts to keep and teach the language, and how it is connected to nature and basket-weaving and other aspects of life.

Ramona's story of first contact with white people—told in the style of a typical Washoe oral narrative—went like this:

My grandmother said, when the white people came, they saw them because there was a trail you know where you go over [Highway] 88, over that, it was just a little trail. And she said the white people came over with their wagons and you know how they brought some cows with them and they came on horses. And they were surprised to see white people, you know, and they had their hats on and you know how they used to dress, and when they saw them she said they were so surprised they just stood and watched them, you know, when they passed by. That's the first time that she saw white people, she said, when they came over on their trail. . . .

And she said that's when she saw them, when the white people came. . . . And they settled, and she said when they came to see them they brought . . . them gifts, flour and some other stuff. That's where the first time they start learning how to eat the white man's food, is what she told me. . . .

Washoe elder Ramona Dick (born 1933 or 1934),
shown here in Nevada, 2007.

And some of the men started to kinda help, you know, the white men, when they were starting to settle in, and that's how they worked and they got, like, material and the beads and stuff that they started to use, that's how they came into that, you know, the beads that they used. . . . That's when the Indians started working for the white people when they, you know, start building their settlements, wherever they picked their lands. I didn't see it, but that's what she told me, that's what her grandfather, and when she was with her father, my great-grandfather, and her mother, when they all saw the white people when they first came. So, you know, they got to see that, I didn't, but she told me that they saw the white people when they first came.

From that moment, cultural change crashed in upon the Washoe with lightning speed. Ramona Dick's lifetime spans memories of first contact and traditional acorn collecting, on one end, to near complete assimilation into modern American society on the other. Much of this acculturation was foisted upon the Washoe; the children were sent to boarding schools, and their language choices coerced. To understand why the language had been largely abandoned, Alan asked about Ramona's experiences in elementary school:

ALAN: And were all the people at the school Washoes?

RAMONA: Yeah, they were all Indian kids.

ALAN: So did they all speak Washo then?

RAMONA: No. There was a lot of kind of older ones, well, a lot of the younger ones, too. But our teacher always told us, you know, that we couldn't talk our language, we had to learn English. That's what they always said to my sister when she went to boarding school in Stewart. She said they were told not to speak their language, because they were there to learn how to speak English. My father said when he went to school here, him and his friends, he said, they all talked Washo and they would laugh 'cause they would say things funny and you know, the teacher didn't like that, he told them not to do that anymore [*laughs*]. But I think the reason why a lot of the Indian kids never really kept up with their language was because they were told not to speak their language.

ALAN: But your school didn't do that to you?

RAMONA: Well, we spoke out of the school, but not in the school. When we went out for recess or lunch or wherever we'd get together, it was kind of fun to talk. A lot of the kids didn't really know what you were saying, so it was kinda fun, you know [*chuckles*]. But they always thought, you know, when you speak your language they think you're talking about them. I think that's why they

didn't want you to speak your language. . . . We all talk
Washo, and then we would laugh and people that come
in, you know, think we're talking about them and they'll
say, "What did they say?"

We also interviewed Danny about Washo's future in his generation. As Danny told us: "The way I see language now is that
we're kinda grasping at straws, trying to save what we can. The old
people, they're all going. We just had two of them pass away not
too long ago. . . . They're the ones that should be teaching this. I
don't feel I should be the one going out doing it. And the people,
they don't want to learn, or they don't have interest in our culture
and our language, it seems like. Only a little bit over here and a
little bit over there. And, it seems like, they're waiting till the last
minute, and by the time they wanna try to learn it, it's gonna be
too late."

"It's different for me," Danny said with a sigh, "'cause I've
always been interested in my culture. But there's a lot of the non-
native influence in the younger people, and they don't wanna learn
or do, like, how they used to do. 'Cause the way they used to, like,
get food and stuff like that, it wasn't easy. It was hard work. And
sometimes they don't like how it tastes, like our acorn biscuits.
It's kinda bitter if you don't . . . you have to acquire a taste for it.
When I was little I used to spit it out," he said, laughing.

All the time we were talking, Danny held in his hands woven
strands of straw and bark that he braided for basketry. I asked him,
"How do you connect traditional activities, like basket-making, to
language-learning?"

"It's all the same," he replied. "We talk about the baskets, what
kind of different baskets they are, the tools that you use, what the
other stuff is called. And when I teach a basket class, I don't like
them to speak in English. The words, like for an awl when you

make a bowl basket, that's called a *mibi'*, and that's what I teach them to call it. And your knife is *taowi'*, and that's what they gotta call it. So every class I teach, is all, there's language there, because our culture and our language is all one and the same, you can't have one without the other."

Alan asked Danny, "If you were an elder for a day, and it were completely up to you how to go about trying to revitalize and preserve the language, what do you think would be the best way to go about doing things like that? What's your vision for Washo?"

"Hmmm. We'd need an immersion type thing. My brother had an idea that you take some teenagers and put them in a house with two elders that spoke the language and just have the elders talk to them in nothing but Indian. That would be the fastest way to learn it. 'Cause the way I learned to talk Washo was real hard. I learned it one word at a time, in the beginning. And just in the past two years I started putting it together. And then it's a certain way that you've got to put it together—you don't talk like you talk in English. And then there's little, just little sounds that changes the word or changes the tense or whatever. The more I hear it, the more I understand it and I speak it better. So when I'm around my elders and we're out by ourselves I try to have them talk to me and I talk to them or I ask them, 'Would you say it like this, or how would you say it?'

"Growing up," Danny recalled, "we used to have our slang words and stuff like that. What we called the 'dirty words' when we were little kids." He laughed. "They're not dirty words, they're just body parts and functions and whatnot. But when you're little, you think that's bad.

"They taught us to count in Head Start . . . body parts and stuff like that. And then I went away to Reno and I came back when I was in high school, and these kids, they didn't even know how to count. When they were trying to talk about a nonnative person and say *d'bo'o,* they said it real funny. I remember, like, 'What'd you say?' Just how they said it. And I said, 'Oh, you mean *d'bo'o*'. 'Cause I grew up saying that, and it sounds crazy when they said that to me.

"It's frustrating," Danny said about the attitudes of his peers. "I wish that people would try to preserve it now while there's people that still talk it, grew up talking it. 'Cause when it's gone, it's gone, and you're not gonna get it back. Those CDs that we have from Jacobson's collection, they're all in Indian. If you don't speak the language, you're not gonna know what they say. And they're gonna be of no use to people next.

"Lately, my aunt Dinah's been making me pray. And I don't feel right doing that, because we're supposed to stand behind our elders, and so I always tell her, 'No, you're supposed to do it, you do it and I'll go along with you.' And, it's really, like, I feel real loneliness, when I'm praying. When they're not there with me, I don't know, it's just kinda like, well what am I doing?"

I wondered whether there was a particular place or occasion for Washoe prayers. Ramona had told us the day before that they prayed to the pine nuts when collecting them. I asked Danny about it.

"The way they used to do it," he explained, "was when they felt the need for it. Usually when you wake up in the morning, you wash your face and you pray. Or when you go out and gather something, you gotta talk to that, whatever it is you're gathering, and you talk to it and tell it why you need it. . . . It's whatever comes to you at the moment. But it's usually just, like, so we'll feel good and get along and be strong and not sick and stuff like that. But, like, if you're praying for something specific, you'll just talk about that."

Wrapping up the interview, I asked Danny if some things are easier to talk about in Washo than in English, or maybe vice versa, easier in English. I thought perhaps he could identify ideas or concepts special to Washo but alien to English.

Danny did not hesitate: "Jokes. When you tell a joke in Indian, it just sounds really funny, it's really vivid. And then if you translate it into English, it don't sound right. And then, like, to get mad, that's best to talk in English when you're mad, 'cause our language don't really have a lot of stuff for that."

Leaving the Washoe land, we marveled at how much the elders and Danny had shared with us in just a few short days of interviewing. I recalled the laughter—the ability of the Washoe to laugh at simple things like the mispronunciation of words, and also to see irony in profound things like the destruction of their culture, their acorn trees, their Lake Tahoe by an invading culture. Ramona recalled that someone had once asked her if Lake Tahoe could be saved. "Yes, if you get rid of the white people," she reported having said, in jest, but also revealing a deeper sense of responsibility for what has happened to the Washoe. As Danny noted, indifference and lack of interest can kill the language, and few young Washoe seem to share his sense of urgency. But Danny's energy and vision can also go a long way. Since he is a young man, Washo may still be with us, not only in recordings made by concerned linguists like Alan but also in Danny's mind, and on his fingers as he weaves baskets, for decades to come.[4]

HIDDEN IN PLAIN SIGHT

Lots of people in Pennsylvania speak Lenape every single day, when they say local place-names like Pocono, which means "a stream between mountains"; Neshaminy, "two streams"; or Wissahickon, a "catfish stream" that runs through Philadelphia.[5] Without even knowing it, these daily commuters read and speak ancient Lenape words, many describing local rivers and landscapes. In contrast to the millions who unknowingly utter Lenape words, only a handful consciously speak the language.

Lenape has already been declared extinct by experts, and the tribe itself is fragmented between disparate bands in Oklahoma, Pennsylvania, Canada, and Wisconsin. Among these groups, contested claims to authenticity sometimes arise. The Oklahoma band points to its historical pedigree and official status as the survivors of forced migrations westward from their eastern homeland. But some Lenape stayed behind, hid, blended in, intermarried, or assimilated. Remaining in the traditional homeland of the Delaware Valley, their descendants also claim Lenape bloodlines. Some of the Oklahoma Lenape folk discount their eastern cousins, suggesting that they have a lesser claim on Lenape identity. But miraculously, and hiding in plain sight, the Eastern Lenape have managed to keep not only their traditions but also their native tongue in their hearts and minds.

Even while leading scholars declared it extinct, Lenape persisted. Chief Bob "Red Hawk" Ruth grew up not far from Philadelphia with a secret: He speaks Lenape. As assistant Lenape chief Shelley DePaul describes it, Bob grew up in Norristown, Pennsylvania, on a farm. His father was Native American, and his mother was not. His family stayed fairly self-contained in their home area. "Lenape family units comprise a community which shares the same beliefs," Shelley notes, "and so in Bob's community, elders would travel for miles, because they were close to his family, and they would teach and persevere their culture. . . . The Lenape people that speak the language know important words like familial words, prayers, and directions."

Bob Red Hawk belies the pernicious myth of the "vanishing Indian" and shows that Native American cultures have not disappeared, as some may have wished, but have evolved. As they become newly assertive and confident in their cultural values, their neighbors may be surprised. Most Pennsylvanians believe that there are no local Indians. Even people who may have attended

Lenape High School in Medford, New Jersey (the school website shows a blonde cheerleader wearing an Indian feather headdress), may suppose that other than a school mascot, all the rest lies in the dust of history. How surprised would they be to hear Chief Bob stand up in Philadelphia, right on the campus of the University of Pennsylvania, and offer a prayer in Lenape?

Though the official count of Lenape speakers is only about three, that number is now growing, thanks to a bold experiment being carried out at Swarthmore College by Shelley DePaul. As a former schoolteacher, Shelley has devoted years to compiling and studying all available archival records of Lenape, often written in illegible (except to specialists) phonetic symbols. She traveled many miles to collect knowledge from the elders, organizing it into textbooks, committing it to memory.

"What I'm finding from most families that still maintain the language," Shelley says, "is that they maintain important words, such as the words for the directions, the word for creator, certain prayers. They know familial words for mother, brother, father."

Decades of dedication led to Shelley's current ability to converse in the language, to say prayers, blessings, plain old everyday talk, and even bad words. Shelley also worked with Bob Red Hawk and others to ensure Lenape's adaptation to 21st-century life. As Shelley notes: "There has been modernization of the language by creating new words to apply to technology or modern things: 'brain in a box,' *dumhokus,* for computer; *shukal* for sugar. There are two ways the Lenape have created words, to borrow the word and just change the pronunciation or to make up a completely new word."

In 2009, a select group of Swarthmore College students enrolled in Shelley's newly formed Lenape class. For the first time ever, Lenape was being taught at an institution of higher learning in the Lenape homeland, the Delaware Valley. It was a

Shelley DePaul, assistant chief of the Lenape Nation of Pennsylvania, teaches Lenape to students at Swarthmore College, 2009.

historic occasion. The table in the seminar room was piled high with cultural artifacts—baskets, animal pelts, bead necklaces, and the like. The students grappled with the immense complexity of Lenape verb forms. Their efforts did not go unnoticed by the Lenape diaspora, and they had a positive impact. Shelley recalls telling the Lenape in Canada and Wisconsin about the Swarthmore students' efforts: "I've shown the work that the kids are doing and they [the Lenape in Canada] were amazed! [People] think Native Americans often have this defective attitude like, 'No, our language is just gonna die,' and it brings tears for them to see—and I'm tearing up right now because I'm amazed at the work that these kids are doing. . . . So it does feed back into the community the work that they've done."[6]

Even this modest effort to reclaim and propagate Lenape was not without controversy. Scholars who insist that Lenape is extinct have criticized the effort, saying that the Pennsylvania Lenape are

259

not the "real" Lenape, pointing out that the Pennsylvania branch of the tribe is not federally recognized, or suggesting that it is a mixed or impure form of the language. These critiques aside, I believe this bold effort is exactly what is needed to bring languages back from the brink of extinction. What better place than a room full of young, bright, enthusiastic minds to extend the life span of the Lenape language? The fact that college students want to learn it will also have a positive effect on the tribe itself, as tribe members struggle to gain federal recognition and to reconcile their everyday lives in modern America with their ancestral traditions.

HOCKEY SPOKEN HERE

Even for languages that are not yet down to single digits of "last speakers," the role of key individuals who promote and nurture the language is crucial. I have met many such individuals over the years, some in places you might not expect.

A Tim Horton's restaurant in Ann Arbor, Michigan, was where I heard Anishinaabemowin (also called Ojibwe) spoken for the first time. Howard Kimewon, a genial Anishinaabemowin elder of 60 or so, kindly arrived a full hour early for our scheduled meeting, then waited an extra 30 minutes as I struggled to find the right Tim Horton's (a local fast-food franchise). He showed no impatience whatsoever at my tardiness, greeting me warmly in Ojibwe. I glanced around at the most banal of modern American landscapes: doughnuts, weak coffee, plastic furniture. Anishinaabemowin could not have been more out of place here, yet it seemed utterly natural when Howard answered his cell phone and began chatting in it. I listened as the sibilants of the language tickled my ear.

Howard is a true linguistic survivor. He has made great efforts to keep up his knowledge over the years, going out of his way to seek out elders for conversation, to be corrected by them, to learn. He has overcome the shame he felt as a youth, maturing

260

into dignity and pride as an elder and teacher of the language. His teaching methods include such activities as demonstrating traditional Anishinaabemowin woodworking (making a corn grinder out of a log) while exploring all the Anishinaabemowin words related to that activity.

Later, I received a text message I could not read, but it began with *Boozhoo*, which means "hello." Who would have thought Anishinaabemowin—with its long, complex words, requiring a lot of typing—suitable for messaging! All that effort to send me a message I couldn't fully read! And yet this powerful gesture introduced me to the language in a gentle way, as I was forced to contemplate the beauty and complexity of the words on my iPhone. The lowly text message, and Howard's willingness to put his language out through all possible channels, may indeed be a key to saving it.

Dr. Margaret Noori, a linguist and promoter of the Anishinaabemowin language, frames the question this way: "What would it truly mean for our society to have people speak these languages as part of their personal and professional lives, right now, in the midst of our history?" She reports that a panel of Anishinaabemowin elders convened recently in Michigan to talk about what it means to them. Many of them approved of new, creative uses like translating the lyrics of popular music, comic books, social networking, or sports terms, as ways to inspire young people to participate. Keeping the language alive "gives all young people the opportunity to think differently," she notes. "Native and non-native students can understand one another better by learning the language of the land they now share." A heritage language is part of the glue that helps keep the native identity intact, and may even help in preventing suicides or other social problems.

Margaret is busy populating the Internet with her language. She regularly posts Facebook notes in Anishinaabemowin, such as *"Aapchigwa n'gii bishigendaan pii Gwiigwaa'agag gii maamwi-zhoozhooshkwaadwewaad Bkejwanong KchiAnongoog!"* which she translated as "I really liked it when the Wolverines played hockey with the Bkejwanong All Stars!" The "Noongwa e-Anishinaabem-jig: People Who Speak Anishinaabemowin Today" Facebook page she created with Howard Kimewon and Stacie Sheldon now has nearly 1,000 members who visit to chat, ask questions, or hear new songs and stories.

What better use of this ancient Great Lakes–centered language could there be than to promote hockey? In fact, hockey has long been a favorite of the Anishinaabeg (people) and is one of many keys to the language's newfound vitality. Recently, several members of the University of Michigan hockey team have taken Margaret's Anishinaabemowin class. All players leave the class with respect for the language and culture, and some with a renewed sense of cultural pride. National Hockey League player Travis Turnbull, now with the Buffalo Sabres, is an example of an athlete who has embraced his heritage. Recently, Travis and several teammates spent a day with the youth of the Bkejwanong First Nation. For native kids, hearing an NHL player promote Anishinaabemowin was a much more powerful inspiration than anything a teacher will tell them. If hockey players think it's important, it is! Recently, another teammate, Brandon Nurato, now with the Toledo Wall-eye, texted to let Dr. Noori know he'd been teaching teammates to count in Anishinaabemowin.

Margaret has a foot in two worlds: she is a professional academic who holds a Ph.D. and teaches at a university, and she is a tribal member and cultural activist with a deep sense of responsibility. As a scientist, she advocates documentation of languages as they disappear. But she believes this work has to be speaker-centered, not scientist-centered, and putting language into archives should be much more than just "building a graveyard." "How does this work impact communities," she asks, "native and nonnative, in ways that support global diversity in a next-generation way?"[7]

COLLATERAL EXTINCTIONS

In my book *When Languages Die,* I wrote: "When ideas go extinct, we all grow poorer," to introduce the notion of the "human knowledge base." In that same book I explored many different systems of knowledge, such as animal and plant taxonomies, calendars, mathematics, and geography, that are uniquely encoded in languages. This may seem to be objectifying language as merely a vessel to convey ideas. But I want to emphasize that ideas and knowledge are not just facts floating around in people's minds. They represent an exchange of thoughts and experiences between intimates and strangers.

An accretion of knowledge, like a giant midden of shells, is what French philosopher Pierre Teilhard de Chardin referred to as the "noosphere"—the sum of all human beliefs. It is living, in the sense that any complex system has a life, an existence beyond one temporal moment or one mortal mind. It grows and emanates from a speech community over long stretches of richly lived lives, deeply felt experiences, midnight musings, and daytime ponderings. This entity of interwoven ideas outlasts any single speaker. It cannot be disconnected, shut down, or silenced, except by the extinction of the language itself.

Some do try to fetishize language as a thing to be placed under a microscope and examined or on a shelf in an archive to be observed. The crucial work of language revitalization reimagines language in all its situational humor, glory, and banality. How were people cussed out, scolded, admonished, admired, inspired? What were the last words of good night, the first greetings of the day? Language mediates all human interactions, and all facets of knowing, whether making love or feuding bitterly, invoking the gods, cursing enemies, or asking someone to "pass the salt."

The loss of a language both foretells and causes the loss of a distinct culture and identity. As elderly speakers pass, the language is disconnected from daily lives. Fewer and fewer of the everyday social interactions are conducted in it, and the elders experience a creeping silence. They know the particular loneliness that only linguistic survivors—or perhaps the mute—can feel, as they are silenced and invisibilized. This can happen at both ends of the age spectrum and everywhere in between.

Anthropologist Bernie Perley, a member of the Maliseet First Nation in Canada, writes eloquently of the bitter childhood experience of linguistic alienation, of coerced muteness:

Why don't I understand Maliseet? My first language is Maliseet. . . . When I started first grade, I did not speak English. The one memory I have of first grade is sitting in the front seat of the school bus. The bus driver, sitting in his seat, was twisting around to talk to me. His mouth was moving and sounds were coming out of his mouth. I did not understand anything he said. It was a shock to realize that everything I experienced in my life up to that point was rendered meaningless and irrelevant. Being a solitary Maliseet child in a largely white elementary school was alien enough. But to have my entire worldview muted and rendered meaningless made me feel silent and vulnerable. My mother made the decision that day that I would learn English because, and I quote, "If my son is to survive out there, he'll have to master English." [8]

Bernie and his mother were not alone in making this entirely rational calculation. Yet he would come to regret it years later, as a prominent Maliseet intellectual and activist, finding himself unable to understand the elders. The choice made by young children and their well-intentioned parents, as Professor Perley describes it, is not merely to "master English," but simultaneously to renounce Maliseet.

Many people all around the world do manage to master English without abandoning their own Mandarin or Hindi or Inuktitut. The world is full of bilinguals—so why do children in this case irretrievably shift from heritage to global tongue, never glancing back or bringing along the ancestral wisdom? The answer may lie in Bernie's statement about being a "solitary Maliseet in a largely white elementary school." The pressure to conform and assimilate can be so intense that there is no quarter for the old ways.

Children are coerced out of their heritage, their religion, their identity. These are what Perley refers to as the "collateral extinctions" of language loss: "We have already lost Maliseet place-names. We have lost evidence of landscape transformations described in our oral traditions. We have already lost much of the esoteric knowledge of medicines. Now we are losing the ability to conduct everyday social relations in the Maliseet languages." Sounding a note of cautious hope, however, he continues: "These collateral extinctions need not be forever. . . . We need to reintegrate all these facets of Maliseet experience so that we can continue to experience Maliseet worlds."

HOW TO SAVE A LANGUAGE

How are globalization and technology affecting the viability of small languages? How can hip-hop, text messaging, and YouTube help save languages? What are the technological barriers and conduits for small languages, and how are clever speakers leveraging these? What is the global future of the smallest tongues? Is there reason for optimism?

There are many leaders and pioneers in the domain of language revitalization. And there are probably as many different notions about how to save a language as there are last speakers and their descendants. I've devoted over a decade to talking personally with hundreds of last speakers and their descendants, as well as other interested observers of language death. I make no judgments about what works; all I am sure of is that a language cannot be "saved" by outsiders. Scientists and other outsiders can assist or enable, but the decision to keep a language alive, and most of the hard work required to implement that decision, must be undertaken by the communities that own and cherish the languages.

The following list gives some tactics that I have seen being employed by actual last speakers of languages I have met. I simply present them here, without making any judgment as to their effectiveness. Every situation is different, involving a subtle interplay of attitudes, politics, and practices. We have far too few success models to draw firm generalizations about what works. But in some cases, these strategies can lead to a dramatic revitalization. In other cases, they help to sustain a language or arrest its decline. In yet other cases, they have no effect or may even hasten the disappearance.

These first two strategies reflect a tension between two processes I call "visibilization" and "invisibilization."

Keep it secret, private, and restricted. This practice protects the language as a type of intellectual property that is proprietary, owned, and not to be shared or taught to anyone who is not entitled to learn it. This seems odd to many of us, but small groups do have a much clearer vested interest in owning their own knowledge and, by extension, their language. The extreme version of this strategy has been used by some groups, most notably the Hopi, who, as we saw earlier, reportedly shut down a planned immersion kindergarten program because it was discovered that a few non-Hopi children were enrolled. This is an unusual strategy, though given the strong ideology of ownership, it may help to perpetuate the language. On the other hand, it may ensure its rapid demise. Many communities enforce secrecy by protecting their language from outsiders to a lesser degree. The Kallawaya of Bolivia enforce language secrecy in their own community by teaching the language only to men, and they share it with outsiders only under special circumstances and with limitations on what knowledge can be made available.

Make it public, visible, and freely shared. As intellectual property in the public domain or creative commons, teach it to anyone who is interested. This strategy is typically how large languages behave. You don't need anyone's permission to learn English, and there is no sense that anyone owns it. But many small and endangered language communities also practice this idea. The Welsh put Welsh names on local street signs. The Lenape of Pennsylvania, as we just saw, want everybody to learn the language, and they delight in the fact that people have to learn Lenape words when they read or utter the names of local rivers. The Lenape do have some knowledge they consider sacred or secret, but in general they want to put their language to public use. They have made a strategic decision to increase its visibility, since for so long it was hidden from sight.

Keep it strictly oral, only spoken. Do not export it into any other media such as writing, computers, text messages, or street signs. All languages were once oral, and some have adopted other media such as writing, typing, and messaging. But others are aware that meaning is lost in this technological transition and have made a strategic decision that the language should not be written. Even when languages do adopt literacy, they may have only one book (typically a Bible translation) available and may choose not to produce much other written material, thus keeping the oral character of the language primary.

Make it literate, write it down. Push it out in written form through all possible new domains and technologies. Expand its footprint by adopting it for Facebook, text messaging, and road signs, regardless if anyone takes it up or not. By achieving a permanent presence, a language extends its usefulness and its longevity.

Elevate it, promote it, express pride in it. A positive attitude toward a language is the single most powerful force that will keep it alive, especially when that attitude is transmitted to the youngest members of the community. Whenever I meet Richard Grounds, who is a linguist and a speaker and promoter of the Yuchi language, he grasps my hands and greets me warmly in his tongue. Similarly, when he calls me on the phone, even if he only talks to my answering machine, he speaks first in Yuchee, then English. He does so with such warmth and conviction that even though I don't understand a word, I feel I have been truly blessed. Richard, like my Ojibwe colleague Margaret Noori, who puts her language on Facebook, leads by example. They show what it truly means to embrace, promote, and elevate a language, putting it out into the public ear regardless of whether it is understood by the hearers. Though I don't understand what they are saying, the message is loud and clear: "We love and value our languages, and we respect both them and you by sharing it publicly."

The opposite of this would be to put it down, to disparage it. Many consider small languages backward, obsolete, old-fashioned, and unsuitable for modern life. They may call it "just a dialect" or a "patois." Negative attitudes toward a language emanate from many sources—often official educational or political establishments, amplified by the press and popular culture. Regardless of the source, these attitudes quickly become internalized, and speakers will disparage their own languages. Many speakers feel their language is not suited to the modern world or not compatible with computer and Internet technologies. But at the same time, others insist that they are suitable and make great efforts to bring their languages across the digital divide.

Replenish the language with new words. If speakers are not overly concerned with keeping the language "pure," they may borrow words freely, adopting loanwords and useful expressions from other languages. Some languages eschew loanwords but readily coin new native terms for new objects. As one Mohawk speaker proudly told me, "We call it 'lightning brain box' in our language, not 'computer.'" Languages that readily coin new words can enjoy a wonderful source of renewal and keep pace with technology. On the flip side, if this is done artificially or imposed from above by a language purity committee, it can have negative effects on the perceived adaptability of the language. A first step is to recognize the need for new words. Nazareth Alfred, a speaker of Australia's Kulkalgowya tongue, told me, "Our language is standing still. We need to make it relevant to today's society. We need to create new words, because right now we can't say 'computer.'"

Embrace new technologies. New modes of communication like texting, chat, SMS, or Skype can be deployed to save endangered languages. Can the lowly text message lift a language to new levels of importance and prestige? My answer is yes, and I've seen some wonderful examples. It's done at the micro level, by individual users, but also by large corporations. Microsoft's new Local Language Program, for example, allows users to customize software to their preferences in nearly 100 languages. Some are very large, emerging ones, like Tamil and Kiswahili; others are small and regional, such as Macedonian. Some were once or are still endangered and undergoing active revitalization: examples include Irish, Maori, and Welsh. Similarly, Wikipedia offers content in about 50 languages, most large but a few small or endangered (Navajo, Hawaiian). I can imagine a time when software and Web content of all types will be readily available in the full spectrum of languages, and how the world of ideas will be enriched. I predict that language localization will be one of the most dynamic trends of the next decades, and I urge corporations of all kinds—but especially those in the information technology industry—to get on board.

Document it. Linguists typically embrace documentation, with the knowledge that even if all speakers die out, a language can, with great difficulty, be reclaimed from written records or recordings. But some indigenous communities feel documentation is exploitative or does not serve their interests. Some resist it as an unreasonable burden on the elders, or as benefiting only outsiders. Some say that having their language only in recorded media would be the ultimate triumph of colonialism—the language would have been captured and placed in an archive; it would be better to have it disappear entirely than to suffer that fate. As speakers themselves take on a greater role in documentation, exerting ownership and control over their linguistic and intellectual property, we can hope for a time when documentation will always show positive effects that support revitalization.

THERE ARE MANY reactions people have to language loss, and diverse strategies for addressing it. Some blame others, assigning culpability to schools and governments. Others blame themselves, feeling they have failed. Some stick to tradition, while others innovate. And all over the world, a growing movement of language activists lobbies, promotes, teaches, records, speaks, and renews.

There are many strategies for saving a language, and enterprising speakers are using all of these methods. We may not know for decades which strategies succeed. But we can observe and admire their efforts, and perhaps as scientists or outsiders contribute to their cause.

GLOBALIZATION: GOOD *AND* BAD

Globalization and technology affect the fates of small languages in surprising ways. Tyler Cowen, in *Creative Destruction: How Globalization Is Changing the World's Cultures,* argues that we are all enriched by the market forces that bring us new goods, services, and ideas. "If we consider the book," he writes, "paper comes from the Chinese, the Western alphabet comes from the Phoenicians, the page numbers come from the Arabs and ultimately the Indians and printing has a heritage through Gutenberg, a German, as well as through the Chinese and Koreans. The core manuscripts of antiquity were preserved by Islamic civilization and, to a lesser extent, by Irish monks."[9]

Cowen's view of the market operates at the elevated level of empires and nation-states, entirely neglecting the thousands of smaller peoples and cultures that comprise them. Occasionally, we find breakthrough phenomena such as Tuvan throat singing, where a cultural product from a tiny nation becomes a globally famous and valued art form. More often, the process goes in the other direction, where art forms valued by large nations become adopted by thousands of smaller cultures who, even though they may improve on the original, enjoy no reciprocal exchange. For example, nothing from Aka culture is borrowed back into American culture as the Aka absorb hip-hop. Americans are deprived, in this one-way cultural exchange, of partaking of the knowledge and cultural richness of the Aka.

More powerful nations wield greater influence; they exert a gravity on smaller cultures. Individuals within these smaller cultures may creatively resist by appropriating, changing, altering, and reinterpreting. A New Guinea tribesman's ceremonial feather headdress may contain bright strips of tin cut from a Coca-Cola can. Tyler Cowen's real argument is that an exchange of cultural ideas (piggybacking onto globalize trade relations) promotes greater diversity and thus a higher quality of ideas and arts. He is making an argument for the value of diversity, and showing that globalization (as it plays itself out in greater trade, enhanced communication, more urbanization, and mixing of peoples) enriches us all. He argues, counterintuitively, that globalization culminates not in a "homogenized pap" of sameness, but rather in a richer, more varied mosaic of ideas. True, we may all end up listening to hip-hop performed in hundreds of different languages, but by that point, it is no longer the same hip-hop—instead, it is a much richer, deeper, more culturally diverse art form.

The downside to globalization occurs when big languages crush small languages and the knowledge they contain. The most common vector for this is national education systems. Where a curriculum planned in Lima or Mexico City or Moscow is imposed on all schools across the land, enshrining one set of received knowledge in textbooks, it effectively discounts any alternative ways of knowing.

An upside to globalization is that small language communities around the world can now communicate and exchange ideas. The Siletz of Oregon can travel to Hawaii or New Zealand to observe a successful language-revitalization effort. The Ho of India can petition to have their bizarre alphabet included into the Unicode standard and can access a Ho talking dictionary website hosted in the United States. Such communities can cleverly leverage all the modern technologies, and they can learn that they are not alone in their struggle.

A fully standardized product—say, the McDonald's Big Mac—is more "global" than a local specialty such as Kansas City barbecue. Why? Because the latter relies on strictly local knowledge. A cook needs more knowledge and skill and expertise, learned through practice and mentoring, to prepare Kansas City barbecue than she does to produce an assembly-line McDonald's meal that was planned in a central facility to be absolutely the same, regardless of locality.

No matter how widely a language may expand, it still becomes localized, because language is endlessly adaptive. There are so many different varieties of English, yet each has local traits that are sometimes baffling to outsiders. In India, the phrase "by and by" is common in everyday conversation, but may be puzzling to speakers of American English (it means "soon"). In Britain, words like "twee" and "right the way" are obtuse to Americans, while an Americanism like "spunk" is a vulgarity to Britons. Even within American dialects, localisms abound. Pennsylvanians tend to say "down the shore" and "yinz," and New Yorkers say "wait on line" or "uptown," while Tennesseans say "fixin' to" or "might could"— all expressions that can cause puzzlement outside the local region. These are all minor local adaptations, and they are not going to disappear anytime soon. Research shows that the varieties of American English are continuing to diverge rather than converging on a norm.

Clearly the forces of localization are powerful in languages, so perhaps we should not worry about globalization at all. In an imaginary future, English will continue to expand, as will Chinese and Arabic, yielding a trilingual world. But at the same time, English, Chinese, and Arabic will branch into hundreds of local varieties, perhaps only connected by a kind of newscaster-speak or written form that is comprehensible across the dialects. We would live in a world of new and superficial language diversity, having lost deep bodies of knowledge when the other 6,997 languages vanished.

The push-back against globalization in the form of language revitalization will be one of the most interesting social trends to observe over the coming decades. Its outcome will have profound consequences for the intellectual capacity of our species, and for the state of human knowledge. As I have followed the lives and stories of the last speakers described in this book, I hear their message loud and clear: We value our knowledge, we value our languages, we have something to contribute. It would be incredibly shortsighted for us, in our Western industrialized societies, to think that because we have put men on the moon and split the atom, we have nothing to learn from people who just a generation ago were hunter-gatherers in a remote wilderness. What they know—which we've forgotten or never knew—may someday save us. We need to hear this message, over and over, in 7,000 different ways of speaking. Let's listen, while we still can.

ACKNOWLEDGMENTS

THIS BOOK IS THE RESULT of years of research that was generously supported, mentored, and assisted by many people. I thank Dr. Gregory Anderson of the Living Tongues Institute for Endangered Languages for years of inspiring collaboration in diverse locales.

The Enduring Voices Project—a joint effort of the National Geographic Society and the Living Tongues Institute for Endangered Languages—made possible the expeditions and research described in this book. The project was initiated at National Geographic by Terry Garcia, Dr. Wade Davis, and Chris Ranier, and funding was generously provided by Lucy Billingsley, Lisa Duke, Joanie Nasher, and the estate of Michael O'Donnell.

Funding for my research was granted by the National Science Foundation, Swarthmore College, Yale University, the Volkswagen Stiftung, the Hans Rausing Endangered Languages Project, IREX, the Genographic Legacy Fund, and the Living Tongues Institute for Endangered Languages.

I extend my heartfelt thanks to people who helped me in various ways during the writing: Garrett Brown, John Paine, Dr. Stephen Gluckman, Jeremy Fahringer, and John Williams.

A portion of the proceeds from this book will support language revitalization.

GLOSSARY

Dialect

Any spoken variety of a language, of no less interest or value than any other variety. As a language changes, its dialects may diverge and eventually become separate languages (e.g., Spanish and French evolved from dialects of Latin). The point at which a dialect becomes a language cannot be determined precisely. Linguists use the criterion of mutual intelligibility (see below) to determine whether two language varieties are dialects of a single language or are distinct languages. But social factors and ethnic identity must also be recognized as partly determining the boundaries among languages.

Endangered Language

A language at risk of extinction. Signs that a language is endangered include a relatively small number of speakers, declining numbers of speakers, and speakers all above a certain age (that is, children are not learning the language).

Grammar

The patterns by which language is formed. For linguists, what is grammatical is based on real-world use. If a group of people use and understand a phrase, it is grammatical for their dialect. This differs

277

from the traditional idea that there is only one "correct" way to speak. In linguistics, only sentences that no native speaker would use (e.g., "John to went my over house") are judged as ungrammatical.

Language Archive
A repository that safeguards recordings of languages in various media and makes them available to users.

Language Death
A popular metaphor describing the situation when a community gradually stops using its heritage language and no longer passes it on to the children. A "dead" language that has been documented and recorded is sometimes termed a "sleeping" language. These languages may be awakened or revived through revitalization efforts.

Language Documentation
Recording of the linguistic and cultural information found in a language.

Language Prestige
Positive value placed on a language or features of a language. Often a language or a language variety is considered prestigious when it is spoken by those in power.

Language Revitalization
Actions and policies to promote and increase the use of a language, with the goal of stopping or reversing its decline.

Language Revival (or Reclamation)
An attempt to bring back a language that has already lost all its speakers, by teaching it to people who will become new speakers.

Language Shift
The most common process in a language's ceasing to be spoken. Speakers almost invariably shift from a small, local, indigenous language to a national or global language. As speakers use the language of prestige (see *language prestige*) more often, they stop passing on the indigenous language to children. This leads to its death.

Linguistics
The scientific study of language, and an academic discipline taught at universities.

Moribund Language
A language that will almost certainly become extinct in the near future because no children speak it as their first language. Such languages as Ös and Chemehuevi, with only a few elderly speakers, are moribund.

Mutual Intelligibility
If speakers of two different language varieties can understand one another, their tongues are mutually intelligible and they are probably speaking different dialects of a single language. If two speakers are mutually unintelligible, then they are speaking two different languages.

Native Language
The language or languages learned naturally in early childhood, also called "first language." This is not always the same as an ancestral language or heritage language, terms which refer to a language that was spoken by a person's ancestors. For example, the heritage language of the Chulym youth is Ös, but Russian is probably their native language.

NOTES

The epigraph is a portion of a longer poem circulated in 2009, written by Prof. John Goulet in memory of Prof. Michael Noonan.

INTRODUCTION

1. Chemehuevi and Johnny Hill Jr., www.chemehuevi.net and www.crit-nsn.gov/crit_contents/government/johnny_hill.shtml.
2. Friedrich A. Hayek, "The Use of Knowledge in Society," *American Economic Review* XXXV, no. 4. (1945): 519-30 (American Economic Association).
3. E. Müllhäusler, *Linguistic Ecology* (New York: Routledge, 1996), 166.

CHAPTER 1: BECOMING A LINGUIST

1. Iris Smorodinsky, "Schwas in French: An Articulatory Analysis" (Ph.D. diss., Yale University, 1996); Scott F. Kiesling, "Dude," *American Speech* 79, no. 3 (2004): 281–305.
2. The institute is now called SIL International (see www.SIL.org).
3. Neil Smith and Ianthi-Maria Tsimpli. *The Mind of a Savant: Language Learning and Modularity.* (London: Wiley-Blackwell, 1995).

CHAPTER 2: SIBERIA CALLING

1. "Castrén," *Encyclopaedia Britannica,* 11th ed. (1910–11). See also Anna Stammler-Gossmann, "A Life for an Idea: Matthias Alexander Castrén," *Polar Record* 45, no. 234 (2009): 193–206.

2. Mendel's original paper on genetics appeared in 1866; a translation appears in Gregor Mendel, *Experiments in Plant Hybridisation* (Cambridge: Cambridge University Press, 1946).

3. This section is adapted from my book *When Languages Die: The Extinction of the World's Languages and the Erosion of Human Knowledge* (New York: Oxford University Press, 2007). A similarly complex system of genetic engineering of cattle according to pattern and color is practiced by the Bodi people of Ethiopia; see Katsuyoshi Fukui, "Co-evolution between Humans and Domesticates: The Cultural Selection of Animal Coat-Colour Diversity among the Bodi," in *Redefining Nature,* ed. Roy Ellen and Katsuyoshi Fukui (Oxford, England: Berg, 1996), 319–85.

CHAPTER 3: THE POWER OF WORDS

1. United Nations Environment Program, press release, February 8, 2001, "Globalization Threat to World's Cultural, Linguistic and Biological Diversity." Viewable at http://www.unep.org/Documents.Multilingual/Default.asp?DocumentID=192&ArticleID=2765.This section adapted from my book *When Languages Die: The Extinction of the World's Languages and the Erosion of Human Knowledge* (New York: Oxford University Press, 2007).

2. Knut J. Olawsky, "Urarina: Evidence for OVS Constituent Order," *Leiden Papers in Linguistics* 2, no. 2 (2005): 43–68.

3. On the hooded seal, see D. M. Lavigne and K. M. Kovacs, *Harps and Hoods: Ice Breeding Seals of the Northwest Atlantic* (Waterloo, Ontario: University of Waterloo Press, 1988).

4. Brendon Larson, *The Metaphoric Web: Environmental Metaphors and Sustainability* (New Haven, CT: Yale University Press, 2011).

5. Benjamin Lee Whorf, *Language, Thought, and Reality: Selected Writings.* Edited by John Carroll. (Cambridge, MA: MIT Press, 1964), 213–14.

6. For recent papers on the debate, see D. Genter and S. Goldwin-Meadow, eds., *Language in Mind: Advances in the Study of Language and Thought* (Cambridge, MA: MIT Press, 2003).

7. The author acknowledges Dr. Stephen R. Anderson as the source of this apt formulation.

8. Steven Pinker, *The Language Instinct: How the Mind Creates Language* (New York: Harper Collins, 1995), 64.

9. Igor Krupnik and Dyanna Jolly, eds., *The Earth Is Faster Now: Indigenous Observations of Arctic Environmental Change* (Fairbanks, AK: Arctic Research Consortium of the United States, 2002), 175.

10. Ibid., 177–78 and following.

11. Conrad Oozeva et al., *Watching Ice and Weather Our Way*, ed. Igor Krupnik et al. (Washington, DC: Arctic Studies Center, Smithsonian Institution, 2004).

12. Ibid.

13. Joseph W. Bastien, *Healers of the Andes: Kallawaya Herbalists and Their Medicinal Plants* (Salt Lake City: University of Utah Press, 1987), 103–4.

14. Mapuche letter to Bill Gates, full text available at http://www.mapuche.info/mapu/ctt050812.html.

15. Bloggers' comments accessed at http://digg.com/tech_news/Microsoft_Sued_by_Indians_for_Translating_without_Tribal_Elder_Permission?t=3972668 and at http://www.jacobandreas.net/2006/mapuche-indians-sue-microsoft-for-language-piracy. I thank Claire Shelden (Swarthmore

College class of 2010) and acknowledge her excellent senior thesis "Linguistic Ownership," written under my direction, as the source of some of the ideas in this section.

16. Peter Whiteley, "Do 'Language Rights' Serve Indigenous Interests? Some Hopi and Other Queries," *American Anthropologist* 105 (2003): 712–22.

CHAPTER 4: WHERE THE HOTSPOTS ARE

1. R. A. Mittermeier, N. Myers, and C. G. Mittermeier, eds., *Hotspots: Earth's Biologically Richest and Most Endangered Terrestrial Ecoregions* (Mexico City: CEMAX, 1999). The term is also defined in an essay by Ralph and Cristina Mittermeier in Colin Prior, *The World's Wild Places* (Richmond Hill, Ontario: Firefly Books, 2006), 126–27.

2. Conservation International, "Impact of Hotspots," http://www.biodiversityhotspots.org/xp/Hotspots/hotspotsScience/pages/impact_of_hotspots.aspx.

3. V. H. Heywood, ed., *Global Biodiversity Assessment* (Cambridge: Cambridge University Press, 1995); Edward O. Wilson, *The Future of Life* (New York: Random House, 2002).

4. Einar Haugen, *The Ecology of Language* (Stanford, CA: Stanford University Press, 1972); E. Müllhäusler, *Linguistic Ecology* (New York: Routledge, 1996), 166; Salikoko Mufwene, *The Ecology of Language Evolution* (Cambridge: Cambridge University Press, 2001).

5. R. Gillespie, "Dating the First Australians," *Radiocarbon* 44 (2002): 455–72.

6. The Enduring Voices Australia expedition team was Greg Anderson, Sam Anderson, Chris Rainier, and myself. We were welcomed and accompanied at every location by local experts and elders to ensure that the work was carried out in accordance

with local cultural and ethical standards. Data presented in this book was freely shared, and informed consent was granted to us by the speakers for its recording and wider dissemination.

7. These were Mary Magdalene Dungoi, in her 80s, reportedly the oldest speaker of Magati Ke; and Elizabeth Cumanyi and Lucy Tcherna, both in their 70s.

8. Although Amurdag had been reported in some of the scientific literature as extinct about 25 years prior, in fact it was not, and Australian linguists Robert Handelsmann, Nick Evans, Bruce Birch, and others had been with working with Charlie Mangulda and another remaining speaker over the years.

9. Charlie Mangulda narrated these first to our local guide Freddie Bush, and then he helped Freddie retell the Rainbow Serpent story to us.

10. We had with us a copy of Robert Handelsmann's thesis *Towards a Description of Amurdak: A Language of Northern Australia* (University of Melbourne, Honors Thesis, 1991). This invaluable monograph reflects a fuller state of the language that is likely no longer in existence, or at any rate not fully recalled by its last speaker(s).

11. R. D. Lambert and B. F. Freed, eds., *The Loss of Language Skills* (Rowley, MA: Newbury House, 1982). See also B. Köpke, M. S. Schmid, M. Keijzer, and S. Dostert, eds., *Language Attrition: Theoretical Perspectives* (Amsterdam: John Benjamins, 2007).

12. An example of recent press about Charlie Mangulda and the efforts of linguists and musicologists to document his knowledge is "The Song Remains Unbroken" by Nicholas Rothwell in the *Australian,* September 21, 2009.

13. Recorded field interview with Neil MacKenzie, July 2007, file L: 00:01:00-8:00.

14. Greg Anderson and I also interviewed Yawuru elders Susan Edgar, her mother Elsie Edgar, and Thelma Sadler, who was

97 when we met her and likely the oldest living speaker of Yawuru.

15. The Enduring Voices team in Paraguay consisted of linguists Greg Anderson and myself, photographer Chris Rainier, anthropologist Anna-Luisa Daigneault, and photographer and videographer Alejandro Chaskielberg.

16. Puerto Diana, Paraguay, May 22–23, 2009. Field recordings by K. David Harrison and Gregory Anderson. Field notes, interview, and translation by Anna Luisa Daigneault. All linguistic and cultural content is to be regarded as the intellectual property of the Chamacoco people.

CHAPTER 5: FINDING HIDDEN LANGUAGES

1. Recordings of the Aka, Koro, and Miji were made mainly in Palizi and Siwu villages in West Kameng District, and in Yangse, Kadeyang, and Kaching villages in East Kameng District, Arunachal Pradesh, India. The fieldwork team consisted of Greg Anderson, Ganesh Murmu, and myself. Many thanks to language consultants Sange Degio, Khandu Degio, Katia Yame, Sange Chopel Nimasow, Anil Sangchozu, Kachim, Gujupi, Sunil Yame, Pario Nimasow, Lupa Sangcho, and Serbu Aka.

The Aka-Miji language cluster includes Aka-Hruso (ca 2,000 speakers), Miji (ca 2500), Koro (less than 800), Bugun/Khowa (less than 800), and Sulung/Puroik (less than 3,000). All these languages are either threatened or endangered. All of them are also poorly known to science. Much of what exists is of varying reliability and usefulness or in secondary sources, often appearing in publications that are obscure and/or of considerable age. See, for example, the following sources: C. R. MacGregor, "Notes on Akas and Akaland," *Proceedings of the Asiatic Society of Bengal* (1884); J. D. Anderson, *A*

Short Vocabulary of the Aka Language (Shillong, India, 1896); S. Konow, "Note on the Languages Spoken between the Assam Valley and Tibet," *Journal of the Royal Asiatic Society* (London) (1902): 127–37; S. Konow, "North Assam Group," in *Linguistic Survey of India*, ed. G. A. Grierson, 3:568–72 (Calcutta: Superintendent of Government Printing, 1909); J. Schubert, "Hrusso-Vokabular," *Mittelungen des Institüt für Orientforschung* (Deutsche Akademie der Wissenschaften zu Berlin) 10 (1964): 295–350; R. Shafer, "Hruso," *Bulletin of the School of Oriental and African Studies* 12, no. 1 (1947): 184–96; R. Sinha, *The Akas* (Shillong, India: Research Dept., Adviser's Secretariat, 1962); I. M. Simon, *Aka Language Guide* (Shillong, India: North-East Frontier Agency Administration, 1970), reprint, 1993, Itanagar; I. M. Simon, *Miji Language Guide* (Shillong, India: Govt. of Arunachal Pradesh, 1979/1974), 198–212; G. van Driem, *Languages of the Himalayas*, 2 vols. (Leiden, Netherlands: Brill, 2001).

Additional Aka data from K. David Harrison, Aka field notes, 2008, pp. 61–64.

2. Dalvinder Singh Grewal, *Tribes of Arunachal Pradesh: Identity, Culture, and Languages*, 2 vols. (Delhi: South Asia Publications, 1997).

3. Queen Elizabeth II vowel study: Jonathan Harrington, Sally-anne Palethorpe, and Catherine Watson, "Monophthongal Vowel Changes in Received Pronunciation: An Acoustic Analysis of the Queen's Christmas Broadcasts," *Journal of the International Phonetic Association* 30 (2000): 63–78 (Cambridge University Press).

4. The Koro work was first presented publicly by Gregory Anderson in 2009 in two talks at scientific conferences: "The Aka Miji Language Cluster of Arunachal Pradesh" at South Asian Linguistic Analysis (SALA), University of North

Texas, Denton, Texas, October 2009; and "The Aka Miji Cluster of the Kameng Region, Arunachal Pradesh" at the Himalayan Languages Symposium, University of Oregon, Eugene, August 2009. Both talks were co-authored by Gregory D. S. Anderson, K. David Harrison, and Ganesh Murmu.

5. The original text of this story is from the archives of the Laboratory of Siberian Languages, Tomsk State Pedagogical University, which were accessed by us courtesy of Dr. Andrei Filtchenko. The author interviewed the storyteller in person in July 2003 but did not reelicit the story, due to her advanced age and deafness. The story was translated into English by the author, Greg Anderson, and members of the Ös community. Copyright herein pertains solely to the English translation; ownership of the original text resides with the Ös community.

6. This story is to be regarded as the intellectual property of the Chulym (Ös) people. A set of original field notes recording this story is archived in the Tomsk Laboratory for Siberian Languages. According to the field notes, the storyteller was Maria Alekseevna Skoblina, who was born 1911 in Tjulapsax village. It was transcribed by R. M. Birjukovich, in Pasechnoe village, Krasnoyarsk Kray, in 1971 (Tomsk archive notebooks tom. VI, supranumbered pp. 573–629). The text was typed up from notebooks in June 2008 by Greg Anderson and myself. We added complete interlinear glossing and translation in July 2008.

CHAPTER 6: SIX DEGREES OF LANGUAGE
1. The Enduring Voices research expedition to Papua New Guinea included Greg Anderson, Sam Anderson, Chris Rainier, and myself, and we were accompanied for portions of the trip by Joanie Nasher. Danielle Mathieu-Reeves went

to Matugar village in 2010 to continue the Enduring Voices project activities there, under the guidance of Matugar consultant Rudolf Raward. Yokoim song lyrics transcribed by Alexandra Israel.

2. William A. Foley, *The Yimas Language of New Guinea* (Stanford, CA: Stanford University Press, 1991). Yimas 1 village: S 04° 40.871' E 143° 33.011', Elevation 106 feet at the Spirit House; Konmei village: S 04° 34.6888' E 143 ° 33.077', Elevation 66 feet.

3. Thanks to Jared Diamond (personal communication of January 25, 2010) for this formulation, a variation of the famous saying by Max Weinreich, "A language is a dialect with an army and a navy."

4. Jadran Mimica, *Intimations of Infinity: The Cultural Meanings of the Iqwaye Counting and Number Systems* (Oxford: Berg Publishers, 1988).

5. Julius Sungulmari, Ambonwari Village: S 04° 36.824' E 143° 36.737', Elevation 42 feet. For an ethnographic study of this Ambonwari village, see Borut Telban, *Dancing Through Time: A Sepik Cosmology*, Oxford Studies in Social and Cultural Anthropology (Oxford: Clarendon Press, 1998).

6. Field interviews by the author with Oruncho Gamango and with Opino Gamango, Gajapati District, Orissa State, India, March 2, 2007.

CHAPTER 7: HOW DO STORIES SURVIVE?

1. Barbara Tuchman, *The Book* (Washington, DC: Library of Congress, 1980).

2. Pablo Neruda, in *The Essential Neruda: Selected Poems,* ed. Mark Eisner (City Lights Publishers, 2004).

3. The Wikimedia foundation, in its 2007–2008 annual report,

also makes the claim that its Wiktionary is "A dictionary and thesaurus in all languages."

4. K. David Harrison, "A Tuvan Hero Tale, with Commentary, Morphemic Analysis and Translation," *Journal of the American Oriental Society* 125, no. 1 (2005): 1–30. Cited extract on pp. 20–21.

5. Small languages, and even not so small ones like Ho, can find it difficult to break into the computer age if they use a non-Latin alphabet or writing system that differs from those used by economically important world languages. For the sake of language revitalization and access to computers by speakers of endangered languages, we hope to see greater progress in ushering the writing systems of small and endangered languages into the worldwide Unicode standard.

6. John Deeney, *Ho–English Dictionary*, rev. ed. (Ranchi, India: Xavier Publications, Catholic Press, 2005), 192–93.

7. Ibid., 1.

8. The Ho origin myth was told by K. C. Naik Biruli (born 1957), resident in Mayurbanj district, Bhubaneshwar, India, on September 13, 2005. It was recorded in audio and video by Greg Anderson and myself. This is an abridged version of a yet unpublished translation by Biruli, Anderson, and Harrison. The "ten months" of pregnancy are lunar months. A version of this Ho origin story appeared in K. David Harrison, *When Languages Die: The Extinction of Human Languages and the Erosion of Human Knowledge* (New York: Oxford University Press, 2007), 202–3.

CHAPTER 8: BREAKING OUT IN SONG

1. Colleagues who accompanied me on the various expeditions include linguist Greg Anderson, anthropologist Brian Donahoe, phonetician Sven Grawunder, sound engineer Joel

Gordon, musician Katherine Vincent, mechanical engineer Afanasij Myldyk, Mongolian specialist Peter Marsh, musicologist Valentina Süzükei, practicing Buddhist lama and shaman Chechen Kuular, and many others.

2. "Greenhouse Gas Bubbling from Siberian Permafrost," *Seed,* September 13, 2006, http://seedmagazine.com /content/article/greenhouse_gas_bubbling_from_siberian _permafrost/.

3. Theodore Levin, with Valentina Süzükei, *Where Rivers and Mountains Sing: Sound, Music, and Nomadism in Tuva and Beyond* (Bloomington: Indiana University Press, 2006).

4. W. H. Auden, "In Memory of W. B. Yeats" (1939).

CHAPTER 9: WHEN A WORLD IS RUNNING DOWN

1. The uniqueness and antiquity of the Tofa bear lexicon represents a working hypothesis, and certainly merits further comparative and historical study. See Gregory D. S. Anderson and K. David Harrison, "Hunter-Gatherers Speaking the Language of Pastoral Nomads," in *The Languages of Hunter-Gatherers: Global and Historical Perspectives,* ed. R. Rhodes et al. (Cambridge: Cambridge University Press, forthcoming).

2. This section adapted from my 2007 book *When Languages Die: The Extinction of the World's Languages and the Erosion of Human Knowledge* (New York: Oxford University Press, 2007).

3. John McWhorter, "The Cosmopolitan Tongue: The Universality of English," *World Affairs* (Fall 2009). Accessed at www .worldaffairsjournal.org/articles/2009-Fall/full-McWhorter -Fall-2009.html.

4. Albert Costa, Mireia Hernández, and Núria Sebastián-Gallés, "Bilingualism Aids Conflict Resolution: Evidence from the ANT Task," *Cognition* 106, no. 1 (January 2008): 59–86.

5. Ellen Bialystok, Fergus I. M. Craik, and Morris Freedman, "Bilingualism as a Protection Against the Onset of Symptoms of Dementia," *Neuropsychologia* 45, no. 2 (February 2007): 459–64.

6. Jared Diamond, *Guns, Germs, and Steel: The Fates of Human Societies* (New York: W. W. Norton, 1997).

7. Tom Colls, "The Death of Language?" *Today,* BBC4, October 19, 2009, transcript available at http://news.bbc.co.uk/today/hi/today/newsid_8311000/8311069.stm.

8. This and the following comments were posted in response to Colls, "The Death of Language?" at http://news.bbc.co.uk/today/hi/today/newsid_8311000/8311069.stm.

CHAPTER 10: SAVING LANGUAGES

1. Nora C. England, "Commentary: Further Rhetorical Concerns," *Journal of Linguistic Anthropology* 12, no. 2 (2002): 142–43.

2. See M. Kat Anderson, *Tending the Wild: Native American Knowledge and the Management of California's Natural Resources* (Berkeley: University of California Press, 2005).

3. Washoe interviews with Ramona Dick, elicited by Alan C. L. Yu, filmed by K. David Harrison, July 2007. See also http://www.kumeyaay.com/2007/09/a-final-say-they-hope-not-tribal-elders-are-helping-a-linguist-compile-an-online-dictionary-of-washo-a-language-close-to-extinction-more-than-just-words-are-at-stake.

4. The preceding sections are based on Washoe interviews with Ramona Dick, elicited by Alan C. L. Yu, filmed by K. David Harrison, July 2007. All Washoe materials are used with informed consent of the speakers and are to be regarded as the intellectual property of the Washoe people. For more

information on the Washoe people and Washo language, see www.washoetribe.us.

5. Terrie Winson, *Lenni Lenape,* http://www.anthro4n6.net /lenape.

6. Lenape language classes at Swarthmore College were organized by Dr. Theodore Fernald and Shelley DePaul in 2009 and 2010, funded by grants from the Lang Center for Social Change and from the National Science Foundation, under the guidance of NSF program officer Dr. Susan Penfield.

7. Thanks to Dr. Margaret Noori for assistance with this section.

8. Bernard C. Perley, "Last Words, Final Thoughts: Collateral Extinctions in Maliseet Language Death," in *The Anthropology of Extinction,* ed. Genese Sodikoff (Bloomington: Indiana University Press, forthcoming).

9. Tyler Cowen, *Creative Destruction: How Globalization Is Changing the World's Cultures* (Princeton, NJ: Princeton University Press, 2002).

INDEX

ABOUT THE AUTHOR

K. DAVID HARRISON is associate professor and chair of Linguistics at Swarthmore College and a National Geographic fellow. He received his doctorate from Yale University. He is widely recognized and consulted as a leading spokesman for endangered languages. He makes frequent appearances before college, high school, and other public audiences and in media outlets such as NPR, BBC, *Good Morning America,* and *The Colbert Report.* He co-starred in the documentary film *The Linguists* (http://www.thelinguists.com), which premiered at the Sundance Film Festival in 2008. The film documents his travels around the world to track down and interview last speakers of nearly extinct tongues. As a linguist and specialist in Siberian Turkic languages, Harrison has spent many months in Siberia and Mongolia working with nomadic herders and studying their languages and traditions. He has also worked in India, the Philippines, Lithuania, Bolivia, Paraguay, Papua New Guinea, and the United States with members of the last generations of speakers of endangered languages. Harrison's work includes not only scientific descriptions of languages but also storybooks, translations, and digital archives for the use of the native speaker communities. He is the author of *When Languages Die: The Extinction of the World's Languages and the Erosion of Human Knowledge.* He lives in Philadelphia.

ABOUT NATIONAL GEOGRAPHIC'S ENDURING VOICES

NATIONAL GEOGRAPHIC'S Enduring Voices project is a partnership with the Living Tongues Institute for Endangered Languages. The project works to identify language hotspots, those regions of the world having the greatest linguistic diversity, the greatest language endangerment, and the least studied languages. The language hotspots model is a new way to view the distribution of global linguistic diversity, to assess the threat of language extinction, and to prioritize research.

Within the language hotspots, the project team works to document vanishing languages and cultures. Enduring Voices also provides training, technology, and resources to support grassroots, community-led efforts at language revitalization.

For more information, and to learn how you can support the work of revitalization, visit www.nationalgeographic.com/mission/enduringvoices.